The Noble's Pauper Children

Marina Radovanovic

PUBLISH AMERICA

PublishAmerica
Baltimore

First printing

ISBN: 1-4137-5941-6
PUBLISIIED BY PUBLISHAMERICA, LLLP
www.publishamerica.com
Baltimore

Printed in the United States of America

Best Wishes!
Mama Rockovara
[signature]

Acknowledgements

Many years have gone by since the first words of this book were actually put on paper. I have decided to write my father's story as a gift to all, a commemoration to my children and to their eventual offspring and thereon, with hopes that history and ancestry will not be lost, nor forgotten. Numerous hours I have spent with my father (with delight) to continue his story.

Travelling through time and igniting painful memories was a difficult and painful task. Many hardships and misfortunes had also interrupted and prevented the continuation of pursuing the completion of the book, at that time. Finally deciding to devote myself with steely determination to complete the book, I had committed myself to the research of the family ancestry that led me to many corners with no results of my inquiries, due to the destruction of some of the archival records during the revolution and previous Communism, at that particular time.

Hours upon hours I had spent searching for anyone who might have knowledge as to what happened to Nikolai Vladimirovich Krasicki, who lived in Stary Oskol, later Kursk, Russia. Upon my incessant search, I had the fortune of meeting (via internet) a wonderful person who helped with locating some documents regarding the position, the status that my great-grandfather had held from 1890 onward. My friend, Sergei Skorniakov, had provided us (my father and myself) with copies of these documents directly from the historical archives of Kursk, where his good friend, Bugrov Yuri, honoured culture worker of Russia, candidate of history and president of the Kursk Historical Society, immediately set to research, in assistance with Larissa Nazarova, the chief of the Representation of Russian Society of Historians and Workers of archives in the Kursk region. I humbly thank them for their dedication to research and their time and devotion to locating the invaluable documents we now hold today. These very important documents had certified the stories my father had heard when he was a child by the artist, by "Judas," and by the newspaper delivery man, to name a few.

Even though within ourselves we had instinctively known the nobility of my grandmother and, to an extent, my grandfather, the verification of my great-grandfather's position of employment and status had sealed the matter. Since then we have obtained from the former Yugoslavia, now Serbia, other relevant documents, such as the death certificate of my great-grandmother, Alexandra Nikolaevna Krasickaya, stating the status of her husband and her place of birth, being Stary Oskol, Russia. Further research is underway, to obtain any more knowledge and any matters dealing with Nikolai and Alexandra Krasicki and of course my grandmother Zoya and other relatives perhaps still in Stary Oskol, or Kursk.

Through patience, prayers and the shedding of many bitter tears, my father and I worked endlessly to compose and accomplish the completion of his tale, of this book.

My family, particularly my sister Vera, had supported me and encouraged me to spend time and many hours working on this book, picking up where we had left off years ago. Fighting back tears myself, as I wrote the words so hurtful, so unimaginable, astonished that such misery had taken place, but a generation above me, I pushed back the thoughts and pursued with determination.

I humbly wish to express my gratitude to PublishAmerica for their support and for the publication of this book. They are a truly a wonderful and kind staff. Jennifer Hendershot, my editor, has been an enormous help in the publication of this book, and I am truly grateful to her.

The moral of this true story is and explicitly hopes to convey that in all sincerity, my father Victor, and myself, never wish upon anyone to suffer such hardships—ignorance, injustice, insults and poverty and hunger, neglected by society and shunned due to the lack of financial and material assets, yet unknowingly insulting and demeaning children who were unaware of their ancestry, of their lineage. The obvious did prevail and was told many, many years later verified by my research and commitment.

My father had told me that he read the book, *Oliver Twist,* by Charles Dickens, and cried terribly. I looked at him. He stated that....True, the story is very sad, but when he had read that book as a child, he thought that Oliver Twist had better luck, in comparison to his wretched state. Even though it was a novel, he envied Oliver Twist.

Introduction

Upon the outbreak of revolution in Tsarist Russia, many aristocrats, bourgeois and some common folk were forced to flee their motherland, emigrating to foreign countries mainly in Europe, China and parts of North and South America.

During the second world war and focussing on the colonies of refugees, many were left homeless and on the mercy of their oppressors. Counts of a fallen Tsarist Russia, princes, some dukes and numerous professors and tutors began establishing, in addition to new lives, organizations and charitable foundations, which fostered the needs of their fellow men pursuing a new home, a new life.

After living the life of explicit luxury, descending to misery and poverty, many were compelled to not only accept their fate, but to employ themselves with such positions that even their servants were superior. One such family caught in the turmoil, regarded as displaced persons, were striving to survive and conquer destitution. Sadly, not all of the members possessed enough stamina to endure the whips of fate, thereby withering and succumbing to bitter poignancy and corruption.

This true story will enable us to visualize the hardships in this harrowing tale of poverty, mystery and suspense and to relive the life through a child caught in an era of war, injustice and destitution and through the cry of a noble's seed.

Chapter 1

She scrubbed vigorously. The more she scrubbed the worn out yellowish floor, the more the tears ran down, washing the dirt and sweat off her face. She was once an amazing beauty. She was working hard, her body toiling, and yet her mind was far, far away...

Zoya's hair was meticulously gathered, and set with a few wisps. Her flair for fashion was apparent in her wardrobe with dozens of brightly-coloured gowns, some sparkled some not, hanging in a kaleidoscopic arrangement. She and her sisters always followed the latest trends, thereby constantly burdening their seamstress with plenty of new orders. Zoya's auburn hair framed her lovely white face, and her green eyes emitted warmth and compassion. Being graceful in movement and genteel manner complimented her tranquil demeanor.

She strolled by that light, sunny day, completely unaffected by the day's cumbersome worries of how the cook forgot to buy the proper spice (the key ingredient) for the recipe needed for tonight's special dinner. *Another soiree, so what*, she thought. She pretended not to care, but the slight curl of the lip at the corner of her mouth betrayed her. She might see the captain again, and even be agreeable to a dance of Mazurka with him. She wasn't certain yet, and then immediately began to conjecture what he might look like that evening, and what gown she should wear. With all that rolling in her mind, she immediately summoned her maid, Anushka.

"Annnuushkaaaa! Where are you?"

"Here I am, my lady," bowing as she rushed to Zoya. Even though Anushka was her maid, the similarity of age between them made them more akin to friendship, thereby permitting Anushka to speak her mind at times. And this was one of those times. Anushka casually disclosed her knowledge regarding the captain, and of Zoya's attraction to him.

"My lady...I think you would look splendid in the turquoise gown this evening, and maybe permit the captain's gazes to fall on your sister Nina for a change."

"Anushka! How could you?!"

"My lady, I just thought that..."

"Nevermind what you thought. I shall wear the soft, peach gown and, Anushka, bring me the appropriate jewels. Must I concern myself of the captain's gazes, Anushka? I believe he has a right to look at whomever he wishes!"

"Yes, my lady, you are right."

Anushka knew better, but she also knew her place. To continue the discussion would only cast a distance between them, and she was not about to jeopardize that for any captain.

Nina desperately tired to outdo her sister Zoya. Since Zoya was their father's favorite and had numerous award for her paintings, and how could she not, after all she had the best teacher who had arrived from Moscow. He previously taught the Grand Duchess Olga. Anyhow, Nina was madly in love with the captain. He was charming, and his boyish good looks were simply not to ignore! When he might accidently catch her looking at him, his ice blue eyes melted her in an instant. That, and his preferred background made him a perfect candidate for a husband. Nina, comfortably thinking that she had the advantage of seniority, had missed the embracing glances between the two...Zoya was in love, as was the captain.

The soiree came, and left, and the outcome produced an engagement, and a date for a wedding. Zoya was exuberant, simply mad with joy. Nina tried to console herself with a new beau, an officer who had offered her a dance or two. Not as dashing as the captain, but handsome just the same. The house was hustling and bustling with activity, keeping all busy with wedding plans. Nina, though jealous, couldn't help getting caught in the excitement. She was given a duty all her own, and she pursued this task with much love for her sister.

The wedding was spectacular in all its splendour. Exactly what Zoya wished for, and exactly what was to be expected. The dazzling display of ladies in their silk and satin gowns, dripping with diamonds that hung around their necks, arms, fingers and hair. Not to say that the men were unnoticed, for they were attired in uniforms, and proudly protruding their chest, decorated with award and ribbons. Carriages were coming and leaving under the soft illumination of the entrance. The valets were in perfect harmony, and in unison performed their duties assigned to them. Even they had rehearsed for that special day. Zoya and the captain had decided that their abode would be with her parents, at least for the time present.

"Zoya! Zo...yaaaaaaa!" She heard her mother calling her with her high-pitched voice, with the heavy emphasis placed on the last syllable of her name, as only the well-to-do know of doing.

"Yes, Mother?"

"Zoya, please gather your sisters in your room. Your father and I must speak to you promptly."

"Yes, Mother," replied Zoya, with a worrisome look on her innocent face.

She raced (though she didn't run, it wasn't permitted unladylike and her heavy gown would

not permit it) through the half-lit hallways, which always smelled of dark, damp wood. She briskly walked by enormous portraits that hung on the walls, and expensive imported vases, so carefully

displayed, and of course, a gilded velvet chair here and there. She found her sisters, Nina and Tamara, at the other end of the palace, laughing and giggling.

Zoya entered the room, but didn't bother to inquire of the cause of their merriment, for the look on her mother's face had troubled her more.

"No...absolutely not! I will not leave home! Never!"

"Zoya...we must leave. We have no choice, dear. We must save ourselves."

"I don't want to go!"

"We know, dear, but the situation leaves us no alternative," Zoya's mother softly replied.

"I'm afraid it's not an option for you, dear," said her father in desperate attempts to conceal his quivering chin.

Nina and Tamara were more dumbfounded than vocal. They saw that Zoya had the protest well under hand, and the countenance they expressed implied that they completely agreed with Zoya, thinking that it was understood. Their nods and joined eyebrows confirmed their inclusion in Zoya's screams of "no" and "never."

"Dear, I have arranged that your sisters, mother and yourself travel by train to Crimea. Of course, you will be escorted by the guards. From there you will go by means of boat to Constantinople, where the three of you will work as nurses for the Red Cross and help the injured soldiers.

"But..." Zoya exclaimed.

"Dear, it is final," her father answered.

"Will you come with us, Father?"

"No. I have matters here to tend to obligations, and I wouldn't leave the Tsar. You must all leave, and quickly. The maids at this moment have started collecting your belongings, and Anushka is waiting for you, Zoya. There is not much time."

A court counsellor rubbed elbows and mingled with the elite, the creme de la creme. Governors, palace consultants and high-ranking officials were just a part of everyday life in the grand salons of the Russian palaces. Sparkling gems cascaded their brilliant light throughout the room with each turn or whisk of the hand of the aristocratic ladies who adorned them. Little did Nikolai Vladimirovich know how horribly the revolution would affect his loved ones, particularly his daughter Zoya.

They worked as Red Cross nurses (as most ladies of high rank did in those days when necessary) in Constantinople. The injuries they were subjected to were of paramount disgust to them, but somehow, swallowing their weaknesses, they persisted in the ongoing care of the injured. They worked tirelessly, and were fervently obedient to their mother, Alexandra, until...a White Army officer wandered in with an injured hand that needed immediate attention. Zoya raced to the scene. Not only did Zoya tend to this officer, but had finally married him. When the revolution broke out, her beloved captain vanished, not a word, nor a trace of him, thus their marriage was annulled to Nina's secret satisfaction, though she did feel for her sister's grief.

Zoya and Andrei lived and worked in Constantinople for ten years, and there they had their first three children: Vechislav, Alex and Olga. When they heard that King Alexander permitted refugees to enter Yugoslavia, they decided to embark on the voyage and begin anew. They packed their meager belongings, whatever little was left, and with not knowing their destiny or fate, had begun their travel to Belgrade, Yugoslavia. Hence, Zoya's miserable life begins, as does little Victor's tragic and poor childhood.

Chapter 2

Under the balcony in the square courtyard were two measly rooms in the suturen (sub-level) where we lived. The landlady whipped out a box, which had earlier contained her new wood stove for her summer kitchen that, incidentally, was right next to our home.

I was squirming around in this large cardboard box, and shivering while listening to my father's hollers and screams. I trembled of fright, lest they find me. It was dark, and the night had already blanketed the city, but it wasn't cold. The new home of mine, this box, provided me with shelter, and even in the event that a sudden wind might blow, I felt safe. While inspecting the interior of my newly-found sanctuary, I unavoidably heard the thunderous roar of my father's voice. "Those barons and aristocrats will not educate and up-bring my children in their villas! I will slice them with the axe you see here before you!"

Lord, I thought, now I was scared even more, and recoiled in my shelter. What had happened earlier was...

In front of our home, but a few hours ago, two sophisticated-looking gentlemen, clad in exquisite suits and hats, and bearing walking sticks while clenching onto their gloves in one hand, were accompanied by two very pleasant-looking ladies.

The ladies also wore such fine dresses and hats, that it all bewildered me. They stood as if cemented to the ground, wide-eyed and shocked with disbelief at what they were hearing from the mouth of the crazed man, who was wildly shouting at the top of his lungs at them, "I will cut you all up before I let you cross the threshold of my apartment and take my children! You have no authority to do so! They will never attend your school again! Leave, I tell you, so that my eyes don't see you here!"

All the while he was waving the axe in the air, above his head, as if it were a baton. Both of these gentlemen stirred, then leapt in front of the ladies, lifting their canes in self defense. One of the men ordered the ladies to, "quickly return to the carriages!"

With a frightful sigh the ladies obliged and scurried to the carriage, as fast as their little feet permitted. Before they retreated the gentlemen carefully examined the madman's return to his home, where his rage continued.

Mother had collected her children around her as a hen would gather her chicks. The tears were mounting in her eyes. She quietly answered to my father's mean yells, "Why do you do this?"

"Quiet!" he shouted back at her, "I have my reasons. I have my orders."

He sat exhausted on the kitchen chair. I guessed all that anger had flushed him of his energy. When he sat down, he slowly released the axe, and allowed it to drop on the floor beside him. I very quietly weaseled out of my mother's embrace.

Our little kitchen consisted of a small iron bed in the corner of the room, and a wood stove that was used for cooking and heating the room alike. A small credenza, which is where my mother displayed our petty belongings, and a wooden table with four chairs, furnished our modest abode. The only light we had in the kitchen was a bulb hanging from the ceiling in the middle of the room with a long, dingy string dangling from it to turn the lights on and off. Covering this bulb was some kind of colourful paper, which served as a shade. On our ceiling we had a sticky track of tape held by thumbtacks, as was practised then, and meant to catch the flies that buzzed angrily when their legs got stuck on the tape.

Mother sat on the edge of the bed in the kitchen, holding my youngest brother George on her lap. My older brother Alex sat on the floor to the right of her legs. I joined them, and sat on the floor to her immediate left. Our sister Olga was content sitting behind her back. Mother's head bowed low causing her short hair to fall upon her face. She had cut her own hair that morning, complaining that it was too burdensome to brush anymore. From beneath her apron I snuck a peek at Father who looked so large to me. In reality, he wasn't that big of a man, but was it due to his demeanor that made him seem like a huge tyrant to me?

Father had pulled the string and the flick of light came on. I took advantage of this momentary serenity to discreetly leave the kitchen. I entered the bedroom, and because the windows were low I was able to leap outside to the solace of the night.

It was quiet, though a song could be heard in the distance. I thought, not everyone is miserable. Some men spoke as they strode by, which was broken by a cough, or laugh, which slowly faded away into the night. The sky was lit with bright stars, and how studiously I admired them. I turned around and saw my trusty shelter, my box. With much relief I crawled into the box. The scent of paint from the new stove hadn't evaporated yet. How nice it was here, I could sleep there. I gathered my knees together, and thought about the day's events, pushing away my father's complaints regarding the cost of rent, and how he must pay for it.

Today's supper consisted of dry, stale bread, provided by the begging my brother and I did. This bread was cooked in boiling water, and Mother had thrown in some bacon, which she picked up from the garbage behind the butcher's shop. It was green, but she scrubbed the mold off and the spoiled part off, and threw whatever she salvaged into the pot. For dessert I had a rotten pear, of which I also had to cut off the soft, dark brown areas, and then proceed to eat it hoping it would take away the nausea I felt after dinner, and change the taste in my mouth. I fell asleep, tired but safe in my little nest.

I awoke to whispers heard directly above my head, and ever so gently pushed the cardboard flap ajar to peek at the owners of the whispers. To my surprise, I discovered it was the same two gentlemen from yesterday's episode. They didn't know I was in the box, and I wasn't about to let them find out I was there, and listening! I concentrated to hear and discern what they were saying.

Nothing...I understand nothing! "Oui, oui," and other foreign words, although some sounded familiar. Wait, that accent...yes, yes! Now I know, it's French! Mother and Grandmother spoke that when they talked to each other, and told secrets after realizing that we were there with them. Usually we, mainly I, was so quiet in the other room, or on the bed in the kitchen (supposedly) asleep, that they thought they could speak in Russian without restraint. Upon the realization that we, or I, was there, the conversation quickly transformed to the French language. I did understand a little after listening to them many times repeating the same words again and again in French, then in Russian, then French, thereby providing me with a type of lexicon.

Luckily, the two whisperers continued their discourse in Russian: "What is up with that man?" one of the sophisticated strangers said.

The other replied, "Your excellency, you have seen the documents at the meeting of the council, therefore you and I should not be astonished. That is why we are here, to save the madam as decided at the meeting.

"Have you read the documents regarding that certain gentleman who followed the family out of Russia to Constantinople and tried on several occasions to dismember the family, but not out of loyalty, rather to steal all of the notable belongings of the family, or rather the madam's? He turned out to be a traitor; he drugged the poor madam, rendering her submissive to that officer, and bound her to him in matrimony.

"Thus, understanding the severity of his actions, he attempted to separate them, unsuccessfully mind you. He managed to confiscate the majority of the madam's treasures. Wether he shared his profits with the lower ranking officer or not is not in our knowledge, but the communication between the two remains mysterious. We managed to apprehend this man, who called himself a baron, but shamefully lost him. He escaped when he went to relieve himself in his apartment, and disappeared through the bathroom window. Four of us had broken down the door, but unfortunately he already left. In his apartment, we searched through his papers, and found some evidence of his betrayal: receipts of payments he received from his people, and for the jobs he rendered. Simply shocking."

"Yes, I know...I read it all as well. That baron, so to speak, was actually planning a complete annihilation of the family. Amongst the papers found was one letter containing strict orders from delegates in Russia that imposed the immediate and necessary destruction of N.K., and his entire family.

"N.K. was gaining considerable ground, authority and post in Russia, which did not suit the delegates, nor their plans. In subsequent letters, we learned that N.K. was murdered, but his wife and two daughters survived him. There is no mention of the third daughter Tamara who resides now in France. Apparently, the wife and two daughters had considerable amounts of diamonds, gems and other pricey items. Though, that not being the issue involved, but rather the knowledge the young Madam Zoya possesses such as concealed important information, which evidently is also substantial to this self-proclaimed baron as well."

"Dreadful," replied the smaller of the two sophisticated men.

While I was floating in this newly-acquired information I tried hard not to sneeze, and succeeded. Suddenly the main orator announced, "Have you seen the disgusting evidence found where it is noted by the officer she wed, that he continuously administered Valium to her, which a bribed doctor prescribed to her, here in Belgrade? Further reports from this miserable officer to the 'baron' describes the effect of the drug. He claims that she often becomes unconscious, and speaks incoherently. He continues to write that he will soon proclaim her 'not of sound mind'…insane, if she dared to say anything.

"Judging from all this, she might know of something hidden in a small town near Kursk, something that her father N.K. had informed her of, amongst other secrets. We had found some coded messages, which revealed some sort of connection to the Tsar."

"True," the taller gentleman replied, and stated, "our mission here is to save the madam, excluding her children for the time being, as you have seen the rage last night by that officer or mad man. The children bind her to the crazed fellow, thus making it very difficult for us to fulfill our duty."

Everything was spinning in my head, and I'd lost track of time. Was it day or night? Even of where I was, for I was completely and thoroughly absorbed in the discussion. They were free to speak there, knowing nobody was home except for me in my box. It took me a considerable amount of time to grasp this data. I was astonished at how this whole discussion partook above my head.

"Come, let us go now," he mumbled, and cleared his throat. "We are unable to do anything now, the baron has his own people, too, that protect him, and advise him. We must verify further documentation, and evidence, and continue our manhunt—to put the baron down, perhaps this officer, too."

I returned to the apartment via the window once they had left, and after considerable deliberation decided to continue my slumber, and rethink all this later since no one was home. Mother was probably ill again last night. The thought in my mind just before falling into a deep sleep was the strange dialogue between the two gentlemen, and if it weren't for their lost keys (which I had heard them claim and discover), I would be spared of this grievous knowledge.

Chapter 3

Days and weeks flew by. My older brother Alex and I were daily visiting the Russian church, not because of our religious fervor, although we did believe, but to beg for alms from the local parishioners and other wandering persons. Later on in the evenings we were subjected to methodical frisking and searching of our persons, which my father eagerly awaited. Finger breaking and the shaking of our torn garments (which Mother so lovingly patched, and yet there were holes) was an expectant procedure, and we began to accept this.

Whatever little money we had was immediately taken without question. We dared not to withhold (if he found it that is) any money, cigarettes, lighters, or food, for there would be a penalty we all feared. I usually wondered, where was the money we delivered involuntarily? Where was his money? Why must we always be hungry? Why don't they buy us food? That daily supper of hot, boiled stale bread was already detestable to me.

Whether it was late summer or early fall, the sun was still being kind and warm. Humble celebrations were heard coming from our kitchen. I was joyfully sitting at the kitchen table, watching Mother's attempts at cooking. She was creating our most favorite dish—kasha. This time the kasha was made with some type of squash, which Mother again found behind the kiosks at the piazza.

From our little black stove we heard the bubbling noise of

the mass that was cooking and spattering the surrounding area. She wrapped a thin, torn tea towel around her arm, and proceeded to stir the meal. "Oh, how this spatters," she proclaimed in an air of a concerned and busy housewife. Father was observing from his chair and immediately retorted, "Of course it spatters! What do you know?! What do you know of cooking! Nothing!"

"Yes, nothing. I know nothing," she softly whispered while stirring.

"You! A noble! Ha! Indeed, some noble you are!" He laughed at her in a sardonic manner.

He had never ceased to belittle her, to downgrade her. She unwillingly accepted all his piercing comments, for she knew very well what devastation would ensue if an attempt was made by her to fight and save her pride.

Father mumbled a few more insults at her, and in the same breath informed us of the cause of our special meal today. "We are having company...my friend from P— is visiting us, and you—" he shot a look of warning at Mother "—you prepare the samovar!"

That was the first time I had seen our famed samovar. So often this mysterious object was mentioned in conversations, but never seen. Well...today was the day this apparition was to manifest itself, yet another cause of excitement and joy.

In front of our dwelling, a tiny wooden table was set up to hold the famous samovar. I sat on the step and vehemently observed my mother's work. She was preparing the samovar by adding something unknown to me through a small opening, which resembled a chimney. She appeared distant to me. I assumed she was ransacking her mind to determine what friend of Andrei Alexeievich's was coming, and she suddenly shuddered. Perhaps she shuddered because she recalled her question to him while she commenced on the preparations of making our pathetic home somewhat decent. She had asked him in a trembling tone, "What guest Andrei? What friend?"

Needless to say, his remarks were not fit of repeating. She was silenced. She proceeded to pour water into the samovar. I was amazed, and didn't stop looking at this samovar, not even to think of what its production was.

"Oh! The long-awaited guest arrives!" exclaimed Father, upon entering the courtyard from our home, which consisted of taking two small steps. We were all assembled outside, and sitting on large rocks strewn in the yard. Each of us were given a cup of hot water from the samovar, and then we added the concentrated tea (made earlier) to our water. Combined with a transparent piece of lemon, and a lump of sugar, we poured the tea onto the saucer we were provided with, for the tea was too hot to drink from the cup. We sat there biting off some sugar and sipping tea. When Father was home we would usually take tea like this before retiring, save for the samovar.

When we had completed the traditional customary tea, my father invited his friend for a walk in the garden. The expression I exhibited bordered wonderment and sarcasm. What garden, I thought? We have no garden! The landlady had a few pots of flowers, some wilted, which she had arranged at the other side of the courtyard near some bushes. Since when was my father interested in flowers anyway? My childish curiosity led me to a new endeavor—the knowledge of their needed walk. I coyly snuck into a large bush, big and wide enough to hide me. I was overcome with curiosity. What amazing flower does the landlady have in the yard? I musn't move, nor breathe for fear of them noticing me. Of all times, a bug decided to crawl up my pant leg, tickling me incessantly. I didn't move; the bush might quiver and give me away. I peeked through the branches and saw them coming toward me.

Noticing my father's anger by his waving arms while he explained something to his friend, I clenched my teeth and decided to let the bug go where it would, I have to suffer now. The branches in front of my face were no compensation. My knees were sore from the stones beneath them, but I was brave and held out. I started sweating...Father was approaching me, the bush, coming closer and closer. He turned his back to the bush and I breathed a sigh of relief. First I captured the irritating bug, and threw it. Then I moved the stones from underneath me. I was now comfortable and ready to listen. I studied Father's friend; he was short and stubby, unshaven, and owned a rather mean countenance.

"Say, what do you think of the tea, my friend? Did you like it?" my father asked.

"To the devil with you, and your tea! You know precisely why I came here. It was not for the tea!

"Yes, I know. Forgive me, but what do we do now?"

"What do we do now, you ask? How could you permit the general and the countess to baptize your son a few years ago? Are you aware that they had formed a secret council and have constituted plans to destroy the baron? They know of his betrayal to N.K., and know he worked with N.K. in Russia, and also knew that he discovered some concealed information of importance. Now he is engrossed with ambition to dig out the rest. How foolish of you to befriend the general and the countess. These discrepancies are costly!"

"No, I have not befriended them, but...it was necessary—" and the friend interrupted my father angrily.

"—Look, we hired you to disclose everything from her...information, locations, etc., and you have spent so many years recklessly, with nothing to show for it. What have you done for us?" The friend was becoming agitated and glared at my father sternly.

"No....it is not as you think," uttered my father in defense. "I have submitted documents and plans, which I had tucked away in a box I built beneath the roof of the shack you see there. I will not compromise with the baron, for he did not comply with the word he gave me. I will give him what I find when he fulfills his promise to me."

After a few moments of silence, my father began again. "I beseech you not to tell the baron what I am about to tell you. I had found some papers in some kind of coded language amongst her things. I stupidly asked her sister Nina to look at them for me, thinking she could decipher the code or language and innocently provide me with information. She remarked that those were poems written by her father, and that he had a habit of writing poems in a different language. She further commented that she would gladly take them home and translate it for me."

Now the friend of Father's was turning beet red with indignation, and beads of sweat were forming above his eyebrows. I thought he was going to strike my father at any moment. The friend managed to keep his composure and continued...

"Is it possible that you could be so reckless and naive?"

"Listen, understand me. You can see that my wife speaks nonsense now. The drugs I gave her had had such an effect on her. Her ramblings are consistent and incoherent. How can I disclose any kind of information from such a woman? Tell me, how?"

Father had such an innocent look on his face imploring his friend's sympathy.

"Andrei, she is of quality. We have heard all about her from the baron, who visited their home often. She is noble. Zoya is highly educated and received numerous awards for her talents. You know...she could tell us many things if only you knew how to maneuver, or better yet, manipulate her. Find a method of persuading, without drugging her that much."

The friend wisely nodded his head as he uttered the last statement.

"I know, I am aware of her past. She attempted to tell me about it, but I don't have the nerves to hear such things, therefore I increased her dosage twofold."

"I am telling you, Andrei, for your own benefit...decrease the dosage, find out more!"

"Agh, how tired I am," my father complained, and quietly continued... "Her mother, the old hag, visited us too often for my liking. As soon as she noticed me, she would snatch her bag and leave. Running, I tell you! When they were together, they would converse in French, laugh and be merry. I despised her, and she me. I understood a little of their conversation. I am educated as well you know. I was forced to learn French, but wasn't keen on the subject, thus I left the class."

Thinking he made a favorable impression, while boosting his own ego, he actually did quite the opposite. The friend was losing his patience with Father, hence he started loudly, but stopped when realizing the importance of their discussion. He then continued speaking, still angry, but more subdued, "You must try harder I tell you, harder!"

"Well, at least I am rid of the old lady. She died, and we had her buried at the local cemetery."

"I know, we know of that. We were immediately informed, and ordered to conduct a search of her home for any relevant items and of use to us...

"Tell me something, Andrei...how often is she conscious or unconscious for that matter? Does she have any friends she might have confided in?" the friend inquired with a wrinkled forehead.

I was ever so quiet, lost, in their discussion, and eager to hear more; they continued...

"No, no one," my father answered.

"I see. I still cannot understand how you dismissed the mistake of the godparents. She might have confided in them, and who knows how much at that."

"Maybe. I am not certain. I had heard that the countess had left for New York. As for the general, well, I don't know."

"We know of the countess' departure. The baron is quick on these matters," the friend reflected.

"Does the baron know of the general? I am very suspicious of him, you know. I had encountered him one day on the street, and could not relieve myself of his company. He was questioning me persistently—asking about my wife."

"Yes...yes indeed, you are suspicious of the general, but perhaps you alone are withholding matters from us." The friend raised his eyebrow to add leverage to his remark.

"To be truthful, I must sometimes rethink my priorities. Do you, my friend, wholeheartedly trust the baron?"

"That is not of your concern, Andrei. You are to lessen the dosage of the drug you administer to your wife, and allow her to come to her senses; thereby you might actually gain some knowledge and credit beneficial to you, and us."

"Are you insane? If I do as you request, I surely risk being apprehended, because of her probable notification to the authorities. Do you think that if they apprehend me, the baron and yourself would be spared?"

"Stop!" The friend was now visibly shaking, and stuttered his reply to Father... "You mustn't speak that way. Do you realize that with those threats you uttered, the baron would demolish you without batting an eyelid?! Mind your words, and speak as a man.

"Come now, enough talk for tonight. Let us go back to your home. I will contact you with further instructions upon my meeting with the baron," and with that they walked away.

The friend was wiping his forehead with a handkerchief, and Father had folded his hands behind his back, walking slowly, cautiously.

I was stiff as a statue. An hour must have passed during the course of their talk. I strolled to the street and stretched my arms and legs back to life, turned around and went home. I entered the room through the usual entry—the window, and crept into bed. Hundreds of words and ideas were racing in my mind, each fighting for precedence. The shack, I must go there, and find this box Father built that bears such value.

Hurt, confused and amazed would define just a few of the mixed feelings simultaneously presiding in me. My poor, dear mother, she was not well. She often collapsed onto the floor, and us children being weighed with perplexity watch our father dash to her, tie her up (at these times I felt like jumping him), and carry her to the bed.

My siblings and I encircle the bed, all clad in dirty, ripped clothes. On some of us they were too big, and on some too small as we stood and watched in bewilderment. We cried, we hugged each other, and Father would yell at us to leave. Our littlest brother George would continuously cry and scream.

I was immersed with those recollections while flicking a bed bug off my shoulder. We had an abundant supply of these bugs. Mother would often be heard as she killed them during the night. We awoke to smears of blood on the walls and dried blood on our faces and bodies. The stench of those dead bugs was disgusting. What a nuisance they were, as were the fleas and lice. Looking around if there were any more bugs, and assured that I was alone in bed, I dozed off into a sleep.

The sound of giggles and gentle talk of a sweet childish voice welcomed my day. I suddenly remembered all that happened, and of how long I slept...I slept through the day and into the night. I suppose all that excitement was very exhausting for me. I went into the kitchen, a good five steps, and saw my mother sitting and hugging the portrait of her father. I also admired that portrait. He was handsome, had light brown hair, and wore a uniform. A large cross was beneath his chin and he was sitting behind a desk. She was hugging, and swaying, and crying, while whispering something that I couldn't understand, because she was chanting something so softly in a sing-song way. I didn't want to interrupt her, out of fear of her collapsing.

I went outside and found the pretty little girl, the owner of the sweet voice I awoke to. The weather was fair, but that didn't amuse me, nor did anything else in the courtyard except for the pretty girl, who was still playing and singing and didn't notice me right away.

I had a crush on her. She was very pretty with golden blonde locks and happy, blue eyes. She was always clean, and garbed in such pretty dresses with matching ribbons in her hair for that particular dress for the day. She was the landlady's daughter.

Besides playing, she was enjoying fresh, white—indeed— white bread spread with homemade jam. My eyes nearly jumped out of their sockets. My mouth watered uncontrollably. I scared poor Danica (that was her name). I know I did, because she jumped back. I must have looked like a hungry wolf, a carnivore that was dressed like a pauper, barefoot and all. Her mother noticed us outside, and quickly called out her name while motioning her to come in. As she went she flung her treat to the ground. Like a scavenger I attacked the food, eating without breathing, gulping and savoring every bite, the bread, the jam and the dirt off the ground that stuck to it. After this delicacy, and quite content, even at the loss of my pretty friend, I continued to my intended direction.

Walking solemnly along the sidewalk, down the street to work, to beg, for dinner, my head hung low, bumping into the occasional post, in deep contemplation. So much...so much had happened since that friend of my father's from P— came. Vechislav is gone, Olga is gone...and our father...is somewhere, but not home. And where, oh where is our mother? Who took our beloved mother?

Chapter 4

I was sitting on a foot stool, resting my head on my hands and scrutinizing my Auntie Nina. She was applying her make-up with such thought and care. Mesmerized in this whole procedure, I examined all the contents on her dressing table—the perfume bottles, the brushes, make-up and other toiletries. Auntie was busy, lovingly picking up, using, then gently returning the product to its place.

The dressing table laden with her personal goodies was an appurtenant fixture to the remainders of the abode. Her small mansardi (as commonly called) was clean, cozy and constituted a worn out, yet smart sofa, a table with four chairs and other corresponding knick-knacks sporadically placed, emitting a homey feel. A colourful rug covered the wooden floor and one hung directly above the smart sofa. Her apartment had a unique partition, which Auntie made herself out of curtains that hid a tiny area where she would prepare her single-serving meals. This she would do on an electrical iron hot plate. True, she did have a stove, but that stove was only to be used as a heating device, not otherwise, and was duly constructed to conform to this rule. Understandably, the landlord had installed these mini stoves appropriate to the apartments. Thus, her partition hiding the culprit—the iron hot plate, for all were obliged to diligently adhere to the code of conduct, whereby the premises were for sleeping in and nothing else.

The city apartment buildings were basically constructed in

such a manner that stoves were placed in designated locations beside a wall, which concealed the interior chimney shaft. The cylinders probed through the wall, into the shaft where all the cumulus smoke of the building exited. There weren't buildings with central air in these common dwellings, but the inner city's buildings did possess them, whereas they would have a large oven or furnace that required constant feeding of wood and coal and constant cleaning. Thus, there were workers for that particular task. The tenants of the more common buildings were assigned a small locker in the basement, placable for their supply of wood and coal.

Our stove at home provided dual services: to cook and heat. Beside every stove was usually found a small pail containing the day's supply of wood and coal, and near that was a tiny broom (brush) and dust pan to conveniently sweep up stray ashes.

An indication of cleanliness and dexterity was measured by the shine of the stove's cylinders, which became a focal point in every home. A black chemical paste smelling of turpentine was used on these cylinders and by rubbing them and polishing them to a lustrous shine. This waxy base was referred to most often as "blackener." The wealthier folks would even have this paste applied to the tops of their stoves, showing that they were in a position to do so and able to afford it. Yet another task for the servants, who were reprimanded severely by their masters if the stove was not up to par after the daily inspections.

Russian stoves were one step ahead, they offered triple duty. It was an appliance to cook on, heat the abode with and a bed to sleep on, on those freezing northern nights. Those stoves were built with a platform on the top, providing a bed when a mattress was thrown on top. I heard of these unusual stoves from the many stories of my parents.

The better situated had "kameens" built for them (a type of fireplace). Its construction consisted of a wall specially made for the kameen and bearing a recess within it, which held the actual fire. Stretching from the floor to just below the ceiling, this kameen was strategically placed so as to evenly disperse the heat throughout the home. The kameens were a valuable commodity and signified the owner's success. The facade of the wall was made of expensive porcelain tiles, sometimes imported, which further validated the owner's progress. At the foot of this structure was a sheet of copper meant for decor more than purpose, nevertheless it served for the occasional stray cinder or ash. This item was also to be kept in its highest sheen possible. Woe to the servants.

Visiting Auntie Nina's home required agility and perseverance to name a few. The climbing of the three long flights of stairs to be exact. On each floor's landing was a button on the wall meant for pushing the lights on, thereby permitting one to envision the next set of ascending stairs. If at some time I were slow to reach the second landing and push the next button, I was forced to crawl the remaining steps and search the wall for the button in the unwelcoming pitch black atmosphere.

"Vitya, stop staring at me! Don't you know that it is very impolite to observe a lady's preparations?" Auntie declared and shook me from my recluse of serene observation. Profoundly overwhelmed at the skill apparently vital to the art of make-up application and how beautiful her already pretty face looked with this enhancement, induced me to become glad and suddenly proud of my Auntie.

"Come now, I will give you your dinner, then you can retire for the night," she softly informed, realizing that she had startled me earlier. I happily ate the provisions in front of me, consisting of soup, some potatoes and a meatball cutlet. Ahhh...what luxury, I thought. All this was followed by a crisply sheeted bed, boasting an actual pillow! So unlike the rags we use at home for pillows. Auntie put together a few boxes in the pantry, a thin mattress on top and, behold, a bed! Before I lapsed into a deliciously sweet repose, I recalled the bragging of my brother Alex when he would visit Auntie and how I can simply now claim the same.

I greeted the next day in a cheerful mode, satisfied of rest and hunger. Surveying the surroundings, I spotted Auntie still asleep on the sofa. She must have had a busy night working selling flowers, I thought. Auntie's residence was on Dalmatinska Street and the cafés she frequented were two to three kilometres in distance. She resided in a more newer development of the suburbs. I assumed she travelled to and from work by trolley streetcar, which luckily was heated during the winter months by a stove in the centre of the vehicle. I often rode on it, but not as a paying passenger; I clung on to the rear of the car as a magnet! I practised this with passing fiacres also, depending on my intended direction; either or would suffice. There was a sprinkle of the occasional odd car, here and there, but the general public chiefly relied on the two aforementioned forms of transport. I often rejoiced in the coachman's or driver's oblivion to my presence and, consequently, I was mobile.

The popular café or tavern, Russian Tsar, was Auntie's main target of profit. Its exterior was brightly lit and had a true Cossack standing at the entry, not as a precaution—nonetheless useful should the need arise, but as a relevant fixture in symmetry to the ambiance intended. His bright uniform with a golden satin track running along the sides of his trousers, which were neatly tucked into a shiny pair of leather boots that reached the knee, endowed him with a majestic aura of a time gone by. He wore a papaha on his head. This tall, woolen hat called 'papaha' was exclusively manufactured for the Cossacks.

The procedure to manufacture such an important accessory required the caesarean section of an impregnated sheep and removing the tight, shiny black curls of the unborn lamb. This they called "afghan's wool" and it was very expensive. On the Cossack's papaha was a Russian crest bearing a double-headed eagle.

The Cossack's second purpose was to courteously open and shut the doors for the distinguished patrons of the café. The discerning crowd was prevalent with their satin top hats, luxurious fur coats and precious jewels, lest their protruding chins in the air displaying their importance to the deplorable onlookers be unnoticed. Their ostentatious manners wreaked of honor and prestige that they bestowed upon likewise to the onlookers as to the café's owner himself as if privileging them with a favour of an audience.

Within the doors of this magnificent café was a plush, scarlet red carpet, and when followed, would lead to the smiling matron who wore the traditional Russian rubashka. When referring to this garment, one must never omit the word "Russian" for the significance of the garment is lost. This shirt was made of Japanese silk and other fine materials, embroidered and worn loosely tied by a golden rope at the waist (depending on the owner). The Tsar was often seen fashioning the Russian rubashka. Seamstresses were always occupied producing these shirts alone to accommodate the many demands.

The hosts escorted the genteel crowd through a room filled with exaggerated laughter as the song "Mimoza" was being sung by the renown singer that gained her fame with this famous song and by her canary voice. The lingering aroma of expensive cigars and cigarettes merging with the sweet scents of French and other exotic perfumes was commonplace at the Russian Tsar.

Forgetting the pretext of their assembly, the newly-arrived patrons were induced to enjoy an admirable evening. White damask tablecloths blanketed the tables and were laden with an array of crystal stemware, highly polished silverware and an elegant lit candelabra, providing a semi-dark atmosphere, adding to the charm of the tavern. These splendours awaited and welcomed the expected honorable diners.

Many a waitress were hurriedly dashing about catering to the visitors with their famous "piroshkas" and "borscht" that the city raved of. Upon whisking by, the windy fragrance of the sumptuous meal did not interfere with the café's own traditional scent, rather complimented it. The staff at the café were rushing to and fro, nearly prostrating themselves at the feet of their guests, knowing a generous gratuity was based on their achievement of hospitality and service.

Based on mutual agreement between my Auntie and the owner of the café, Auntie was permitted to visit each table and offer an exquisite rose, or any favourable flower matching the lady's dress or demeanor, for sale. Immediately, the gentlemen would provide payment, paying no mind to the change of his bill, thus not risking his cavalier disposition to his companion, or any possible observer in the café. Auntie was grateful to the owner for allowing her to sell flowers there and in return he received compensation: a percentage of her earnings. I later understood the faultless, paradoxical achievements and notably better establishment of Auntie's to our exiguous lifestyle and living quarters, which now was incredulous to me. This profit-pouring hot spot was located on the intersections of King Milan and Great Milosh streets.

Two blocks from this café was the notable King's palace,

where two immaculately dressed guards, all in white fur hats and a protruding white feather, stood immobile at the sides of the doorway. Adjacent to this splendor was an artifact known as Parliament Building, where at the front stood an ample statue of a galloping horseman. Indeed, there were many noteworthy places to visit if one had the opportunity and money to do so.

I was walking absentmindedly along Dimitriya Tutsevicha Street, when I struck an iron post with my forehead. That smarted! I stopped, shook my head and resumed my solemn walk. This street led directly to the outskirts of the city onto a hill, which was famed for the natural spring of the most delicious, ice-cold water. They named this spring after an historical even. It was called "The Third Uprising (Revolt) Against the Ottoman Empire Spring or Faucet" (the name is much longer when translated in English).

Continuing along the road, which led me straight home, I watched the city workers repair and replace some cobblestones on the road with hammers and cudgels. They toiled to level the stones, brought by the ox and wagon. Meanwhile, other city workers were trying to manipulate the large pipes aligning the sides of the road. Their goal was to bury the pipes, which the natural spring's water from the hill ran through and supplied the residents with fresh water. These pipes stretched as far as the Danube River.

Observing one of these workers, who was melting in the heat of the sun and who snatched a dingy rag from his back pocket to wipe his greasy forehead, I watched him smile as he heard a man cry, "Boza, Boza!" Immediately the workder turned around and acknowledged the street vendor who instantly poured him a refreshment of Boza from the tap of his mini-barrel while nodding his head. How lucky he is, I thought.

Boza was a drink made from cornmeal flour, sweetened with sugar and other spices and cooled with crushed ice. I terribly wished I could afford one and envied him bitterly. Vendors knew where the money was, while never refusing a passer-by added to their successful sales.

Corn on the cob, roasted or cooked as to the purchaser's specifications, and sweet popcorn balls, the size of an adult's fist, glazed with coloured sparkling crystal sugar that some fortunate child had the opportunity to enjoy, was another vendor's product. There were djevreks, too. These large, hot pretzels had chunks of crystal salt on them and were among the popular street treats. Boza was not to be found in restaurants, nor stores, only on the street. It was homemade and sold proudly by the chef himself. The middle to lower-class citizens had these enjoyments more often than any. I stared at them eating and drinking and, in particular, the popcorn ball that glistened its sweet colourful savor in the sun and happily painted the face of the lucky child.

It was truly a handsome street. The posing trees provided their large leaves as canopies, shading pedestrians from the sweltering heat and burning sun. I strolled past rackety, low houses, and some of them possessed a small barn in their backyards, where a few running chickens and maybe a moping pig could be envisioned. The owners of the houses, most often employed by the city, were the chief providers and laboriously supplied the bread and butter to their families. These houses were so old that one could comfortably note in a phrase of their equivalence to the times of "Maria Theresa."

There were many stores that provoked admiration, particularly a well-established bakery that I visited every now and then. This fine bakery sold delicious fresh bread, baked in the twilight hours by the baker, who lovingly set the loaves aside for the day's sale. He sold bread by the kilo and if it weighed more than the requested amount by the customer, he would nonchalantly cut off a piece and chuck it to the floor where I would be waiting, like a mouse to snatch the piece. And how wonderful that was! Previously, the baker had prepared a sufficient amount of bread, rolls and other baked goods to be delivered by horse and carriage to the core of the city as was common to do. Servants would be chatting with each other and patiently waiting for the arrival of the baker and goods to be taken to their master's breakfast table. This service was exclusive to the wealthy clientele.

Finally, reaching home, I ran through the courtyard remembering the bump on my forehead and I was in no need of any encounters with nosy neighbours to question me. The kitchen door (our entry) was open, for we never locked the door, nor needed to. I merrily grabbed Father's beret, which he forgot, and to my benefit, and placed it on my head to conceal the bump. Not a moment went by when I heard Mother's voice. She was having a confrontation with the landlady. That old witch, I thought. Mother entered after she had agreed to talk to me and discipline me. The landlady viciously complained of my running and gladly reminded Mother of the strict rules concerning such courtyard matters. She had no alternative but to agree, shaking off the annoying landlady.

Mother carried some fishnet bags in her hands, which she dropped abruptly when noticing the beret on my head.

"Vitya! Take off the beret instantly! You know the rules. No hats allowed indoors!"

Numerous inquisitions befell upon me when I removed the beret. Between, "how did you do that? Tell me what happened? What were you thinking?" I tried to maintain an innocent composure.

Mother furiously began tumbling through the drawer of the credenza. She whipped out a metal spatula intended to treat by its cooling effect and shrink the bump on my head, which was now a rainbow of colours. Mother rigorously believed this old-fashioned remedy, while I on the other hand was tugging away from her grasp, caused by the additional pain of this remedy.

Incessantly, I pleaded with her not to tell my father about my mishap while she was busy nursing my head. I knew of the two previous convictions, and Father's rule of thumb was that as soon as three unpardonable demeanors were collected, the humiliating and painful punishment of us bending over the kitchen chair, bare of course, and whipped with the belt, would begin. We had to stand in line for this!

Mother was not concentrating on my implorations; she was devoted to diminishing the sore on my head. Recalling my previous actions now in sequential line and forwarding the ultimate sentence was Danica: Yes, she was the pretty girl, with long blonde hair and blue eyes in the courtyard. She knew very well of her fairness and that I was attracted to her. Thus she would coquettishly stroll by our window hesitatingly and tease me. Her bread was the cause of my conviction. She had cried to her mother that I ate her bread and jam, even though she dropped it to the ground first, before she ran inside to her mother's calls. That, in combination with the restrictions of us being together and the prohibition of her to be anywhere near us, by her parents, concluded the first misdemeanour.

My second mistake entailed my profound interest in the mechanical and technical functions of the newly-acquired-and-installed French toilets. This new device, so envied by all, was the cause of gossip throughout the neighbourhood. When these toilets were being installed by workers, onlookers would stop to marvel at the masterpiece. Naturally, by the gate was the landlord who accepted all merit and honour for being one of the first in the neighbourhood to own such a thing. He was ridiculously intoxicated of himself, for his head swelled, and from all the smiling he oozed saliva from the corners of his mouth. That did not deter my probe and inspection. Hence one day I was to satisfy my curiosity, at least partially in respect to those much-talked-about French toilets!

Entering the outhouse near the back of the courtyard, key in hand and with strong determination to solve the question that so bewildered me, I opened the stall. The fourth one being ours, I stood there gawking and inspecting the masterpiece. The tank (reservoir) was hanging off the wall above my head. There was a thin chain to pull and flush the toilet. Good. But there was only one pipe! The water goes up to the tank through this pipe and then comes down the same way? I was amused and simultaneously confused at this system. Decidedly, I climbed onto the seat of the toilet, and grabbed the top of the tank with my fingers while pulling myself up to uncover the mystery of the pipes.

During the course of my acrobatic endeavours I disengaged the tank from the wall and came tumbling down. The tank, the water and I, unitedly. Needless to say, I was soaked. I ran from the scene as fast as the wind would take me. Anywhere, but not there.

I found myself at the piazza. The piazza was nearly vacant of its vendors and customers. All had left, but the very few that take forever to pack their merchandise and leave were taking their time, waving to each other and bidding adue. I hid under the kiosk. I sat there for hours. Night fell. I immersed myself in the burdensome task of resolving the problem. Money...plumber...I have neither. I ransacked my brain for any possible solutions that would save me from Father's scorn and, worse, belt. I finally resolved to bear my judgement, be brave and head home.

The lights were on in the kitchen of our apartment. I peeked in as a burglar would, through the corner of the window. Mother was holding George in her arms as he lay fast asleep. Father sat there shaking his leg at the kitchen table and his pants demonstrated this by their quiver. His eyes were ricocheting from rage and fury, like poisoned darts.

"Where is the bandit? Where is that little bandit? He has many answers to give me, very many I tell you!" Father remarked in a loud, hostile voice.

Forgetting my composure, I coughed and Mother noticed. Her immediate glance toward the window assured me. She directed me with her eyes to the bedroom, signalling for me to enter through the window, while diverting Father's attention with trivial questions that suddenly seemed very relevant, "Andrei, why did you not buy the extra milk I need for George?"

Thus, I was saved by my mother's quick thinking. Later, I had heard that Mother had informed my father that I was asleep the entire time in the bedroom and that I must have crept in earlier that evening.

The antagonism between my parents, clearly visible to many, formed an additional barrier between them and procured inhibition to any sojourner. It was quite obvious that they were not meant for each other. She was warm, kind and intelligent and he cool and cunning. Even we had noticed the irony in his voice and patronizing methods he utilized toward her. We had trouble understanding what particular qualities they shared aside from us children, that brought them and kept them united.

Anyhow, returning to the two previous errors of mine that were now enhanced by this third error: the bump, naturally including the fact that my carelessness and leisure and (duly noted by the obnoxious landlady) of running in the yard would unfortunately catch up to me. I knew that, but decided to think about more pleasing thoughts; hopefully it would help me fall asleep...

Grandmama and Auntie Nina were at our home one day as I recall, the cause being no other than my father's absence. Auntie quickly pulled out the samovar (yes, I saw it once more!). Grandmama sat down tiredly as elderly people have the tendency to do so, with a sigh. Her old, yet graceful, face still shadowed a once serene and noble beauty. Knowledge, experience and wisdom were defined by the deep-set wrinkles that appeared as honourable and well-earned trademarks of the difficult years abroad.

My siblings and I merrily gathered around the table and fought over the chair next to Grandmama's. I won. We began sipping our tea from the saucers (as mentioned before, for the tea was too hot, thus we used the saucer), nibbling on a lump of sugar and fully prepared for the forthcoming emotional conversations.

Auntie had taken the portrait of Grandpapa off the wall and we all knew what discussions were about to ensue.

"Agh, my dear girls, my sweet girls. What lives you lived before. Such a contrast and bitter judgement that you and I are here and not with your father." Grandmama began the usual wiping of tears, followed by sniffles, followed by nose blowing and then remarked, "What a wretched fate we have. You know, children of mine," now she was addressing my siblings and myself, "your grandfather, yes...he was such a good man...*sniff, sniff*...a very good man. He often visited the Tsar's palace and was personally awarded the honour of the cross of

St. George, you see here!" She pointed to us, with her finger on the portrait of Grandpapa. In the same disposition, she commenced, "What is of my Tamara? Dear God, what is of her? We only received two letters from her and then she stopped writing. She does not reply to our mail. Why was she that stubborn to go to France on her own?"

We all were respectfully silent, until Mother broke the lucid trance... "I remember...I remember when the governess and tutors gave us lectures in French and other languages and art. All the dances we had to learn—quadrille, polonaise, mazurka...for what? In vain were all those lessons I tell you. Of what practicality and benefit is it to me now? I also miss Anushka," she whispered as she stared at her mother, in anticipation of an agreeable answer.

"Enough! Enough of that, Zoya," snapped Auntie, then she continued. "You wanted all those classes and lectures and lessons in art!"

"True. And Nina...you were envious!"

"If you must know, Zoya, my envy didn't lie in your praiseworthy art, but with the captain, whom you were insouciantly fascinated with."

"Nina, I didn't plan to marry him, but...you see, I..."

"Children! Stop that!" Grandmama intervened and the subject was dropped.

Grandmama commented that they must try to forget what happened then and only remember and acknowledge the bravery of their father, including the captain, who vanished during the battle in Russia. The ending of Grandmama's statement produced and induced a torrential downpour of tears, sniffling, head shaking and shoulder shuddering, while we (my siblings and I) sat there with our mouths hanging open in synchronization and resting our heads on our hands engrossed in their discussions and displays of emotion.

"Zoya! Where is that Andrei of yours?" Grandmama growled, while sniffling. "You are left here with all these children, my dear Zoya, and you are forced to wash other people's laundry and floors and scavenge the piazza for discarded food. Where is he? Where, Zoya?"

Mother sternly implored Gradmama to silence by putting her finger on her mouth and casting her eyes on us. Grandmama turned silent, she was indignant, but silent. She looked at the floor, she understood that she said too much.

Father had already practised coming and going and we were becoming accustomed to his ways. Unfortunately, my eldest brother Vechislav was gone. I heard that following one of their many heated arguments (Father's and Vechislav's). Vechislav had no option, but to leave. I also heard that he was residing with the church's custodian. Mother, steadfast in her belief of his return, as all mother's tend to do, would systematically, after supper, walk outside to the gate of the courtyard and wait as minutes and hours ticked by.

I followed Mother the first few times, curious where she was going, and found her standing there at the gate, all raggedy in her black skirt and torn and thinned hanging shirt, which hung on her more with each passing day. Her head followed the motions of the night, passing vehicles and pedestrians. A few shouts would bounce in the darkness of the night and she would turn to look toward the noise, but all in vain. Her favourite, her firstborn, didn't come back and never would. This she did every night, each time returning with her feet dragging and her head bowed low to her chest, sobbing bitterly. After many of her loyal attempts of waiting, she had grown tired, ill and hopeless.

We very seldom saw Vechislav and had become adjusted somewhat to this matter, whether due to our constant burden of providing food, or our new concern...Olga.

It was a dark and gloomy day, forlorn and heavy of misery. I was not in a much better state, lacking ambition for the day's work or begging, though very necessary for our survival. I heard George's cries in the next room, the kitchen. I went to inquire as to why his cries were not tended to.

I saw only him. George was on the bed, crying. I picked him up and looked around for any tell-tale signs of the reason

George and I were alone. Nothing. While pondering, I assumed that Mother had left for the piazza, but that didn't explain Olga's absence. A rapping on the window of the door stirred me from my thinking. I opened it and saw our familiar neighbour: Auntie Katya. She really wasn't our aunt, but it was unheard of that children address elders by their names, thus were expected to add either aunt or uncle preceding the name of the person.

Auntie Katya walked into the kitchen, while surveying the room with her eyes, finally resting them on the two of us. The orphans. She inquired of my siblings and I answered her truthfully. "I don't know," was my quiet reply.

"Fine, I will take George, and you, Vitya, remain here." With authority she proceeded to take George out of my enveloped embrace and left with him, closing the door behind her.

Auntie Katya lived near the end of the courtyard, right next to the laundry room. This served as a convenience to her, but in the summer months the additional heat wasn't welcoming. In this laundry room there was an over-sized pot where clean clothes were cooked in boiling water as to disinfect. The busy housewife, handkerchief tied around her head, would busily stir the stew of garments whose domain it was now. She lifted the smoking items with the long stick and placed them in a colander to drain and cool, ready for hanging outside.

On laundry days it was well known that children were not to be seen in the courtyard. This was standard procedure. A child lost in play once knocked over the stick holding up the line of clean clothes, causing the clothes to fall and become dirty. The owner of the clothing would dash outside and begin cursing through clenched teeth, then look at the culprit and admonish him. He was forced to collect all the clean and dirty clothes and re-rinse them all. The extra labour was then reported to the landlords and very strict regulations were suddenly imposed regarding laundry day rules in the courtyard.

Auntie Katya, whom took George from me, was a middle-aged woman. Not pretty at all, rather frightening. Her two pools of ebony dark eyes and raven black hair scrunched beneath the black handkerchief that matched her black attire, summoned a gloom and eery countenance. She was dressed all in black due to her mourning of her husband's passing. Luckily we (I) knew her and was not scared of her appearance at our door.

I decided to exit our home of continual mystery and breathe some fresh air. I began walking toward the gate of the courtyard and unintentionally brushed the landlady with my shoulder. She was either cleaning, or arranging something and was stooped over. I, not being tall yet, was able to brush her with my shoulder and startled her. She stood up and turned around to look at the cause of her interruption. Quizzically she looked at me and suddenly manifested a pleasant and charming appearance, while she inquired, "oh, Vitya, how are you today, dear?" I believe the shock on my face was not concealed and quite visible. I had never experienced such an encounter with her. I witnessed her pleasant attitude toward others and knew her attitude toward us, therefore, I assumed it was quite natural for her to own two different and separate sets of stances for two different sets of people. I had never expected such a display of courtesy toward me.

She asked, "Where are your siblings?" Then the slap came, "I'm sorry about your mother, Vitya."

I believe I had an instantaneous shower of sweat and was burning of horror.

"Don't worry, dear, she will be well. They will take good care of her at the hospital."

Finally, I realized that another seizure took place and Mother was taken to the hospital, but by whom? I turned to ask the landlady—who had already left after patting my head—but the question remained unanswered.

It was too late. I left the courtyard and began to think...Father is not here anymore. He must have decided that he had done enough damage to my poor mother. Vechislav is not here, thanks be to Father, and Olga is gone, but where? And how did Mother take herself to the hospital? I walked tripping on the loose stones on the sidewalk and bumped into my brother Alex.

"Alex! I have to tell you..."

"Vitya, if you only knew what luck I had. I found a job a few streets down, selling papers, and you—"

"Stop, Alex, stop! I must tell you, let me tell you first."

"All right, settle down, tell me."

"Well, you see...George is gone and, and...Olga is gone and—"

"What? You are mumbling, Vitya, I can't understand you, slow down. Here, let's sit on the curb and you slowly tell me."

"Fine. You see...this morning I was alone with George, then Auntie Katya came and..." I proceeded to inform Alex of all information I had.

"Hmm....I think we shall go directly to Auntie Katya's and find some answers, Vitya."

We both stood up, firm in our resolution, and continued to Auntie Katya's home. We arrived at Auntie Katya's and, thankfully, she answered our never-ending questions that we poured on her.

Olga was taken by those gentlemen and ladies whom we had seen earlier at our home, who Father chased away. They took her to the White Monastery. Why? We don't know. Auntie Nina was at our home last night. She stopped by after selling her flowers, to check up on us knowing that she could now, for Father wasn't there to prevent her. Mother lapsed into a frantic seizure and Auntie Nina had her taken to the hospital. Not such comforting news, nevertheless, we at least had some kind of knowledge now.

Mother was in the general psychiatric hospital located in the midst of the city. On occasion, I would visit her, but my visits were curtailed by more burdensome chores. My hunger and the roof over our heads had to be looked after. I wasn't certain if Father had taken care of the rent and I wasn't in a position to ask the landlord, out of fright and worry of his answer. I spent many spare moments reflecting on matters of survival and the impending winter months.

Chapter 5

Mother's return home was pleasant to us, although we still had the fear looming over our heads if she were to be seized with a fit again. Father's existence was verified when he might have decided to show up a couple of times, only to depart again to some destination known only to him. Alex and I continued our usual pauper ways. Begging for alms, if lucky working and the days went by in such.

School no longer imposed an obstacle to our sustenance. We did rarely visit though and that we did only because of the breakfast offered. The school gave breakfasts to the poorest of children, thus we were able to have something in our stomachs, at least in the morning, but as to the matter of the evening; that was a dilemma. If we did decide to attend school bright and early for breakfast, we were obliged to attend the rest of the school day, which sometimes involved a whipping of the hand, due to our ignorance and to our incomplete homework assignments. A hefty price for a breakfast, plus we needed to feed our sick mother and George, too, therefore attending school was not always the wisest choice.

George was returned to us by Auntie Katya after a few days of Mother's arrival home. Hence our need to work more; it was selfish of us to attend school.

Strenuously, Mother would go to get us food from the butcher shop. She did return at times with bones and the skins of ham not needed and discarded by the butcher. She happily prepared this meal for us and we were truly grateful to her for her efforts. Not long after the splendid evening of dining on bones and skins and following our return home from our usual begging, Mother had suddenly reproached us. She was glad, however, since we had delivered some dinars to her, but she warned us of the new law that she had learned of when she visited the butcher shop.

The government affixed a notice on shops prohibiting begging as Mother told us, "I, my children, had the dishonour of having this notice pointed out to me by the butcher. He gently warned me by pointing his finger to the fresh notice attached to his window and proceeded to quail my cries of sorrow with some bones and skin. Therefore, my dears, do not attempt to enter these shops and beg, lest you be arrested."

"Mother," we both simultaneously answered her, filled with determination to prove her wrong in her assumptions, "Mother, listen, we are no longer begging, but working! We are able fellows and we shall earn our keep. Don't worry."

She looked at us standing there, dirty and raggedy, yet smiling, and lovingly said through her tears in a monotone voice, "My day will come...the day will come."

"What day?" I implored, but she didn't answer me. She began, "Nevermind, dear, just nevermind..."

Alex and I had heard on several occasions the repetition of those words, spoken as a premonition of some kind, of an unknown event that would alter, change and correct all injustices, poverty and ignorance. We pondered Alex and I, but were more involved in the monotonous burden of hunger and its appeasement.

We were faced with injustice with every turn we took. Our attire provoked ridicule and scorn from our peers. Our grumbling stomachs spoke before we had a chance to, provoking giggles. We were even shamelessly ridiculed by our miserable teacher in school, who hit us at any given opportunity, though he had a bagful of that. To disgrace us, because we were poor and hungry? Such cruel insults were added to our sufferings, to our injuries. We were cast aside by our peers and treated as aliens. Them being one step above our destitution by owning a pair of shoes, and we did not. Or that some had even owned two pairs of pants and we didn't. Thus we were condemned by peers, teachers, onlookers and regarded as paupers and street urchins of the lowest possible class. Such prejudice from such a society, I thought...I cried.

We struggled in our mission to survive. We had no play. No such thing, no time. We did observe on occasion the joy of the children playing and laughing, but we hesitatingly walked away to our destination of employment. We were diligent in our quest for food as the lioness is to feed her cubs, or as other carnivores are in the task of providing for their offspring. Gradually we became oblivious to consternation and were plagued with constant threats of starvation. We sought work, fighting not to succumb to the fate handed us. We knocked on many doors where the owner, noticing our garb, would either brush us away as pesky flies, or with a kind, uninviting smile would escort us out to from where we came in. At the odd time our luck became prevalent and we earned a few dinars selling newspapers, or doing odd jobs for innkeepers. During these times and precious moments we were very proud of our ability and accomplishments and would run home to Mother with our earnings.

Sunday. Alex and I embarked on our journey to the church. On the main street of King Alexander were the streetcars, which for today were our method of transportation. We clung on the back of the car, onto the step, and hung on the air pipes of the streetcars. When we heard *ding, ding,* we knew the conductor pulled the string and would be stopping to let off and pick up passengers. Thus we fell off the car, withdrew, so as not to cause suspicion, and leapt back on when the car began moving.

"Agh, Alex, my feet are sore from all this jumping and leaping," I complained, for we both were barefoot.

We arrived at the church of St. Mark's, a large beautiful,

white church, though not our destination. Behind this church was a little Russian church, The Holy Trinity. Alex and I would mingle in between the devoted parishioners in line for the taking of the Holy bread, which was given after mass. Beside us in line was a raggedy old man with long, greasy hair and a long, greasy beard. He didn't smell very good either, a raunchy smell floated about him. He wore an old torn overcoat where a bottle was peering out of the inner pocket. On his feet he wore some old dirty, grey army boots—probably black at one time, which he had tied up with some rope, lest the sole of his boot is lost. I looked at him and wondered. It was summer, hot, and yet he was dressed in such a manner? I wanted to move from him, but had no way of doing so with the crowd on the left and right of me. Briskly, I pushed my brother Alex in my place and I took his. Suddenly I noticed that people were throwing change in the greasy man's hat, that he held turned upward, to catch the flying money.

Realizing the old man's intentions, I followed suit. I protruded my hand and a very pretty lady put a coin directly in the palm of my hand. I quickly put it in my pocket, then returned my hand in the same manner as before. When, again! I received a coin! The joy! I nudged Alex and whispered to him, "Stick out your hand, idiot." Alex, being hesitant for a moment, finally gave in and stuck out his hand. He, too, received a dinar, but because of his hesitation, the people had nearly left the line and no more alms were given. I looked at the old man, who was also looking at me beneath his bushy and dingy greyish-white eyebrows. He spat on the ground and we ran.

We proceeded to the front of the first church we passed earlier: St. Mark's. We noticed that there were many people standing outside and dressed in elegant and wonderful clothes. The children, too, were smartly attired. Little boys, clean and pressed, and little girls with bouncy dresses and matching ribbons were obediently standing in anticipation. The mothers of these children, upon noticing us standing there, would come and take hold of their child and tug them away from us, not permitting us to think that we could actually join in the fun. We waited patiently. We knew what was happening. A wedding. All the ceremonies were over and the wedding party was beginning to exit the church. Then the maids of honour would exit as did the bride and groom and, finally...what we were patiently waiting for—the best man. The tradition was that the best man would throw a bag of money in the air and allow it to fall where it may, scattering all over the paved ground, where the anxious children (from the wedding party) would gleefully run about to collect their winnings. This is where Alex and I stepped in. We stood like two motionless cats, observing. When the money came down, so did we, on all fours, and we hurriedly collected as much as we could. We worked hard and had our hands walked upon, but that was a minor nuisance to us in comparison to our great acquirement. We were radiant with joy. We had a good day, indeed a good day. We pranced home, jubilant of our success, nearly illuminated because of our prosperity.

I didn't sleep well that night. In the morning, I felt a throbbing pain in my right toe. I got up to look at it and it was bluish-red. I repeatedly hurt that ill-fated toe several times. I found Mother in the kitchen. She was yet again hugging her father's portrait and crying in the same familiar sing-song way.

"Why do you cry now, Mother?"

"Vitya! Did you forget that today is the anniversary of your beloved grandmama's passing?"

She looked at me entreatingly, with her cheeks glistening of tears. She didn't need to remind me—I painfully knew and had tears of my own.

"Yes, Mother, I know my grandmama is gone and not with us anymore." I sobbed even more upon uttering those last words.

Since I needed no preparation, I slept in street clothes as we all did; therefore, I grabbed my books, deciding I would chance to visit the school today. Besides, I was too sad to do otherwise. The usual occurrence at school awaited me without fail: the shunning, the teasing and all, but that passed by, or I didn't let it bother me too much that day.

After school, Alex and I met up and quietly walked to a location we had earlier chosen for the day's pleadings. We had constructed a verse, which we used when we cried for alms: "Sir...please, sir or madam...we have no father, he left us. Our mother is sick. We are of four children, please help us," while our dirty hands were cupped, awaiting generosity. With these statements we managed to make a lot more than simply holding out our hands silently. We, therefore, provided Mother with a plentitude of bread, which she dried in the oven and stored away for future use and for the days Alex and I were unable to beg and work.

My foot, or toe that is, did not cease to bother me. I remembered my grandmama's words when I visited her one afternoon before her passing. Because she caught me limping and inquired of my limp, I showed her my toe and she flew into a panic.

"Vitya! Your toe!"

"Yes, Grandmama, my toe."

"What happened, child? Oh...oh my...oh my." She was racing around me, confused as to what new method was to be partaken in the treatment of my toe. She stopped and mumbled with a final conclusion. "Lard. Pig's lard. That will be the thing. That is the cure!" she professed with an air of authority.

Grandmama began to question me of my family's whereabouts and the usual questions one asks pertaining to the day's events, but I left her not listening and mumbled a good-bye, closing the door behind me. That is how I ended that visit with my dear, dear grandmama.

Now, I looked at this same toe and wondered what I should do? It had taken the form of a purple balloon. I went to the piazza, limping on my right heel. I sat on the curb to rest and thought to ask the passers-by for help, anyone who would tell me where I might find this mysteriously charmed lard. It was hurting and throbbing of pain and I began to cry. Some of the onlookers would glance at me in an implorative way, some not even that. But one kind gentleman stopped after hearing my cries and leaned down to face me. He had an amicable aura to him and his pleasant face confirmed that. "Why do you cry, my child?"

"Look, sir, look at my toe! I have no magic lard and I have no money!" I was now hiccupping with tears.

The kind man, so gentle and sincere, provided me with ten dinars. Silver dinars! Unfathomable! I had never seen such a sum in a silver coin. I thanked him profusely. Now...I thought, I can give this money to Mother to buy the magical lard at the pharmacy. Why, that man must know of the importance of this cure and of its expense. I must have been an eyeful to him dressed in dingy, torn clothes, bruised all over, barefoot and my bonus ailing toe, perhaps the combination constituted sympathy.

I limped and hopped with my silver coins back home, but found no one there. What now? I have the money. I have no method of obtaining this darn, magical lard. I cried again. Wait...I know! I know who will help me, I know where to go! I quickly limped and jumped and hopped to the local cemetery. Far back by the fence was a bright, white cross signalling Grandmama's resting place. I arrived.

I sat by the grave and began my outpour of cries, complaints and questions, every so often stopping to catch my breath. "Grandmama, help me! My toe! Remember my toe...look, it's worse! I have money now; a kind man gave me this money at the piazza, but I don't know where to buy it. You know, Grandmama, the magical pig's lard you told me would help my toe. No one is at home and able to help me buy it. Oh, Grandmama, look at me, I am all bruised, even my head. It hurts me. Mama is hurt, too. Father beat us last night. Tell me, Grandmama, tell me...what do I do?"

I couldn't stop sobbing and imploring Grandmama. As I was telling her of my bruises, I was patting myself as if Grandmama could see. Now I had no Grandmama to hug me and her kind hands were not there to pat my bruised head.

It was dusk, hours went by. I had a very long discussion with Grandmama. I thought it was time to leave the silent Grandmama and go home. As I got up, I had no pain. No pain in my toe! No pain on my body! The bruises, the bruises were hardly visible! I was bewildered and glad. I knew Grandmama would help me. I knew it.

Mother was cooking and Alex was sitting at the table. When I walked in, they both started. "Where were you? Why didn't you tell us anything? We were worried!"

I tried to interrupt them with my answers, but it was of no use. I simply put the silver coins on the table, knowing that it would permit me a moment to explain. They both looked at the coins, at me, at the coins. I told them what had happened. The whole story, the toe, the man, the coins, the magical lard, the cemetery, all of it. They were in awe. Mother examined my arms, back, head and legs. She was dumbfounded. Alex, too. The climax being my cured toe!

Mother was relieved to see me and relieved that I was well, thus she crossed herself. After she was certain of my wellness, she began to laugh as did Alex. I stood there wondering what was so funny. Soon, I found out the magical lard isn't magical at all, it's simply pig's lard and could easily be purchased at the market and was not very expensive either. That day I learned many things, things I would remember for the rest of my life.

Sunday night explains the bruises and Mother's, too— Father's return. During the night, unsure of what time it was, but certain that it was late, I heard some screams. Alex heard it, too. We sat up on our beds and hugged each other, trembling. We heard the door open and shut. Then...my mother was heard: "Andrei, I beseech you, let me in! The children, let me be with my children, Andrei!" and loud sobs were audible. Mother continued her pleas, but in the background we also heard the landlord. He was shouting something, or threatening something, unsure of what exactly, for Mother's cries were much louder. We heard the door open again, some shuffling, then Father's voice: "Mind your own business and family!" he hollered at the top of his lungs.

"Alex, do you think he will kill Mother?"

"Quiet! What's wrong with you, to say such things?"

If Alex only knew what I knew—I didn't tell anyone of what I had learned of before in the garden, for fear overpowered my senses. Now it was silent. As if nothing happened. We looked at each other in wonderment and, as we were preparing to sleep again, we heard the soft cry of Mother's monotone voice: "My day will come, the day will come."

Thus we learnt of Father's unexpected and unwanted return home. For how long, who knows? Time would tell.

We had an exhibit of what kind of love and concern our father had for us, which was generously provided by his belt. Alex and I came home the next day and went directly into the bedroom. That was the usual method when our father decided to visit and invoke fear in us, reassuring himself of his authority, or simply his madness. While we passed through the narrow path between the table and credenza to enter the bedroom, we noticed two white papers teasingly on display on top of the credenza. We knew what those were. Reports from school. We sat in the bedroom, smitten of anxiety. Will he see it? Or not? We waited in terror. He finally summoned us.

"Alex, Victor, I want you here now!"

"Yes, please, Father," answered Alex and I copied, "Yes, please, Father," very politely. We both whimpered and sighed heavily. Poor Alex...he was transparently pale with fright. He walked slowly to the kitchen after the door was opened. I was directly behind him.

Father pointed us in with his finger. The longest, most terrorizing and horrifying minutes ensued. Little George was on the bed and Mother was washing something at the sink. We didn't dare to look at Father; we knew our mistakes and dreaded the mask of terror on his face, which would scare us the more so.

A thundering voice commenced, "Alex, take off your pants and bend over that chair! Now!"

Poor Alex, he had complied, but was shaking and nearly tumbled over. The sound of the flying belt cut through the thick air of suspense and hit Alex hard. Father kept hitting relentlessly as Alex yelled out in pain. Father roared, "If I hear you again, I will double your punishment!"

I sorrowfully looked at Alex, who now had his fist in his mouth to bite and to prevent him from screaming. Father mercilessly continued bashing him and, with each hit of the belt, Mother would shudder and cry.

"Get up now!" Father exhaled. Alex grabbed his pants off the floor and ran to the room crying. Butterflies were fluttering in my stomach. I was biting my lip viciously and made them bleed. I dreaded that painstaking moment of hearing my name thundered.

"Take off your pants," Father said in a half-roar and near shaky voice. As if it were such a noble and hard duty he was administering to us. My eyes fell on Mother, imploring, begging for her rescue.

"Take it off! Take it off!" Father regained his energy. In two hops I was at Mother's side, clinging onto her legs, my head digging into her stomach.

"Mama, Mama," I cried. At once I felt a sharp pain on my back, on my head, on my arms, on my head again. I was unable to hide. Father unleashed his fury and was now raging with anger as he was whipping the belt; like a lasso he twirled it before plunging into our flesh. He now resorted to using the buckle as his weapon. Mother screamed in horror. Mother was caught in the battle and was hit with the buckle as well. I assume for protecting me, or at least trying to. Father refrained from his torturing performance and went outside. I believe the landlord's noisy threats were the reason we were spared from further abuse. Gratefully.

We heard Father shouting outside to the landlord to mind his own business. Mother was now on her knees, sobbing and looking at me, crying and hugging me. I couldn't see my mother's face, my eyes were swollen. I only heard her. Mother was wiping me with a cold, wet cloth of the blood from my head, nose, mouth and ears. Everything was sore, everything hurt. Slowly, limping, I walked into the bedroom.

"Alex?" I whispered in exhaustion, "Alex, where are you?"

"I am here, under the bed," came a soft, nasal voice.

I bent down in pain and slid under the bed to where Alex

was. He tried to comfort me by putting his arm around me. As he was doing so, he accidentally touched my head.

"No, no Alex, don't touch my head, it really hurts."

"Why is your head wet, Vitya?"

"Ah, Mother, she was trying to clean me."

"If she was cleaning you, Vitya, why is it sticky?"

"I don't know, Alex, you ask me too much."

Because of the wicked school, hungry I leave and hungry I come back. I had no more benefit of it, save for the skimpy breakfast. I was whipped at home and at school. I dozed off into a safe daydream while sitting in class, where no one could hurt me—for the time being—and listened to the chirping birds singing outside.

More and more, I became convinced and assured that Father was a capricious, coy and self-caring human. The discussions I heard before had not left my memory, but were stored away safely at the back of my mind when I was consumed in my daily tasks of gathering provisions. I often pondered over Father's true intentions, but not knowing any better, could not condemn him, nor was I empowered to do so. We suffered through many beatings intermittently, Olga being spared of these, for she found a beneficial system. She would grab hold of baby George, thus disabling and deterring Father's morbid strikes.

The lunch bell rang and awoke me from my trance. The children eagerly and gladly rushed outdoors. They ran, hopped and sang, while clinging onto their little lunch bags, so happy. I was not included in these activities. I was an outcast. My new haircut that Mother lovingly gave me last night didn't help matters either, but that wasn't her fault.

I went outside, out of obligation, and proceeded up a hill by the school. I found a little wooden crate and some rope nearby to tie the crate with and form a trap. I had some crumbs in my pocket from some leftover bread of previous beggings. I took these crumbs out and placed a few under the crate and then went behind a little bush, while holding the rope in my hand.

I waited. Quietly and patiently I waited. Hours went by.

School had commenced and ended for the day. I still sat there. Until...a little sparrow flew down to eat the crumbs I set out. I pulled the rope and caught the sparrow. I repeated this procedure a few times until I gathered a few sparrows, which I killed and de-feathered. I had a book of matches in my pocket. I made a little fire and, after cleaning the birds, I threaded them onto a thin branch and began roasting them. There wasn't much meat on them, but enough for me. I was no longer hungry. I ate my meal and noticed it was becoming dark. I descended the hill and went home thinking, I must not tell anyone. No one must know this secret of mine. It is mine alone.

Mother still bore traces of our previous near-massacre and Alex had much difficulty sitting on chairs for a few days. Time had ridden us of some scars, but welcomed new ones of a physical and mental nature.

It was a habit of Mother's to frequent the piazzas furthest from home, the reason being to dodge the neighbours' gossip and because the discarded produce was a better pick than at our local piazza, called Stari Djeram.

Alex and I were well trained in matters of where to go and where it was more profitable, though formidable. It was a dangerous place to be, for us that is. The policemen were acquainted with the vexation of persistent paupers and were prepared to apprehend any noticed delinquent in pursuit of a meal.

Mother's preference was the Tsvetni Trg Piazza—in translation: The Flower Square Piazza. Not far from this piazza was an edifice belonging to the higher-ranking officers' guild. The officers would spend near eternity at this club and, to appease their wives' provocations, would conveniently pick up a bouquet of fresh, fragrant flowers. This piazza was thereby a necessity for the officers, who enjoyed frivolous evenings at their meetings. The piazza catered to the officers and to the higher society alike. The ladies would visit and shop in the company of their servants who were carrying the items chosen by the fussy, wise ladies.

Tsvetni Trg Piazza was in a central location and circled by ministerial buildings. This piazza had significance to me, for it was due to visiting this place that enabled me to have my picture in the national newspaper.

Chapter 6

A year went by after our father's bludgeoning performance, not that we didn't have beatings in between—that was standard—but not as severe as the one that transformed Mother, Alex and I into near approximations of an ornamented Christmas tree.

One morning, after waking us up, Mother sent Alex to school and detained me at home, for we had a mission to accomplish. George was bundled up in an oversized shawl and tied to Mother's back as a knapsack. She had a basket in one hand and me in the other. We set off. Today's journey would be via foot, since we lacked fare for transportation. I wasn't about to suggest to Mother to travel in Alex's and my usual mode of transport—as traffic magnets, thus was I committed to Mother's directions. The scorching sun, no wind and hot air, did not add pleasure to our journey.

We trekked along King Alexander Street to Palmoticheva to Duke Michael Street. Just as we arrived the piazza was closing for the usual daily closure between twelve and three in the afternoon—a type of siesta so to speak. It took us nearly three hours of travel time to arrive.

The greetings and nods by the people informed me that Mother was a familiar visitor there. Mother set to work as if she had punched in a time clock and began to perform her usual task. She looked and found an empty orange crate, looked further and found a rope. She tied the two together and proceeded to visit the kiosks of the florists. There she was provided with flowers unsuitable for sale to the wealthy, picky customers. The florists provided her with these nearly wilted flowers and cleaned out their inventory simultaneously. Mother returned with her flowers, gave me the rope to hold and guard the crate while she continued to shop. Now she was searching for discarded produce, another unwanted item, faulty of bruises or the such, thereby filling our table with food. She had accomplished two tasks at once. Upon her return, where she nodded to me, notifying me of our departure, we headed toward Franko Panova Street.

I was struggling with the crate, now with a section of nearly wilted flowers on one side and a section of bruised fruit and vegetables on the other side. As I was doing so, to my astonishment, a camera flashed before me. Was it because I was toiling, or was it because I looked piteous, or perhaps the combination of the two that inspired the photographer. The next day's national newspaper contained my photograph and a caption that read: *And This Boy Wants to Earn a Few Dinars!*

We stopped at Krunska Street (Coronation Street), where we both sat down on the curb. Mother began cutting off the dry leaves off the flowers that were too wilted, and some soggy stems, with the scissors she had previously pulled out of her bag. Now that big bundle was just a pile. After our rest and her pruning, we commenced.

Passing by the famous Vuk's Monument, we turned to Groblyanska Street. To my ease, the path was now asphalted and admissible for dragging the crate less burdensomely. I was surprised to see Auntie Nina as we reached Dalmatinska Street. Yes, that was where she lived, but I had no apprehension of our meeting. Auntie and Mother greeted each other with a kiss, exchanged the flowers and money, and then the three of us went home together.

Autumn months passed quickly and winter's frost set in. We were blanketed in a diamond sheet of snow. Our little stove worked hard to heat our home and, usually, we left the bedroom door open for the warm air to circulate into. During the bitter, cold nights, the fire in the stove would die down and had anyone left a cup of water on the table, they would find it solidified in the morning.

We were now imprisoned by nature. It was too cold for Mother to frequent the piazza. Too cold for Alex and I to beg as we had not the luxury of owning winter gear. No coats, no boots, etc., such was a fantasy. The winter, thereby, punished us two fold, by its whipping cold winds and by hindering our methods of gathering provisions. We were duly obliged to attend school now. Mother had bundled us in quantities of rags layered upon us and on our feet, which then were covered with plastic bags and tied. Hence, in this hideous and unavoidable fashion, surely to provoke ridicule, we attended school.

One particular day, Mother was very silent. She didn't even notice our return from school. Father was home, miraculously. He was sitting there complaining of his mattress. The hay was too soft and becoming uncomfortable, since he could feel the wood beneath his mattress, he professed. Our mattress, on the other hand, where we children slept, had long ago formed a pile of dust beneath the bed and we dared not to complain of how uncomfortable it was.

In this peculiar aura, Father summoned us to eat. The dreaded hot and boiled stale bread again, which we now sprinkled with a few grains of sugar in order to lessen the burden of appeasing our hunger. We quietly ate and studiously began to do whatever homework we had, the best way we could. It was a sombre evening.

Day turned to night. Father told us to go to bed. Mother had already retired. A horrific, loud scream was heard in the middle of the night. I instantly sat up, rubbed my eyes to adjust to night vision and saw Mother lying on the floor and, of all horrors, Father on top of her. Father yelled out to me, "Give me the rope to tie her hands!"

"Where...what rope?" I stammered in confusion.

"There, the belt of the bathrobe. Bring it here, now. Hurry!"

What now, I thought. I watched in dismay as Father tied Mother's hands behind her back. He yelled out again, "Alex, give me something to tie her feet!"

By now Alex was fully awake and involved in the matters at hand. Alex threw a pair of ripped stockings, or some kind of long and dangling rag, to Father, who used it to quickly tie Mother's feet. I looked at Mother. "Mama, Mother dearest, what is wrong with you? Mama, do you hear me?" Her eyes were turned upward and she didn't recognize or answer me.

My terrible Father, I thought. Did he do this to her? I couldn't say a word to him out of anger. The three of us encircled Mother—Alex, George and I. We looked pathetic in our rags, crying and hugging each other, while staring at our tied mother and summoning her to speak to us. We cried and shook in the nasty cold of the uncaring, brutal winter.

Father was hurriedly dressing while simultaneously instructing, "Alex...you are the oldest here now," between his gasps for air, "take care of George and Vitya. Stay inside, do not open the door to anyone, but me," and he left.

We sat and stared at our mother. We were hopeless in our inability of helping her. We knew that Mother had some sort of lapses, or some kind of illness, because of her sporadic absences. But...this was the first time we had encountered and experienced the tragedy of watching our mother succumb to illness and all the mean, though necessary, efforts of Father's to restrain her and prevent her from hurting herself and anyone in her path.

It seemed to me that a generation had passed since Father's leave. The public telephone was located near the Stari Djeram Piazza and not that far of a distance for him to be taking so long. We were trembling of fright and cold. Unable to speak. Just waiting. A few moans were heard coming from Mother, who was still lying there with her eyes turned upward. It was a scary vision for us.

We suddenly heard scrunching footsteps in the snow outside. We heard a few knocks. We still didn't move. Alex started to get up to answer the door, but I stopped him. "Do you not remember what Father said? Don't open the door to anyone, but me!" He sat down again.

Now we heard an angered rapping on the window of the bedroom where we were sitting and we shook. Luckily, Father pressed his face to the window and, through the frosted glass, we were able to recognize his squashed nose and piercing eyes that so well portrayed his angered expressions.

Father rushed in when we opened the door and began, "Did she wake up?"

"She isn't sleeping. She is still looking up at the ceiling," I answered him, more calm now.

Within minutes we heard some more hurried feet crunching outdoors, followed by quick, brisk knocks on the door. A policeman entered, a man dressed in civilian garb and two men in white overcoats carrying a stretcher.

Our mother was a saint to us. She was kind, noble and loving. She wouldn't hurt anyone. To witness such a terrible incident, her falling, her screaming, the tying of her hands and feet as one would do to a criminal, had imprinted on us a most horrifying and tragic memory that was to remain with us forever.

The doctor examined Mother. He looked at her, nodded his head while instructing the two men in white overcoats to lift her onto the stretcher. We watched in horror as our mother was being whisked away out of our home. Once the two men and Mother left, the doctor began asking Father a series of questions.

Father had started from the beginning, which became very interesting to us, for we missed that part. He stated that Mother had come to the kitchen to take George, who was already asleep, and put him in his crib in the bedroom. They exchanged a few words as she left the kitchen. He then (as did Alex and I) heard a scream. He told the doctor that he found her flipping on the floor and proceeded to restrain her, with no time to turn on the lights (which later Alex did).

George, naturally, was awoke by the scream and the noise of all the commotion, but unusually had not screamed as if he knew that it would cause added aggravation, and as if he knew what was happening to our poor mother. He sat there quietly and waited, just as we did.

That day we left for school hungry and exhausted from lack of sleep. Alex was attending his first year of high school as I was ending my last year of elementary school. I knew I would get punished in school that day, for I would be napping during class, but didn't and couldn't care less.

When we returned home, we found Father sitting, clasping his head with his hands, in deep contemplation.

"Where's George?" I inquired.

"He is at your Auntie Nina's house," he answered without looking up at me.

Alex and I tidied up whatever there was to tidy up after the night's incidents as per instructed by Father.

For dinner...the usual...boiled bread, or as commonly referred to as "popara." Argh! While I was picking at this concoction in front of me, the thought and picture of Mother in her vulnerable state had never left my mind.

Finally...school's end. That burden was done with, at least for now. I was thrilled I wouldn't have to see that despicable teacher anymore. How I wished revenge, but other affairs diverted my attention.

Mother was home again, after a prolonged absence. She still didn't seem to be that well, but much better than what we had witnessed earlier. I was outside now, in the courtyard, up in a tree. I sometimes gave in to my childish needs, hence my location in the tree! Besides, I thought, I had some time to spare before going out to beg.

It was a nice, warm day, begging of only leisure activities. There I sat, giving in to the day's requests. I spotted the landlady talking with the neighbour, Mrs. Mara. I paid no mind to them until I heard the word "Zoya.'" My ears sprang up as a cat's upon noticing a mouse. I strained to hear better now and payed attention to what was being said.

Mrs. Mara was a large, hefty lady who had a tendency to wear a kilo of make-up on her face. She leaned her elbow, hugging the fence with one arm as she listened attentively to the landlady who was all red and beaming with her melodramatic explanations. "Yes, yes, Mrs. Mara, that is how it happened...indeed."

Mrs. Mara was nodding her head up and down in agreement and added, "You know...I think it must have gone to her head the fact that she had once lived exuberantly and lavishly, and look at her now, a beggar, a cleaning lady. And...her children are no better, for they have been seen begging for food also."

The landlady now was nodding her head. I was fuming. I plucked a handful of unripened walnuts and, with vengeance, threw it in their direction to break up their insulting gossip. The landlady stirred. Mrs. Mara just looked around to see where the walnuts came from.

The landlady then said to Mrs. Mara that she must return to her guests, which she was successfully blocking from her view. When she turned to go inside, she looked up in the tree and said, "Vitya, you mind where you throw those walnuts, child!"

I assume she thought I was collecting them to eat later on. How did they know of my mother's past? The gossip travelled faster through the invisible grapevine than the walnuts that I had thrown on the offenders.

We no longer needed to beg for food. The miserable irony of Mother's seizure enabled us to receive charity without begging. A couple of weeks upon Mother's return we were visited by city officials and the Salvation Army—granting our pathetic home, pathetic property and our degrading forbearance an election of support from the aforementioned organizations when the policeman and doctor had answered our call.

Thus we received wood, coal and supplies of food and clothing. I—we—were ecstatic. Not only did I have this, but was honoured of being enrolled in the Salvation Army! I did not know the difference between an army and the Salvation Army, therefore, I was honoured and proud. I bragged to the few friends I had that I was a soldier and had the possibility of being drafted! Oh how I daydreamed. Perhaps I would even become an officer to the pleasure and pride of my grandfather's if he were only here.

Our days were much lighter now. Our school grades improved dramatically and were not as burdensome. Why, even the teachers seemed nicer and I was all the more courteous to them. I passed the grade successfully.

Winter was not as harsh as previous ones had been known to be. Thanks be to the social services and the Salvation Army for lightening our load and burden and enabling us to study. We attended school regularly and were prompt and, most importantly, properly attired for the weather. We looked better, felt better and were of a better disposition.

Spring had arrived! The blossoming flowers were amongst us; the grass became green again and the trees began budding their flowering fruit, awakening from winter's slumber. A joyous celebration awaited us: Easter! In addition to that, we were also looking forward to the camp that the school provided for the less fortunate children and we were on that list. It was splendid, yes splendid.

Mother had prepared the traditional kulich (sweet bread with raisins and covered with white frosting and colourful candy sprinkles) and had coloured some eggs a few days earlier. Today was Sunday, Easter. She was preparing us for church. We were happy and were joyously abiding by Mother's rules without objections. Everything seemed joyful, sunny and beautiful; the day, the occasion, the overall ambiance spruced everyone's mood. I sat on the kitchen chair waiting for Mother to finish dressing George.

At once, a loud whistling noise was heard above our heads coming from outside. What was that? We all looked at each other, questioning the same thing with our eyes and expressions. Suddenly another one...whistling above our heads.

Father jumped back inside our kitchen, for he had previously gone out to chat with a neighbour. "Get down, now!" he yelled out at us. We fell to the ground. We didn't question why.

The ground shook and vibrated concluding the whistling sound and the horrific "boom." An earthquake? I knew of those, but this did not sound familiar and the tremors were not to this degree.

Father roared out again, "Down! If you feel you can't breathe, grab a rag and wet it and then hold it to your face. It looks like we are being hit by the Nazis." With that, he walked outside.

"Andrei! Andrei! Don't leave us again. Not now!" Mother was imploring. He went out regardless. The whistling noises becoming incessant with the crashing-booming sounds as the earth shook beneath us.

Father returned to the dangerous outdoors in an attempt to gather more information regarding the attacks. He hopped back in quickly and with a tone of severity had instructed us, "quick! Grab the pots, the kettle, anything that holds water, and fill them. I heard we will be losing the water supply soon!"

We scurried around our tiny kitchen like frantic mice, grabbing whatever pots, kettles and jars and whatever else that would suffice. As I attempted to fill my pot of water, the water gradually ceased to flow, filling my old stained pot to the half.

More thundering noise was heard, more whistling, more shaking of the ground. Each new strike became louder, sharper and deadlier. We were terrified. We fell to the ground again, this time without Father's directions and we knew that the war had begun.

I dared to steal a peek outside and saw the once sunny blue sky now darkened with black cumulus smoke and in some areas of the heavens was a pinkish hue directly above a raging blaze of targeted structures. The bombardment and explosions were continual. Father left again to join the group of men gathered at the opposite side of our gate to the courtyard. Meanwhile, Mother had thrown a couple of old and torn blankets on the floor and placed some rags for pillows. It was decided that we sleep together for the duration of this bombardment. For safety and security reasons and, simply, because we were all scared.

When Father returned, he found us sitting on the floor, huddled on top of the blankets. He sat tiredly on the chair, wincing from all the running he did back and forth. He noted that he could not understand this bombardment. The city had proclaimed itself a free zone, that is, a zone free of military defence and populated with only civilians, to the league of nations. Regardless of this claim, the city was heavily bombarded.

The smoky, black day turned to a pinkish, whitish night. After some rest, Father rejoined the group of men continually discussing and observing and offering their opinions of the situation. I decided to venture out and join the men, now heavily immersed in conversation.

They were completely absorbed in the situation and their discussion as they all faced toward the core of the city and the blazing sky above it, that they didn't detect my presence. Once I joined these men, I felt less vulnerable and more secure in regard to the bombardment, which was slowly fading. The air was heavy of smoke and smelt of burning wood, amongst other things.

"Today I listened to the news on the radio and heard that some persons had vandalized a few libraries," one neighbour said to the other as the others held a fixed stare at the sky.

"That, you know, was not very pleasantly accepted by our bordering countries," the other implied, while adjusting his hat on his head, then buttoning his sweater. Another member of this crowd, a retired colonel who had fluffy, snow white hair, a fluffy white moustache and a pipe protruding from his mouth, further lamented, "Yes, it will be bad, very bad. For the city, for the people."

Father looked at him sadly and added, "True. I have been through this before. It is as you say," and Father heavily pulled a puff of his cigarette.

One of the men commented, "We have no electricity," while another added, "We have no water either."

"That is not a problem, gentlemen," said the colonel. "I have a well in my yard, you may use it. I also constructed a bomb shelter two metres into the ground. It is very safe and you may all come if the bombardment continues."

The night's fall was unanimously welcomed. The bombing subsided and the night was silenced. At once, Father noticed me and asked, "What are you doing here? Vitya! I specifically ordered all of you to stay indoors! How dare you disobey!"

I looked up at him assured that I would not be reproved due to our new situation. I studied my father while we were standing out there and childishly began scrutinizing him. He wasn't tall. He was of average height as the other men were. Oddly, he always seemed tall to me.

I walked back home and, as I took a few steps, I overheard over my shoulder one of the men say, "When did that rascal join us?"

My entry at home was welcomed with an outpour of questions, worrisome looks and the such.

"Vitya! Where were you? How could you have disobeyed and left?"

"With Father," I answered affirmatively, and not waiting for any response I went into the bedroom to reflect upon the discussions I heard and the historical events that took place that very day. Easter day.

The next morning we arose to commands of not to leave the house under any circumstances! Father started the fire in the stove and began preparations for tea. He was interrupted by a strong, angry knock on the door.

The landlord. "Shut off your stove at once! All we need is the smoke from our chimney to attract attention and possible bombardment! He angrily demanded and left, huffing and puffing.

What an idiot he is! The entire city is being consumed and burning in flames and he worries for his building! Suddenly, I remembered the colonel. I wondered how it was that he had already built some kind of a bomb shelter? In the ground? I didn't know what that was and I was also amused of how quickly he accomplished it, just in time! Did he have special access to information pertaining to the bombardment and of the time it would occur, since he was a colonel?

The remainder of the day was boring. We each took turns going to the outhouse, all the while looking above our heads, lest a bomb was to hover over us and whiz by. Distant whistling and thunder was heard, though not in our vicinity this time. Mother occupied herself with mending our mended clothes. Father visited Aunt Katya and rather often at that, to Mother's chagrin, but ironically, to our benefit.

The following morning Mother and Father were already up and discussing. "I am going to go to my sister Nina today."

"No, you will not. You are not going anywhere."

"I must go to see if she is all right. I need to know, Andrei," she softly said as she was tying a handkerchief around her head.

She left. The day was murky and threatened of rain. It became darker now in our already dark home, for we were sub-level to the ground and had a balcony overhang above us from the apartment directly above, and that did not improve the situation. The sun seldom penetrated through certain tight angles and if lucky a poking ray of sunlight on rather very sunny days would illuminate a speckle of a corner of our home.

It was a dark, foreboding and sombre atmosphere. Father began collecting the blankets off the ground, since he decided it was no longer necessary for us to sleep on the floor. We had circumstantially adjusted to the new situation.

For supper that evening we ate half-baked potatoes, for fear of the taunting smoke emitting from the chimney, if we dared to fully cook the potatoes, lest we provoke the landlord. We sat there afterward in contemplation, while nervously scratching ourselves. We hadn't bathed in over a week now. Our bathing ritual was somewhat of a circus.

Father would bring and display his prized possession and eventually ours, an assembly of wood with strips of metal sheet lining the joints of this item, enabling it to contain water. Though prized, it eerily resembled an upper lid of a wooden coffin. Nevertheless, we had a tub. Mother would boil water in a large pot on the stove, mixing it later with cold to form a comfortable temperature for bathing. Father had privileges of being first to bathe. He washed and then the rest of us took turns, patiently waiting for the other to finish. By the time the last person entered the soiled water, it was useless even to bathe, but they did so anyhow, for by touching water they assumed that they were clean.

Mother returned from her visit in the late afternoon-early evening and obligingly informed us that she did not find Nina at home. "I barely managed to climb those flights of stairs in the darkness. I finally reached her door and banged on it as hard as I could, but to no avail. She did not answer."

"She is probably at Sonya's," Father replied with an air of unconcern.

Sonya was a general's daughter. She lived with her father in the outskirts of the city. She was a friend and a co-worker of Aunt Nina's. They sold flowers together sometimes. Sonya, too, was once better situated as Auntie Nina had been and as my mother. Sonya's dream was to attract an officer and marry off happily. For now, she was still single and pretty I might add.

Mother then proclaimed, "Yes, Andrei, probably at Sonya's

house, to stay with her father. They do live on the outskirts of the city and perhaps it is safer there. Indeed, they must have invited Nina to their home!"

Mother was content with this idea. Father, completely uninterested, decided to change the course of the subject. He began questioning Mother of the city's condition. When she began to describe the scenery she had witnessed, she became upset and shaky and her voice was crackled. With all the data we had collected by listening to Mother's accounts, Alex and I resolved to go and investigate the matters for ourselves tomorrow morning. The city was in turmoil and we wanted to see it.

In the early hours we did as we planned. We went to commence our investigation. The main streets had electrical wires hanging and drooping all over them. Craters left from the bombs were a circumference of ten metres and three metres deep, sporadically embedded on the semi-deserted streets. Homes bore shattered windows, broken eavstroughs, missing shingles and doors. Curtains were swaying, hurling out of the windows forced by the wind as if to call attention to the destruction of that particular home. A splash of people here and there were noticed on the dust covered sidewalks. Some were collecting their scattered items; some were salvaging theirs, yet some were taking advantage of the desertion by looting stores.

An array of confused people, busy and cursing all the while, including the looters who seemed perplexed at the state of the city, even if they were taking full advantage of it; ironically. We observed a few groups of people walking steadily, carrying blankets, suitcases and other belongings, in a mechanical trail stretching as far as the eye could see. We had stopped an elderly woman who seemed approachable and asked her where were they headed. She bitterly answered while shaking her head; was it from age or discontent, we weren't certain.

"You see, children, my family is pulling me to the village with them, out of the city and out of danger's way. I have no choice, it is my fate."

We continued walking, opposing the oncoming colonies of people heading out of the city as we aimed into the centre of the city. The damage was colossal. We were shocked. Amidst scattered, charred debris, we observed dead horses along the sides of the road—dogs, too.

We stumbled on fallen debris as we gazed at the ruins. Some homes or stores had no roofs at all and all of its contents were gaping in the open smoky and smelly air.

"Alex!"

"What?"

"Let's go to the piazza!"

"What piazza, Vitya?"

"Baelonova Piazza!"

"Fine," agreed Alex.

Since we were not far from Baelonova Piazza, we arrived there swiftly. Strolling along King Alexander, crossing Beogradska Street, observing and commenting on all the burnt and some unrecognizable stores. Burdensomely we walked in the middle of the street in attempts to avoid the hurdles, the sidewalks being piled with mini hills of stone, wood, glass and other materials.

Bypassing the craters in the road, we glimpsed at a streetcar now vertically aligned, about to travel upward, one would think, giving the entire circumstance an added degree of eeriness. More and more people we encountered along the way, none of them bearing smiles; all had serious expressions upon them as they knew of the vital need to escape the attacks, the bombardments. Their children were holding onto their mothers' skirts and other trivial, childish possessions in the other hand so important to them, a safeguard.

We arrived at the piazza. By now we were accustomed to all the debris, the ruins, the charred and still smoking embers in the piles of destruction. The piazza was not spared of the fate of the rest of the city. Kiosks were in shambles now, some still burning. We picked up a piece of wood, which was not entirely burnt and was probably a part of a table or kiosk at the piazza. We poked through the piles we saw before us.

"Look! Look here, Alex!" I said excitedly.

"What now, Vitya?"

"Potatoes! That's what. And they're cooked potatoes, too!"

"Yes, Vitya. It is!"

Obviously...we ate. We found a meal, courtesy of the bombing! How ironic. Nearby we found some material—what it was previously, who knows—but it served a purpose now. We scooped up the potatoes and wrapped them in the rags to take home.

We took another route home. We had experienced looking at the damages on the previous streets and now were investigating other parts of the city. Passing by the once beautiful botanical gardens and toward Karaburma we encountered more dead horses. A sad and dreadful sight. They were now becoming swollen and disfigured. It was the third day since the first bombardment. The third day of Easter.

We mused at how we hadn't met any policemen, or any other figure of authority for that matter. Where were they all? Were they afraid? Were they gathering orders from the government? It was the last thing on our mind really, but who could help but wonder.

Alex was lucky that day. Our new route provided him with a gift that he always yearned for: a bicycle. Someone had abandoned their bicycle; it was leaning against a post, nearly to the ground. Alex took it. He had authority to do so. He was older and should I have objected to this, I would have payed for it dearly. Therefore Alex rode and I ran behind him.

We came to Tsvitcheva Street. "The bakery, now!" I yelled out in front of me to Alex who was enjoying his ride, despite having to swerve at times to avoid the new obstacles of the road. What joy, I thought to myself, I might be able to take a djevrek at the bakery, which I had only dreamt of before. Alex heard me, because he nodded in agreement and stopped abruptly.

We ventured into the bakery and looked around. It was shattered, but not as severely as the other stores. No one was there, it was abandoned. Odd. How easy it was now to enter these stores and not be brushed away as pesky flies. We noticed an opening in the ceiling and heard some ravens. They were delighting in their feast of the bakery's commodities as well.

Beside the window were some covered baskets. We took the

cloth off the baskets and discovered dough that smelled of yeast. What a feast! Alex was gathering and scooping the flour that was spilled all over the floor. He put this in a container he had found. I motioned him over to my side of the store, questioning him as to how we would carry all this home.

"In the cloths, silly."

"Right." Why didn't I think of that?

We shook off the flour and other dust off our dingy clothes and proudly returned home with our find.

Our plight home was troublesome. We hauled our newfound treasure home. Alex on his bicycle and I behind him. A couple of times we received help from passers-by, sympathetic to our cause, and who helped poor Alex out of the bomb craters as he rode into them accidentally, tumbling over with our fortune. Ironically, even though we received help from these courteous people, we were ever so cautious and took great care hiding our food, lest they be taken away from us two scrawny lads.

Our return home was met with more dead horses, dead dogs and debris, which by now unfortunately were becoming a standard fixture on the streets. It was nearly dark, the sun becoming tired of shining on such atrocities had solemnly and hesitatingly became a recluse, pinkening the sky as if reminding all that perhaps the next day would not be as cumbersome.

The first words we heard upon our entry into the kitchen were Mother's complaints of us smelling like smoke.

"Mother, if only you had seen all that we have seen!"

We spoke of our adventure and Mother listened attentively, but working all the while scraping the dough off the cloths. In no time our miserable kitchen smelt of fresh baked bread, making our pathetic home somewhat cozier nonetheless.

Father was there. I suppose the aroma of the fresh bread made even him somewhat tolerable and tolerant. He decided on visiting Auntie Katya's house again and again to the dislike of our mother. We were happy. We had freedom (at least temporarily) and bread! This third day of bombardment ended in such manner. We retired, with mountains of thoughts of what the next day would bring.

The flour we had brought home, that Alex so greedily gathered off the floor, had produced grains of dirt and sand between our teeth as we ate the bread in the following days. We didn't mind all that much, since now we had bread, and that was good. Bread was a luxury, not only to us, but to many.

The devaluation of money was astronomical during the war. Two weeks prior, 100 dinars could purchase 200 kilos of bread, where as now one orange would cost 100 dinars.

We no longer received help from the social services, nor the Salvation Army. The war situation had intervened and interrupted this charity. Alex and I were once again forced to rely on our own devices. The usual: begging for food, begging for work.

Father was a man of mystery. Sometimes he came home, more often he did not. We had adjusted to this style and seldom did we discuss his whereabouts, or why he was not home in the first place. Whether he was home or not did not benefit us and actually lessened our worries of getting beaten by the belt.

He casually visited us as if it were most natural and normal that he didn't reside with us on a full-time basis and he couldn't care less whether we had our daily bread, or any provisions for that matter. He gave up on his obligations, which basically meant the payment of rent. He rarely had provided for us in the first place, therefore, he left us to our own means, which now included payment of rent.

That day Alex decided on targeting Tsvetkova Piazza and I would target downtown for possible provisions for today's menu. Mother and George remained home. We left with high hopes of obtaining food for us. Mother pecked us on our cheeks, then began her usual scrubbing of the very scrubbed, thinned-out, yellow, wood floor. She was paranoid and obsessed with the notion that if the floors were not to par, bugs would gather more frequently. Sadly, they still called on us, regardless of our squeaky clean floors.

Chapter 7

We left Mother to her chores and devoted our time and energy to the collection of food or money. The mist of the morning rain gently washed our faces and refreshed us for the tasks we were to partake in. This refreshing mist would smell delightful, was it not for the smoke and other rancid stenches which were now enhanced with its dew and made it more prominent and noticeable and reminded us of the war that pursued and of our days at hand.

It was now common practise to walk in the middle of the road, everyone did. The sidewalks were impassable and also threatened of any possible ruins of falling upon the head of one that was brave enough to use the sidewalks. The safer mode of travel was to walk in the middle of the road; indeed one still encountered and had to jump hurdles over debris and bypass craters, but was safer nevertheless. Obviously, streetcars and fiacres and the occasional car were not in use, at least not on the streets that were impossible and heavily destructed. Walking would be the only feasible alternative to the impassable roads.

Trekking along King Alexander Street and proceeding to Beogradska Street as I turned the corner I noticed a group of people gathered around this once very busy store. In front of these people and blocking the entrance to the store was a pile of black, charred rubble. The rubble was made up of broken glass, charred wood and the usual mixture of contents that bombing brings together. Somewhere in and through the pile of rubble was a small opening, large enough to permit a single person to crawl and squeeze through it and enter the dark, vacant store. On the ground there was a sign, which once hung proudly above the window depicting: *Jovan's Grocery Store*, where customers would purchase their daily requirements and necessities. Now, it was open and free to all, provided they were thin enough and courageous enough to squirm their way in, into the ruins and dangerous structure that looked like it would collapse at any given moment.

I noticed an obtrusive woman exiting this hole into the street and pulling some sort of bags behind her as she crawled out and stood up amidst the admirers, their applause and taps on the back. Upon visualizing this lady's assets, the mass of the crowd began pushing and shoving each other, including the lady who proved it safe to venture in and loot. They became rambunctious and violent while yelling as if that would enable their entry through this tiny hole that brought so much wealth easier. I, too, not permitting this fortune to falter, began to nudge and penetrate through this hoi polloi and was reprimanded for doing so!

This tall, heavily built man with a sprouting stomach and sporting an unclean dingy, grey moustache, bellowed out, "Hey, you! You there, young man! Where do you think you are going?" He looked at me quizzically and nearly laughed at me, I imagine due to my scrawniness, nevertheless he made certain that his question was to be taken seriously by the sudden joining of his eyebrows. He was a greedy man, it showed, and he didn't seem like the type who was vigilant of concealing this. He shoved me aside like a mutt as he pushed through, stomach first, for he was a large man and somehow that gave him superiority. How he thought to fit into that hole was beyond my imagination, regardless...I was not about to be defeated. I continued my endeavour with more steely determination now!

"Listen, young man. You are not allowed to go in there. Do you hear me!"

"Sir, I am going in."

"Where do you plan on going in?"

"There. Through that hole." I pointed my finger to my intended destination.

I ignored the rest of his and other's protestations, which were sprinkled with profane remarks, and diligently pursued my goal. While we are all scrambling to get to this hole, this gateway to various goodies and treasures, a sudden, loud shriek was heard exerting from the hole.

Suddenly and remarkably, the entire avaricious group dispersed in all directions, leaving me standing there confounded. I watched them run and scratched my head and rubbed my eyes, for their sudden departure caused a small cloud of dust to form off the ground. Where they suddenly rushed off to, I didn't know, I preferred to concentrate on obtaining the much needed items that were within that treasure cove of a store.

I was debating on entering this hole, however, now so free to approach, or leave for fear of what lies within, because the treasures inside also were a part of that screechy noise that made everyone dart into every direction. Hmm...The hunger outweighed my fear. In addition to my own hunger, I also knew that I was not the only one to appease, but my family also.

Cautiously and astutely, I began my entry into the unknown. I felt my way through the rough, dusty entrance, gaining a few scratches along the way. It didn't take me long to reach the opposite side of the hole, and finally I stood up amidst clutter and in a room painted in grey, cement ash colour. There were not many colours in there and it was dark. The dust painted the entire contents of the store in one murky, depressing colour.

Canned goods, rubble, preserves in jars, rubble, confections, rubble surrounded me, even though they were dusty grey, I could discern them. It was semi-dark, with beams of light protruding through whatever entry permitted it to.

I heard a shuffle and then some groaning. My eyes needed a moment to adjust to the darkness and then to follow the moaning I heard. I did a brief survey of the area first, for my being there in the first place was to acquire food. Shelves were torn off the walls, beams were now angularly standing, dust and debris was everywhere. The air was stale and ashy.

Now I clearly heard whining implorations, thus I followed the sounds. On the floor, beneath some rubble and a large heavy beam, was an average middle-aged woman. She was covered in dust and soot. Her once neatly braided hair was dishevelled. Her face was smeared with wet dust, was it from tears, or from the sweat of her pains that painted her face, or a combination of the two. She spotted me, her eyes emitting a glossy, tearful expression from her joy of possible salvation. I was lost in this unexplainable treasure before me: Food and lots of it. I couldn't help but gawk at the inexplicable items sitting there in front of me, waiting to be taken home! Her wincing shook me back to reality. I shook my head and tip-toed over to where she lay, careful not to promote another avalanche of beams and whatnot.

"Little boy, please, come. Help me! You see that wall on the ground, it fell and knocked over this beam on my legs. Can you help, little boy?" Her voice was scratchy and she breathed heavily as she spoke to me.

"How?" I answered her in a faded tone of voice. I looked around and wondered what I could use to coax this beam up off her. I extemporaneously lifted (or at least tried to) the beam. No. It didn't budge. I was not as strong as I thought. The lady groaned in regret, or pain. I picked up a thinner plank of wood and put it beneath the beam, then I found a brick and put that under the plank, forming a type of see-saw. I used all my weight on the other side of this see-saw and with luck and much sweat, lifted the beam a few centimetres above her.

As I was doing all this manoeuvring, I yelled out, "Move your legs, ma'am, wiggle your way out."

"I'm trying, my boy, I'm trying! It's difficult...It's painful!"

"Keep moving, I can't hold this beam up much longer! Sit up and rock yourself out!"

Just as I was about to give, she pulled her legs out. I fell back panting, tired and sweaty. She was breathing heavily on the opposite side. Now she had to get up and soon, because the creaks we heard were not too promising. She managed to slowly pull herself up. On one leg, then the other, all the while holding onto that plank we used to save her. It was now her walking stick, her crutch. Luckily, she hadn't broken any bones, but was bruised and scratched immensely. But a moment passed and we heard another wall of shelves come tumbling down and its items were scattered about directly where she was lying earlier.

In relief we wiped our foreheads. She was slapping herself on her legs, on her behind and arms in a desperate attempt to rid herself of the dust. Her face was still painted, she did look funny.

"Little boy…Come here. What is your name?"

"Vitya."

"Vitya, thank you for helping me. How did you know I was in here?"

"I heard the scream. We all did. Everyone else ran. I thought to come in and see what is the excitement about." I didn't want to come right out and say that my presence in that store was solely due to my growling stomach and my obligations toward my family. Although, I think she knew, hence her presence there and the same motivations!

"Pigs! That's all they are. Pigs! They forced me to come in here first and investigate. A lady followed behind me and she took all that I gathered and fled upon hearing the creaking sounds and tumbling of cans. She stole my food and ran without looking back, leaving me behind."

I observed this austere woman, dressed in a dusty, green shirt and a more greyer now, knee-length skirt. She was truly indignant.

"My name is Helen. I apologize that I did not even tell you my name, dear."

"That's all right," I answered.

"Vitya, I commend you for the fine job you've done of saving me!"

"Thank you, Mrs. Helen."

"Vitya, I think now we have to get to work here, before we are inadvertently trapped. Grab that pillowcase over there on that box." She pointed it out to me as she began collecting cans and whatnot.

I handed her the pillowcase, (that she had most likely brought in with her for this precise reason) and was instructed by Mrs. Helen to make a knot at the top of it after she filled it. I was also to slide a long, thin piece of wood strong enough for the task, through the knot, to enable us both to carry the burden on our shoulders and transport this free treasure.

Now Mrs. Helen and I were swaying from side to side as we tried to balance this pillowcase between us and had the wood on our shoulders, just like maids carrying milk. She took the lead and we were at the far end of the store, where there was a door. I suppose that Mrs. Helen was quite familiar with this establishment, since she knew of the second exit. I helped her push the motley assortment of debris blocking the rear exit door and she attempted to open it.

"Pigs! They probably went around and locked the door!" Mrs. Helen declared.

I wondered why would they do that? Perhaps Mrs. Helen was in such a state that she would chafe at any trivial matter. I quietly examined Mrs. Helen's next move. She pulled out a large ring with an odd looking key, a kalhaus (as Father would call it, since I saw him carry it before), it was a type of master-key. She unlocked the door and we were out on this narrow path. Before I knew it we were at the side of the store and perceived a crowd of people gathering again in the near distance. In front of the store they stood, completely oblivious to our surveillance of them.

"Vultures, pigs! They are too late! They came, but too late," Mrs Helen reiterated.

It took us an hour to arrive at Jovana Risticha Street, walking slowly and balancing the pillowcase between us. We came in front of a gate. Again, Mrs. Helen pulled out her kalhaus and unlocked the gate. We walked by some barricaded, obviously vacant homes. Its doors and windows sealed shut by strips of wood, announcing that no one lives there anymore. We walked casually as if this is the most natural thing to do: Mrs. Helen being taller than I and our balancing act with the pillowcase full of heavy jars and cans! We finally reached an obscure dwelling, which was partially barricaded (Mrs. Helen did this intentionally to ward off any unwanted intruders, she confessed to me). She shoved the hanging eavestrough and slid the diagonal piece of wood, so that it now hung on one side of the door and we entered upon her unlocking it. Smart lady, I estimated...

The facade of her residence practically foretold the interior's decor and cleanliness. The rooms were not large, akin to other regular and modest dwellings, nothing extraordinary. Judging by Mrs. Helen's demeanor, it wasn't a prelude as to how her home would look, in fact it betrayed her. Even though she was dusty from her experiences at the store, it seemed that her attire was previously clean, or new, or both.

Items of all sorts were scattered about: papers, some dirty pots and pans and clothing (whether it was clean or not, only she would know). A purring black and white cat announced itself upon hearing her master enter, supposedly reminding her that she needed to be fed. We dropped our pillowcase on the table. Mrs. Helen, now very polite, seeing that I am her guest, had asked to me to sit. I sat on the edge of the very dirty bed, covered with very dirty blankets and pillows and tried to rest as I gazed at her whitewashed walls. I was shocked to see all the canned goods, preserves of all kinds (only what I had dreamt about and sampled from that little neighbour of mine Danica), now all on display, tempting my hungry eyes. I decided that Mrs. Helen, considering her inventory, must have been a regular at that store, even many others in the duration of the war to date. Mrs. Helen evidently proved to be competent with her skills of survival.

"Vitya," she broke my pondering, "I will give you some of these goods for you to take home. You have a family also to feed as you stated."

I had earlier informed her of my family during our long walk home and due to her inquisitions. She was a prying, nearly intrusive woman, I decided. I took care not to tell her too much, after all, who knows...it's war time and people are desperate. I'm certain she had no intentions of robbing me, but if I told her how I managed to exiguously provide for myself and family, she might rob me of my idea, my system of enterprise!

"Thank you, Mrs. Helen, I would be grateful." I smiled. She packed some cans, some jars, flour, lard and some other confections and I merrily departed from my new friend, hardly waiting to arrive home abounded with my fortune. I had never had so many canned goods and so many jars of preserves! It was excruciatingly heavy, but I gained strength at the mere thought of consuming and sampling the food and sharing it with my equally hungry family.

Alex was sitting at the table with George when I entered triumphantly, eagerly awaiting their demonstration of joy at my return with this unexpected wealth. Mother was in the other room, but quickly came when she heard my happy greeting.

"Where have you been?" Alex asked in an angered, yet worried tone.

"Are you blind? Do you not see all this?" and I dumped the goods onto the table. Their eyes sparkled at the new found riches. Mother immediately began sorting and stacking the items in an orderly fashion, while Alex began to interrogate me. George was content with playing with the cans as Mother would quickly grab them from him, lest some become damaged. Of course, I had to retell the whole incident from the beginning, careful to depict all the dangers and how I was courageous and saved the trapped woman, Mrs. Helen. They listened, nodded and were genuinely proud of me and amused at my twofold accomplishments.

"What did you get, Alex?" I calmly returned the inquisition that befell me earlier.

"Nothing. There wasn't anything to find, everything was gone. There were all kinds of people there, Vitya. Peasants, merchants, even the higher class, it was a strange assimilation. I witnessed a peasant selling a glass of water to a city dweller for ten dinars! They are taking revenge on them." Or us for that matter.

The peasants never did tolerate city folk and always felt like they were disapproved of, humiliated and mimicked, or simply demeaned by the urbanites. Now the ball was in their court and they were taking advantage of it. They had land and livestock...meaning food!

"You know, Vitya, I passed by Dedinye" (a very illustrious part of the city, known for its wealthy inhabitants), "and it wasn't touched by the bombardment. It's preposterous! Yet the poorer areas are hit the hardest and have the most casualties!" Alex commented profoundly.

I decided to change the subject, chiefly due to my sudden realization...

"You know, Alex, it's been over a month since Father visited us."

"I know."

"Maybe we should ask Auntie Katya about him?"

"No. She wouldn't know anything."

"Well, we should ask Mother then."

"No. Vitya, it's of no use. She is languishing. She is quiet, sometimes too quiet and stares aimlessly and absently at the floor. To bring this subject up with her would not benefit her, nor us."

"You are right, Alex. I was just wondering."

Our day ended; we ate some of the goods I brought home and retired for the night.

"Get up! Get up, Vitya! Now!" Alex was shouting.

"What! What is it, Alex?"

It was the middle of the night when Alex woke me.

"Mother! It's Mother again! She is not well again, Vitya!" Alex now pointed to the floor, where Mother lay helplessly.

After some brief instructions, Alex ran for help. I sat praying and waiting. Auntie Katya was soon amongst us. Not long after that, two men in white overcoats were amongst us as well. Our bitter experience and sadness again...Again, they took Mother.

Auntie Katya sat us down after Mother and the two men left and then she informed us of her intentions.

"I am taking George to the orphanage. You two boys...Well...You two boys will have to fend for yourselves...Work."

Alex and I were not only saddened now, but hurt. She was

taking George from us. What could we do? We couldn't keep him, because we had to work. We had no alternative, but to approve and consent to her wishes.

Alex ventured to ask Auntie Katya of our father's location.

"That is a long story, Alex. Do you recall the neighbours you had living above your home?" After our nods of recognition, she continued. "And do you remember when they slept in your home, too?" We remembered. We were lying on the floor like sardines to accommodate us all.

I heard people in our neighbourhood name this family that was staying in our very tiny home: Jewish. I had no inkling to what that meant. I only knew that we had company. I also recall that we were only permitted to leave our home at night, at that time. Later on, after the family left us, I overheard Father tell Mother that he took them to meet someone at the local cemetery (years later, I found out they were saved from the Nazis by my father). What irony in that Father of mine: A merciful tyrant.

Auntie Katya commenced her explanation to us. "You see, children, after that incident with your neighbours, somehow some people found out and your father was sent to another country," she matter-of-factly pointed out to us.

"Your father left some money to me and I paid the rent for you. Tomorrow, I will take George to the orphanage and you two, well, you know."

Auntie Katya finished her remarks and headed out the door with George. Alex and I stared at each other. We hadn't had much to say. Everything was said and done. We just had to conform, persist and prevail on surviving.

It was such a sorrowful atmosphere in the desolate home of ours. Vechislav rarely visited us. He knew of Mother's lapses, because when we accidentally met him in the streets, while doing our begging (and he would be scornful to us), we would update him of our situation at home as if we were obliged to. He showed interest, but did little to appease and lighten our burden. We still thought of him as our brother and even though he restrained himself of any emotion toward us, nevertheless we loved him. Whether he visited Mother in the hospital or not was unknown to us.

Our morning disposition was as dark, grey and gloomy as the outdoor weather. We knew we had to scavenge again. We knew George is not with us. We knew Mother was gone. We knew Father didn't care. How we managed to maintain willpower to continually seek money and food is incomprehensible, but we did, we had to.

Brutally condemned, abused and humiliated repeatedly and systematically, had promoted in us either an apathetic frame of mind or a supreme force to motivate us in obtaining the never-ending provisions, vital and necessary for survival. Certain that the latter was prevalent, we mechanically continued forward. The assimilation of our abode, commodities and the woeful methods practised for our daily bread, was interlaced with tragic circumstances and morally congruent to the Dostoyevskian era. An enigmatic factor when compared to the opulent lifestyle once existing and relished by my predecessors.

We heard an impatient rapping on the door. Two large men, with serious expressions stood before us. In one heavy breath, they instantly informed us that there is no one to take care of our mother at the hospital and they must return her home. While they were stating their inability to continue the care for Mother, they motioned two other men (again in white overcoats) to bring Mother in. In came Mother on the stretcher. They put her on the bed in the bedroom. We were dumbfounded. We hadn't an opportunity to even inquire of her state, or how to properly care for her, for the men cooly remarked that it was entirely our problem and they walked with a fast pace, nearly running as they left.

"What do we do, Alex? Mother is lying there staring at the ceiling and she is not responding to me?"

"Let her be. She will be fine there," Alex remarked exhausted and full of anxiety.

"Alex, what about George?"

"What about him?"

"Will he be brought back home, too?"

"Auntie Katya probably took him to the orphanage," said Alex.

"We can't do anything, Vitya."

"Agh, if only we had our Olga here to help us. Why did those people that Father chased away take her to that White Monastery? What is a White Monastery?"

"Vitya, stop that. I don't know why they took her, but you're right, it would be beneficial to have our Olga here to help us with Mother."

I wondered how Father could have possibly allowed those two gentlemen to take our Olga, after that display that evening long ago. Perhaps they took her due to the landlord's complaints of our home bearing too many children? Another fact was that Father was absent.

We spent the rest of the day in severe contemplation. Mother fell asleep. We ate whatever was left of the canned goods, which I had brought earlier. I did keep in touch with Mrs. Helen, knowing of her vast collection of cans and jars that created me into a frequent caller of hers. She would be charitable and offer one or two cans, but not more. She had to conserve as well.

On our stove was an old, crusty pot which once contained that morose concoction of boiled stale bread. We didn't bother to wash this pot, for we had no use of it. We decided not to venture out that day, due to our mother's presence and her need of attention. We had to devise a formidable plan of survival. Soon it became dark, we had no candles, nor anything else to provide us with light, thus we retired early.

"Alex."

"What?"

"Should we pray to God to help us?"

"Pray if you wish."

I went down on my knees and folded my hands together as I rested my elbows on the bed. "Dear God, help us. Look at us,

God. Please help us. We really need your help...we really do."
I crossed myself and climbed back into bed.

Mother was standing beside the bed near me and her
penetrating stare and presence awoke me. She was gazing at
me oddly. It was strange. I was scared.

"Alex! Alex!"

"Quiet," he mumbled.

"Alex, get up. Get up now!"

Mother was standing in a puddle. Alex got up after repeated
implorations and nudges of mine. We vehemently attempted to
move Mother out of the puddle and onto the bed. She didn't
budge. We were amazed at how strong she was considering her
physique and illness. Perhaps it was due to our sleepiness and
unanticipated shock that caused our disability. At once
Mother started shouting at us, "Leave me alone, you
murderers. Leave me alone. You killed my father! Stop! Stop!"

Mother had no comprehension. She did not recognize us at
all. Suddenly, I flew back a metre, knocking something over
and stumbled to the ground. Alex was not exempt from this
sudden jolt and violent outburst from our very quiet, loving
and weak mother. She shook us off herself, while yelling at us.
It was most terrible. Alex jumped on Mother. They were now on
the bed. Alex howled out to me, "Get me the rope, any rope, and
quick!" I obeyed my brother.

Mother was now apprehended. I had pulled the rope that we
used to hang our measly belongings, after Alex had washed
them with ashes (tip from the neighbours). Now the laundry
was scattered everywhere and Mother was lying motionless on
the bed tied and we were tired, very tired as she was probably,
too, after that unforeseen and strenuous exercise.

Alex successfully tied Mother, but we still had to ensure that
she would not escape like that again. Therefore, Alex decided
on tying her hands to the bedpost. I disagreed.

"I don't think I want that, Alex."

"I am not asking what you want, Vitya, I am doing it. Hand
me more rope."

"No."

"Vitya, she will get up again. I am not pleased with this either, but we really have no choice."

Reluctantly I found some more rope and handed it to Alex. She was restrained. We sat there, like two heroes...Miserable heroes.

We cleaned up the mess on the floor and sat to rest. It was dawn, daybreak, and we didn't realize how long it took to complete our tasks. A gentle barely audible knock was heard at the door, followed by an attempted turn of the knob. I got up and so did Alex. We opened the door. A young girl stood there. Tired and confused I curtly asked this girl, "What do you want now?"

"I am Olga, Vitya."

"Olga? Is that you, Olga?"

"Yes. It is me."

We immediately hugged each other and Alex joined in. How Olga changed. She was dressed in dingy, shabby clothing, a dress long past her knees. Her blonde locks were no longer there, just very short hair, a crew cut.

"Olga, we thought you were at the White Monastery?" Alex inquired.

"Yes I was. But now they sent us all home. Look at this paper, they gave it to me, it has our address on it."

Alex and I examined the paper, tossed it aside and didn't hide our merriment from her. We were exuberant. She couldn't have come at a better time than now!

"Where is Mother?" Olga looked at us beseechingly.

"In the room, on the bed," I answered her.

She went into the bedroom. Alex and I heard the cries.

"Mama, what has happened to you? Mama, who tied you? Who did this to you? Mama, look at me, talk to me!"

In between her groans and sobs, we heard both our names called out. We glanced at each other and went directly to her. We caught Olga attempting to untie what we strived to accomplish and luckily she couldn't muster it. She looked at us with an unusual assortment of anger, hatred, disbelief, finally grief and pity. We took Olga to the kitchen and in half an hour Olga was informed.

"Olga, we are relieved that you are here to help us. We need someone to look after Mother while Vitya and I seek for provisions."

"How can I help you? I don't know how to cook."

"Olga, just help out with whatever you can and look after Mother."

Olga, silenced now, nodded her head in agreement.

Olga worked hard. She cleaned and cleaned. She made a few unsuccessful attempts at cooking, nevertheless we were proud of her and obediently ate whatever meal she put before us. She looked after Mother as best as she could, which was a load off our minds, for we couldn't take Mother to the outhouse and we couldn't wash her. Now that Olga was home, these two chores were lightened. Olga found some old dresses and skirts of Mother's and she wore them, in spite of them hanging to the floor. She had tied a rope around her waist and was content.

With all that gladness now at Olga's arrival, we were now faced with a new misfortune. Lice. Olga unintentionally brought, along with her good will, lice. Hence her crew cut. We all scratched ourselves to oblivion. We received a thick-toothed comb from a generous neighbour, who kindly directed us how to rid ourselves of the lice. We were to comb our hair, place the lice on a piece of paper and then squash them with our fingernails. We still had the other pests in our home, bed bugs, fleas, centipedes and now lice. The three of us would kill the insects during the night, when they carelessly roamed about in the dark. In the morning the walls canvassed our nightly work, our art.

Our days were filled with exasperation. Whom to beg from? There is no one to beg from. The people, now so accustomed to the war, found methods of placating themselves in every way and form, from provisions such as food, shelter, wood for heating and cooking, to entertainment. Prices were astronomical. People, decidedly, were no longer generous. We were deprived in every manner.

"Alex...where are we going to get food? You know, Mrs. Helen had delicately warned me that her inventory was running low, diminishing, and that I should call on her less frequently."

"The black market!" Alex exclaimed.

I wondered. What in the world is a black market? I manifested a scene in my head of how the black market would look like: Long, black tables, with long black tablecloths and people totally garbed in black and all that in a large black auditorium of some kind. I was truly piqued regarding this black market and of what possible benefit it would be to us? We don't need any black items? What Alex had in his mind, his intentions were unknown to me. In any event, he was older and knew better of all these worldly matters.

The next day we left in the brisk coolness of the autumn morning air, wearing some pants of Father's and shirts that we had found. We naturally tied the pants up with ropes, lest we lose them along the way. We customarily tied a fresh set of rags on our feet every morning, which served as socks. We departed for work.

The city began to reawaken somewhat and spring back to life, be it in a zombie mode. The people were sombrely preoccupied with gathering needs and food for the preparation of the winter months ahead. The gathering of needs was an endless and troublesome task that required non-stop work and contemplation. They resembled busy squirrels in many cases, not paying heed to others, not looking left, nor right, simply busily working.

We had all unfortunately and unusually become accustomed to the whistling noises, followed by explosions in the distance, which slowly faded. The occupiers were now in full command and control. I heard conversations between people clustered into groups and chatting on the streets that now the infamous black market was open. Again this black market! What is it about this black market and how it differs from our regular local market that attracts people to speak of it, including my brother Alex? Some men began commenting on the financial aspects of the war: New currency was in circulation, courtesy of our enemy oppressors. They carried stashes of this money as I have noticed, when making their purchases at the piazza.

We had to produce a system or method of obtaining our provisions. At times I would suggest ideas to Alex, but poor Alex had a slight hearing loss in one ear after his illness last year and he would therefore not always hear my suggestions. I would become frustrated and mumble a few words, which would not be appreciated by Alex. I knew he didn't hear me, for if he had, I would have received a generous slap across my face. I knew when I could complain bitterly and on what side of Alex I may do so.

Alex and I travelled by our common method: hanging on the streetcars. Surprisingly, others did, too. The car itself, acquired new rules for the passengers lucky enough to get inside. The front of the car being exclusively reserved for the enemy occupiers, while the rear of the car, for more distinguished people, whether in relation to the enemy or not, was unknown to us. The general public now fancied Alex's and my old, but reliable means of transport—traffic magnets, thus we had to share the back of the car with others in need of transport. How dare they!

The streetcar stopped in front of St. Mark's Church and went no farther. From there we were obliged to hop and hang on to a passing fiacre. We were sometimes faced with angry coachmen who waved us off and yet some didn't care, or didn't know of their additional tarry. We arrived at the Terraziya and set off to the Moscow Hotel, that is, the Serbia Hotel now, the name had been changed to suit our city's new situation and status. We jumped off when we were close to our destination and began our walk.

"Look! Look, Alex! Over there!" I tugged viciously at Alex's shirt sleeve.

"What!" he angrily answered.

"Look, Alex, there is a man hanging over there on that post."

"Vitya, you are right!" Alex shockingly replied.

"And his hands are tied," I observed.

"Indeed they are," replied Alex.

"Do you think he's dead?"

"Are you an idiot, Vitya? Would he be hanging there alive? Of course he is dead. Look at him."

"Who hung him, Alex?"

"Not his friends for sure!"

I snuggled closer and nearer to Alex for protection.

"Alex...Let's leave now. If that man's friends or enemies notice us here, they might put us there to accompany that man!"

Alex just looked at me.

We cornered the hotel and advanced toward the steep descent along Balkanska Street, to the train station. We observed a coachman whipping his skinny, exhausted horse that was unsuccessfully pulling or dragging a heavy load of wood in the wagon. The whip kept falling on the poor horse as he didn't budge, for the load was too much for him and he tumbled over. Some passers-by scurried to help the horse, not the coachman. Sympathetic to the animal, they began to reproach the coachman, who unconcerned of their remarks, proceeded to place a brick beneath the rear wheel of the wagon to prevent it from sprinting backward.

A smartly dressed lady stood there between the others, she apparently was the owner of the wood, for she began scolding the coachman for piling too big of a load in the wagon all at once, to spare himself a second trip. She demanded that he must take half of it off and return for the rest. He curtly answered her that if he did so, who would keep guard of the remainder of the wood. He then sarcastically advised her that he would do as she requested, provided she remains there with the rest of her wood; he didn't want to be responsible for any wood missing, especially considering how valuable it had become. Somehow they reached an agreement and he poked the poor horse back to his feet and left after emptying half of the wagon. The lady, satisfied of her achievement, continued to stand awkwardly, gawking at the passers-by.

Concluding our little diversion of attention, we continued to our destination: the train station. Finally arriving there after losing time by watching that coachman and lady for a half hour, we noticed many people, of all kinds and classes, coming and leaving. Luggage, bags and a variety of other cherished notables were seen lying on the ground and platform everywhere.

"Now we must hunt for a customer!" in unison we proclaimed as our eyes were darting and surveying the vicinity.

"There! Go there, Vitya! There's an officer in need of help, run!" Alex commanded and continued, "We'll meet here at the square, right there where that lady is selling her homemade dumplings."

Gosh, those dumplings smelled so good and tempting!

"Alex, can you buy me a dumpling?"

"No, with what? I have no money." He pulled his pockets inside out to prove his point. "Now go and earn some money, Vitya! Run! Run before that officer gets away!"

I obliged. I ran as fast as I could with Father's shoes on, which were too big for me, and as I was doing so, I lost one shoe, revealing the rags I had for socks. The darned rags, even they came undone and were waving behind me as I ran. I had to stop to collect my foot gear. With one shoe under my arm and rags tied in a knot around my foot, I ran faster, worried I would lose a customer.

"Please, please," I begged the officer while pointing to his luggage and my back. I assumed he would understand. He said something in a brusque tone and in a foreign language, which I didn't understand. I repeated my gestures and begged. Finally this officer understood and gave me his luggage, which was as heavy as lead. I wobbled as I tried to put it on my shoulder, all the while with the shoe still under my arm, I hadn't the time, nor luxury of slipping the over-sized shoe back on, therefore I walked in this fashion.

Judging by the way the officer was dressed, clean and shiny, his uniform sharply pressed and shoes glistening in the sun, gave me the impression that a good wage was to befall my way. Probably a pack of cigarettes, which Alex would later barter for some bread. Agh, how heavy his suitcase was, what did he have in there?

We came to Balkanska Street. Oh no! Balkanska Street! The pig! Why did he have to choose this street of all streets? We were about to embark on a steep ascent. I was thin, scrawny and not as strong as the officer might have thought. His heavy baggage was hovering over me as a leaf over a tiny ant that toils desperately. I might even earn two packs of cigarettes considering the steep ascent of this street and all the sweat I am sparing him. At once I recalled that poor horse that toppled over from over exertion, I felt that I was not much better.

I dragged my feet upward on this steep hill. The cobblestones made it more difficult, especially since I had only one shoe on. By now the officer was far ahead of me and I was lugging behind him. He would occasionally turn around to see how far I am and briskly clap his hands twice while mumbling something, which acknowledged was a signal to hurry it up.

This officer was a tall man. He looked intimidating and the protruding revolver from the side of his belt didn't comfort me, rather intimidated me. Where is he rushing to I wondered as I tripped on a cobblestone, nearly fell, but regained my balance just in time, because he had turned around again to check exactly how far behind I am.

Oh God help me I prayed. A little more, just a little more. We passed by Queen Natalia Street. I was drenched in sweat and the lice were feasting on my scalp, under my beret. I could not do anything about it, except make silly faces, which made my entire guise all the more peculiar. Finally we arrived at the foot of the hotel. I fell down on my face with the suitcase on top of me. I jumped quickly avoiding the officer's scorn. He turned around and took his luggage. He began to walk away! What! I ran after him.

"Please! Please!" I was now holding my hand open pointing at my palm for him to pay me. He stared down at me quizzically.

"Please!" I pleaded with him and a cold sweat this time showered me. I think even my chin might have begun to quiver. I was desperate. All that work! All that sweating! All that biting by the lice! For what?

The officer was now contemplating. I thought that perhaps my pitiful importunateness would render him generous. He dug in his pocket and pulled out a shiny, golden cigarette case. He opened it and handed me two cigarettes. Two measly cigarettes! My eyes nearly fell out of their sockets. I was crushed. I stared at the cigarettes, at him, at the cigarettes. I was silent.

A stream of invective words escaped me. I cursed and hollered and cried. He did not understand me, but I am certain that he was well aware that I wasn't thanking him. I could not have anticipated such a mediocre payment from such a pompous officer. He openly exploited me. "I can't even buy bread with that!" I hollered at him.

"Nau, nau!" He reached for his revolver as he began to shout back at me. Upon noticing his reaction, I ran. I flew. I didn't look back until I reached the bottom of this steep street and I turned around and saw the white and blue sky at the top of the hill. I sat down on the curb, breathing heavily even though the flight down was much easier since it was a descent and I had no luggage. I put my shoe back on my foot. Then, I took off my wet beret and went wild scratching my scalp. Furiously scraping the lice with my fingernails, "And you must pester me as well!" What will I tell Alex? I sat there and began to sob.

Back at the train station, the people were sparse, the crowds thinned. The days travellers were nearly all at their designated locations. I threw my gazes around me—no dumpling lady; she, too, had left for the day. A man was heard yelling "Boza! Boza!" I sat on the bench and wondered. Thinking of that inconsiderate officer and how I threw the two cigarettes at his feet. I gave an oath to myself, I would never carry these officer's luggage again. Never. Swimming in these thoughts I waited for Alex and I didn't realize that someone was standing behind me.

Chapter 8

I felt someone tugging at my ear and painfully so. "Ouch!" I turned around and beheld a gendarme!

"Sir, please stop, that hurts! I didn't do anything, sir!"

"Scoundrels! That's what you are! A scoundrel!" he warranted as he kept tugging and pinching my ear. "It's scum like you that are taking away the bread and butter from these licenced and registered luggage carriers!" the gendarme stated, while pointing with his truncheon toward the very satisfied luggage carrier, who had one foot on his cart and was smirking at my misfortune.

"We have received complaints from these carriers and you little weasels come here to do their job!"

I was mortified. Not only was I cooled from yet another cold sweat that suddenly hit, but was instantaneously warmed with a warm drizzle down my pants, which later became cool as I was dragged by this gendarme (still by the ear) across the street. Oh, where was Alex, I panicked. *Goodbye, Alex, Olga and Mother. What will become of me I am uncertain. I might even be hanged as that poor soul was on the Terraziye.*

We arrived at the central police headquarters located within the train station. We scurried up the stone steps and found ourselves in a very long and dreary corridor. To our immediate right was a gloomy and heavy looking dark door, which he unlocked loudly and shoved me in. The clanking of the noisy keys assured me that he probably locked me in.

It was semi-dark in this room. A dim, smoky bulb covered

with this mesh wire hung low from the ceiling. I noticed a large, withered wooden desk. A chair of the same value and a worn out wooden bench (where most likely many transgressors had the privilege to be seated) beneath an iron barred window.

I suddenly realized that I wasn't alone in the room. I strained my eyes to observe this person without looking conspicuous and thought, well...at least I'm not alone! I dared to call out, "Hey! Hey you?" I didn't receive a reply, nor a recognition of my presence. Maybe he's dead and a cold shiver ran down my spine. I was never alone with a deceased person! Through this musty darkness and frightening stillness of air, I ventured closer to the apparition. I began to poke him, out of curiosity, out of fright. Oddly, this person seemed familiar to me, in fact too familiar! Could it be?

"Alex! It's you! What are you doing here? Why didn't you answer me?"

"Quiet, you elephant! Does it look like I'm here to sing and dance! You silly horse!"

Alex was vexed and even more so, since I, too, was locked in with him and became his cohort in crime. Not to mention that I disturbed his deep contemplation. I thought he might be happy to see me, but found the contrary.

"All right, Alex, I know you are not here to sing and dance! Did that gendarme bring you here, too? Was it for taking away and interfering with the business of those luggage carriers?"

"Alex, I have so much to tell you. Remember that officer you told me to run after? Well I carried his obnoxiously heavy luggage and he wouldn't pay me! Imagine that! He hesitatingly handed me two measly cigarettes, which I proudly threw at his feet! He then reached for his revolver and well...I ran as fast as the wind would carry me! Therefore, Alex, I have no earnings today. I was waiting for you at our designated meeting spot and suddenly that mean old gendarme grabbed my ear and dragged me here into this room." I cried again...

"Vitya, I had no better luck than you. I was grabbed by the collar of my shirt and thrown in here. I didn't have a chance to spy on the person who hurled me in, even less of any explanations," Alex exclaimed, becoming more mellow after witnessing me cry.

"I wonder what they will do to us?" I thought out loud.

Alex sat sorrowfully. I observed him, I felt sorry for him. He looked pitiful in his garb, with his head sunk low, hungry probably. I thought then, I am no better than poor Alex. We were pathetic.

"Did you eat, Alex?"

"What? No one gave me anything."

"Alex, do you think this is a jail?"

"Hush now, Vitya, quiet. I am trying to devise an escape plan."

"Oh, of course, Alex, sorry. Did you think of anything yet?"

"Quiet and listen to me, Vitya. Get up and go try to turn the door knob. If it's unlocked, peek through the door and determine whether we are being guarded."

"But if it's locked, Alex, then what?"

"Whistle, you donkey. Nothing. Come back here," Alex charged, now fully agitated. "Vitya, if it's locked, silly, you have the kalhaus, remember?"

"Right! I forgot, Alex."

Now I was prepared to assist Alex in our escape. I tip-toed over to the door, ever so quietly and sneakily. I tried turning the knob. Nothing.

"Kalhaus! Kalhaus!" I heard Alex whispering in frustration. I shakily grabbed the homemade kalhaus from my pocket (which I made a habit of carrying in my pocket, should the need arise to utilize it, apparently like in that moment. I borrowed it from Father; he didn't need it and wasn't home to prevent me from taking it. Besides, when I noted the accomplishments Mrs. Helen achieved by the kalhaus, I decided to carry it with me at all times) and tried the door's lock, since it could be unlocked from the inside, luckily. *Click, click.* It unlocked! Alex whispered loudly now, "Good! Now look for the guards!" I opened the door ajar, cautiously trying not to make noise, but these old doors squeaked in protest nonetheless. I protruded my head, enough to enable me to spy on any guards standing there. I looked about and pulled my head back in. "Nothing!" In two hops Alex was beside me and declared, "Run! Now! Fast!"

I believe only the wind was left behind us; we ran as if competing in the Olympics.

In a matter of seconds we crossed the street and flew into a mini parkette. Alex, being older and faster, was ahead of me, but had slowed his pace in consideration toward me. I caught up, breathless. We walked along Nemanya Street when Alex hollered out, "Look, a fiacre!" No more instructions needed. We found ourselves sitting on the rear fender of the fiacre.

The coachman's whip was whizzing by our heads as he whipped his horse into direction. We understood that the coachman was aware of his unwanted tails, thus we hopped off the fiacre.

"Agh, we didn't have such a long ride," I uttered to Alex, who was not paying the least bit of attention to me, but staring off into the abyss.

He didn't say anything, just picked up his pace and suddenly shouted, "Hurry!" I did.

The street we followed had tracks in the centre—street car tracks, although no cars ran this way anymore, for the tracks were sliced apart by the bombs. The copper wires of the cars were not visible either; the enemy supposedly needed those, too. We walked by huge, stone buildings. Some were in ruins, some slightly chipped. These buildings once housed the various ministries of the city, and now stood abandoned. The buildings looked ominous, rousing a sense of forlorn as these structures were barricaded and stood towering in the sky as ghostly shadows preventing any ray of sun to penetrate onto the street, or its pedestrians. The cold wind was felt each time one would take this route and would feel as if they were being pulled forward. Was it due to the draught of the cold air pulling in toward the mouths of the rivers Danube and Sava? I reflected on this, while noticing that this street was treeless. It was a drab, grey, draughty and cold street.

At the intersection of Great Milosh and Nemanya streets were on each corner beautiful edifices harboring the Academy of the Army, now demolished and in ruins. I followed Alex across the street and he, then I, crouched in front of a low iron fence, beneath the streetcar stop number three. We sat there.

Why? I don't know. I knew that this streetcar was now in use and ran to the suburb of Topchidar. A wonderful suburb full of lush green trees and parks. Was he thinking we were going to visit Topchidar? I didn't plunge into questioning. I just mimicked all he did as if I knew of our next plan.

"We will work here now, Vitya." He broke our silence as he picked up a cigarette butt with some tobacco left in it, sufficient for a few puffs, and he commenced to light it. He savoured the cigarette as he pulled a heavy drag of it.

"Give me some, too, Alex!" He looked at me and selfishly instructed me to find my own butt.   "Fine!" I answered insulted. I took a few steps and found another discarded cigarette butt, probably from those supercilious officers I speculated.

"Give me a light!" I exultantly asked.

He threw over the book of matches and I lit my cigarette. I stood leisurely aside, studying the passengers that were gathering for the coming streetcar, while smartly puffing the cigarette butt. Beside me stood an elderly man. He wore a greasy hat and a torn grey overcoat, which hid his very greasy grey pants. On his feet he bore some torn replicas of shoes and his dirty toes poked through the holes. He had thick, untamed eyebrows which looked dirty and grey, suitable to the rest of his attire. An unkept, overgrown beard partially hid his face.

A heavy stench of liquor at once swarmed over my face as he implored me for a puff of my cigarette butt and he held out his dingy, dirty and shaky hand. I gave him the cigarette, with no intentions of recovering it. I deliberated that his hand, nor the rest of him, hadn't seen water since his baptism. He nodded his head in appreciation as I casually stepped away from him.

My eyes now skimmed the vicinity in search for my brother, Alex. I caught him standing with a young man talking. This fellow had a cap on his head, an oversized, faded black overcoat on his person that reached well below his knees. He was clad in a pair of pants that were wide, but short, certainly a perfect fit for the previous owner, but pitifully not the new one. His two thin legs projected from these bell pants that swayed in the wind. His shoes, though, were in much better state of repair than ours I noticed. They were army boots. I judged that his entire garb was well suited and proportioned to his nasty demeanor.

He stole a glance at me, questioning my presence, then directed his question to Alex, "Why are you two here? You don't belong here!" he started as he took a pack of American cigarettes from his coat pocket. Alex and I admired. The fact that he had Camel cigarettes completely forgave his sullen appearance. He calmly demanded us to leave, mainly directing his commands to Alex, but pluralizing. Alex and I began to depart after this long, thin and bleak person threatened to hit us.

"Why does he command us, Alex? Who is he to have such authority? Look at him!"

"Go...Go over there, Vitya."

We were safely out of reach now and we heard the streetcar's approach by its squeaking breaks. We turned around just in time to observe the streetcar full of passengers hanging on the sides like pears on a tree. I immediately understood why Alex brought us here.

Hefty peasant women stepped off the streetcar, with weather beaten complexions and of course, provincial deportments. They carried an abundance of baskets filled to the brim with their hard earned harvest, intended for sale at the piazzas. Some of them carried fresh baked bread which was carefully covered with clean tea towels. As I was poring over all this, I witnessed that tall, thin, scornful lad who scooted us away, carrying a basket over his shoulders and a peasant woman following him closely behind. Right after him was Alex! He, too, was now carrying a basket on his shoulder and a peasant woman was following him! The greasy old man found employment as well. Hopefully, I was next.

I came up to a peasant woman who had a brightly coloured kerchief wrapped around her head and most naturally, I proceeded to grab the basket out of her hands. To my astonishment, she pulled it back and began cursing. I was in a disarray. I was not about to be the only unemployed person there, thus I, too, began pulling her basket. We went on like this for a few minutes. I beseeched her to allow me to carry her basket like the others did. She gradually relented. I was happy. Now I merrily asked this lady, "Ma'am, where exactly are we going to?"

"Tsvetni Trg."

"I know where that is, ma'am, my mother goes there for flowers," I wisely remarked.

"No, son, not to that piazza, but to the Kalinicheva Piazza."

Agh, that's a long trip from here! We ascended back along Nemanya Street, and the basket began to irritate my shoulder.

"Let's go this way, dear," she guided.

We went along Slaviya Street to Krunska and turned right. To break the silence, I began to discourse, "You know, ma'am, that on Krunska Street a bomb had targeted a children's hospital. Tiny limbs, being of arms and legs, were scattered about everywhere and visible to all."

"Child! What is this you tell me?" She was alarmed and frightened now.

"Yes, ma'am. It was a dreadful sight. And you know, ma'am, the annoying loud sirens the city gets are very irritating to us. Daily we listen to them, when it sounds three times it signals that we are in danger. When it is once and long, it is the end." For some reason, I found it my duty to inform her of "our" city's events.

"Oh my, oh dear child! Let us hurry, child!"

Am I ever dumb. I had to mention those things to her and now I have to run with this basket on my shoulder, since I did a marvellous job of frightening her.

I sweated along Krunska Street. It was a scenic route, lined with mature trees. It housed the foreign embassies. Gratefully the road was asphalted, thus we arrived more swiftly. I gently placed her basket on the ground in front of her and patiently waited for my payment.

"What does it cost?" she asked me as she was fumbling through her bag.

"Ma'am, bread please."

She took another large bag off her shoulder and pulled out a large loaf of round bread called "pogacha." She broke it in two and handed me half of it. My eyes gleamed at this delicious

MARINA RADOVANOVIC

reward before me. Again, she searched in her large bag and out
came bacon and a knife. She cut off a generous piece and
handed that to me, too! Oh the joy! I shivered of happiness and
hunger. I took what she gave me and bowed ever so humbly,
nearly to the ground. My joy was unsurpassed. Lucky were
those peasants that had much food, harvested from their
fruitful land.

I decided to return to the third (that's what it was dubbed,
for it was streetcar stop number three). If I was this fortunate,
I might score again! I broke off a piece of bread and chewed
merrily. It was made from fine flour, how it was sweet to me. I
couldn't sample the smoked bacon, I had no knife, only the
kalhaus. I put my precious bundle within the inside of my coat
pocket and gladly thought of how we will all have a splendid
dinner tonight.

When I reached the third, Alex was nowhere to be seen. A
slight drizzle of rain began to pester. Should I wait for Alex? If
another streetcar arrives, I will most definitely acquire another
customer. With that, I noticed another streetcar approaching
and began to rejoice.

There were but a few passengers and no peasant women
with precious baskets either. No one carried anything in need
of my assistance. "Perhaps the train hasn't arrived yet?" I
mumbled this out loudly with hopes of some passengers'
assuring answers. No one said anything, but went off to their
destinations.

What now? I looked across the street where a skeleton of a
building remained. I crossed the street on the semaphore
where traffic lights (put up before the war) used to be. The
bulbs were missing, someone had certainly needed them. I
climbed the wide stone steps of the skeletal building and found
a stone in a corner to sit on.

The cold autumn drizzle turned to light rain, thus I was wet.
I was lucky we weren't hit by the usual autumn storm where
any human caught outdoors would be obliged to hang on to a
nearby post or tree, lest they fly away with the wind. Despite
the emptiness of the streetcar, I persisted and waited for

another one and Alex simultaneously. But, neither arrived.

I had a good view from the angle I sat in, providing me with an unobtrusive view of the intersection. I hoped for Alex's quick return. While sitting there, tugging at my shirt which I found in the garbage as well as my pants. I conveniently wore them over my old clothes, which proved to be warmer for these chilly months. Father's clothes, that I previously wore, hung too much on me.

I studied the state of the city and its inhabitants. The birds were not as chirpy as usual. The streets nearly abandoned, save for the urchins, looters and brave souls. A few crows loomed over the city of ruins. I felt chilly. It must be, because of my feet. I took off my shoes, one by one and unwrapped the now soaked rags. Wrung them thoroughly and returned them on my feet, all the while spying on the intersection.

At once a most beautiful vision emanated from the dark, gloomy and damp day. A lovely lady dressed in a black suit, with an enormous, widely brimmed, black hat was walking in my direction. In one hand she held an umbrella, in the other, the hand of a little girl. Such a pretty girl, she wore a beret on her head, matching her neat coat. Her shoes were shiny and lacquered in black. Her golden locks fell upon her red coat. She strikingly resembled the girl from the fairytale "Little Red Riding Hood." To me and my grief, they seemed like a burst of sunshine on the dull and poignant day.

I followed them with my eyes and rested them twenty metres ahead of me. The beautiful lady bent down and whispered something to the little girl, while pointing her finger at me. Why? Why are they here standing and pointing at me? What have I done now? Where should I go? Is she another authoritative figure? Or is she married to one? God, help me. I have nowhere to hide! I must run! Should I? I didn't do anything, or steal anything. Why should they be standing before me and gawking at me?

I was now fully perplexed in this circumstance. Agh, it was no use. The little girl was but three steps in front of me. The closer she came, the more I realized how pleasant she was. She was hopping merrily up the steps, entirely insouciant.

"Hello!" She smiled like an angel sent from heaven. I, on the other hand, felt chagrined at my appearance and stature. She then pushed her hand forward at me and in her little palm were five hundred dinars! The new dinars, minted by the occupiers. I gazed in astonishment as an escaped tear betrayed me and rolled down my cheek.

I had my hand on my chest and inquired of her, "Is that for me? That is much too much for me." I quivered.

A warm, heavenly voice emitted from this angelic being singing, "Yes," while smiling serenely.

Should I take it or not? It was a dilemma. Look at me. A vagrant. A street urchin. Look at her, so beautiful, pure and heavenly. I mused and looked at the lady standing below us who was smilingly nodding her head in approval of their offer to me. I took the money from the palm of the little girl who stood there patiently.

"Thank you, thank you!" I reiterated.

The little girl, completely satisfied of her noble deed, had turned around and bounced back down the steps to the lady, I assume her mother.

I couldn't believe it! I was speechless and beside myself. I had not anticipated such an occurrence. I was waiting here for work and Alex and look! Out of nowhere, five hundred dinars! Sent from heaven! What a gift! They waved goodbye to me and disappeared. I was thoroughly exuberant, touched and ashamed at my state. I left with my gift.

I had bread...bacon and now money! I had no patience whatsoever to wait for Alex. I must share this wealth and joy with someone.

I skipped through Great Milosh Street. I was wet, but didn't care, I floated lightly in the rain, eager to get home. I merrily hooked onto a passing fiacre that did not object to my fastening, and in no time, I was home.

Alex was sitting at the table and he had a guest.

"Aleexsss, Ooolgaa! I'm home!" I gleefully announced.

"I know," Alex uttered without looking at me as he was

involved in a discussion with his guest.

I looked over to Olga who was sitting quietly on Father's bed, questioning her with my eyes of this intruder. She ignored my imploration. I asked where Mother was as I placed the goodies on the stove.

"In the bedroom asleep," she mumbled. She seemed intimidated by this guest of Alex's.

I looked at the two of them at the table. Alex then commented, "Vitya, this man knows our father. They were together in another country. Father had sent him here with this tub of lard for us."

"Oh, I see." I peered at the stranger and allowed my gaze to fall onto the tub of lard, located on the floor right beside the man's feet.

"You know our father, sir?" I courageously asked.

"Yes...I do." He spoke no further, but in his place, I heard a growling.

"Don't be scared, Vitya. He has a dog," Alex laughingly stated, when he noticed my fear.

"I have to go now," the man informed as he stood up, then bent down to the dog (that was under the table) and said something to him in a foreign language. He yanked the tub of lard from the floor and in two large steps was nearly out the door. He stopped abruptly and hung onto the door frame as if someone was pushing him out. He turned around and in a perturbed manner commanded, "Do not feed the dog. Do not take the dog outside!" With that, he left.

What kind of friend is that of Father's? He not only had the audacity to take our lard, but left his dog! With instructions to us!

I began questioning Alex of this unusual stranger, who gave good reason for Olga to feel intimidated. He looked like an officer, though he had no uniform. Odd. Alex didn't find it necessary to retell their conversation. Thus I began, "Alex...I waited for you at the third. Why didn't you come there?"

"I couldn't. I was busy. Look, I earned two packs of Camel cigarettes!" He proudly displayed them on the table. I smiled, I knew I had better...much better.

"Alex, I earned, too!" and I placed the five hundred dinars on the table, gently, reverently. I was nodding my head, waiting for the jubilant praises to launch. Olga stood up at once and Alex's eyes widened and displayed his approval and joy.

"Vitya! You have done exceedingly well today! Now...we can finally pay the rent and not sneak around avoiding the landlord."

We were ecstatic. I requested a cigarette from Alex, from his Camel pack on the table, to celebrate of course, and I considered that I was fully authorized to do so, after my benevolence and delivery of goods.

"Now?" Alex stated.

"Why not?" I asked, realizing that even that achievement of mine didn't provide me with much authority.

"Well...I have to sell these packs tomorrow, Vitya, and buy some bread," he exclaimed.

I noticed that one of the packs was already opened.

"Alex? One pack is opened. I can have one from there?"

"Yes, I know it's opened, because I had one. All right, Vitya, we'll share one."

He then proceeded to shake out a single cigarette from the pack and we smoked in satisfaction, passing it to each other intermittently, and to Olga's chagrin who poured out complaints about the smell.

Olga placed two heaping, hot bowls of bean soup in front of us on the table. She had been earlier at the piazza and sold some of Mother's dresses that were fit for sale and bought a kilo of beans.

"It's good, Olga!" Alex and I chimed.

"Yes. I know," she answered and then took off to the bedroom to feed Mother.

With our bowl of bean soup, we ate the bread I brought and a slice of bacon. What a feast! What a marvellous and productive day!

I looked at the dog on the floor and decided to give it a piece of the bacon's skin. I placed it before the dog (who was called Boy) and observed. He sniffed it, licked his mouth and rested his head on his front legs as he had been doing since his master's departure. I realized that this dog was well trained and fiercely loyal to his master. We completed our meals and with our stomachs full and needs content, we went to bed.

The next morning as every morning, the usual preparations for a day's work ahead. Alex had already left to pay the landlord our overdue rent and then to the third. He was to exchange the cigarettes for bread today.

Olga was busily preparing tea for Mother and us. Olga also had a job. She found employment; she was to wash laundry for a family in exchange for soap, a type of barter, which was good, for we were in dire need of a good scrubbing. Our laundry stank and piled up quickly, since Olga had to frequently change and bathe Mother. Mother seldom left the solace of her bed, thankfully; that was Olga's duty. I was to remain home that day and replace Olga, because she went to work. I had to look after Mother feed her and offer her tea, basically keeping watch on her. I also had to babysit the darn dog that hideous stranger left and hasn't returned for yet.

For the most part of the day, I catered to Mother the best I could. I stared at Boy, who now seemed a fixed part of our furniture in the kitchen. He didn't cease to bewilder me. I eagerly awaited for dusk and the return of Alex and Olga.

Finally, the hours rolled into the evening. Alex returned as promised, with a loaf of bread under his arm. Moments later, Olga returned.

Now it was dear Olga's moment of glory. She proudly placed two bars of soap on the kitchen table. We praised and applauded her and with due respect, for now we had one bar for our own personal bathing and the other for the laundry! I desperately needed to grab that soap and hop into some water and wash away the dirt and grime collected on me. Alex read my mind.

"Not today." The command fell from Alex. I had to oblige. We supped on the left over bean soup, finished off the bacon and enjoyed the bread. After dinner, we had cigarettes to compliment our meal and gratified with the day's outcome bid it adieu.

The sky was turquoise blue, the clouds dispersed and rolled away. We now freely and confidently roamed about, since our rent was paid. The neighbours at first would inquire about our state should we chance to meet them in the courtyard. Later, they would through brief intervals, politely inquire and now not at all. We didn't seem bothered by this ignorance, nor did we attempt to discourse in any conversations with them, in fact we rarely and seldom had encountered them. We would leave early in the morning and return at night; therefore, it was on the odd occasion that we met with those who found no necessity of inquiring. We were aware that we had new tenants living directly above us and as for the landlord...We met with him when he would come to collect his rent money.

It wasn't very cold outside, permitting our door to be open, welcoming the fresh air to swirl inside, ridding the stale aroma of dampness (since we were sub-level), cigarettes and other annoying smells accumulated during the past few days that irritated Olga immensely.

I sat beside Boy. I dared not pet him, for I learned that any attempt would provoke an exhibit of his white, sharp teeth and threatening growl. That dog was a statue! He didn't move a millimetre from the first day of his arrival. I pitied the dog. I settled on becoming his benefactor. A mortal error, I was to find out and experience later.

I came up close to Boy and slapped the side of my leg several times and yelled out, "Boy, come! Come, Boy," continuously padding the side of my leg. Boy's head popped up, looked at me sadly, then returned to his accustomed position. I marvelled at the non-wavering obedience of this dog! I attempted again. Again, he refused. After several attempts, Boy leaped outside in a fury. I accomplished my task!

Boy completed his duty of answering to nature's call. With his tail wagging joyfully he wrapped himself around my legs, circling me, thanking me for his release, for his relief.

Since I considered myself a quasi-master now, I continued my beneficence by pushing the old, dried out piece of skin from the bacon (still on the floor from my previous attempts of feeding him). In one gulp, he devoured the meal, which was followed by noisy slurps of water that I had placed in a bowl in front of him.

A couple of hours later, I decided on letting Boy out again. He went. We both returned satisfied in the kitchen. Boy assumed his usual position and I went to rest on Father's bed. Mother, Boy and I were still alone at home. Olga and Alex were at work, I remained home that day, simply because I decided I was too tired to venture out. What an unforseen mistake that was.

A tragic choice for me and for Boy.

It was dusk. Alex and Olga hadn't returned yet. I napped. Mother was napping after I fed her. While Boy slept, I heard him moaning and I assumed it was due to the absence of his master and his missing him so.

Suddenly, our kitchen door swung open, with no knocks or any indication that we were about to have a visitor. That miserable stranger was back.

"Who's home?!"

"I am," I answered, sitting up on the bed.

"Where's Boy?"

"There. Where you left him," I calmly answered.

He turned the light on, since it darkened outside. The dubious stranger approached Boy.

"Come, Boy. Now!" he roared.

At once I observed this insolent man whipping the German Shepard, Boy, mercilessly. Boy didn't budge. He moaned, but he didn't move. I observed a puddle underneath Boy, who shook in fright before his master. I wondered why was he beating the dog. I thought of jumping to the dog's defence, but by the coarseness and fury of this man, my decision became hindered.

The monster was breathless and flung his cap on the table. He then turned to me, fuming. His eyes were ablaze, his mouth foaming, his hair was standing on end, resembling a porcupine. He was fire, red with anger. He thundered out, "Who took the dog outside?! Who! Answer me! Do you hear...who!"

I was speechless, dumbfounded and visibly shaken. I

pondered. If I said I did, I'd be whipped. If I said I didn't, Olga and Alex would be whipped undeservingly. I was perplexed with all these thoughts flying in my head, certain that I made grimaces during my consideration.

The hooligan blasted, "I ask again—Who!"

He grabbed me by my shirt and in seconds I was lifted off the ground and dangling in the air as he repeatedly questioned me.

"I did," I whispered while stuttering.

I flew to the ground in an instant and fell between the door of the bedroom and the kitchen. He then proceeded to kick me with his heavy boots, in my stomach, with little restraint. Needless to say, I lost my breath. I whimpered, "Mama! Mama!" I looked over to the bed and witnessed Mother's unsuccessful attempts of answering to my pleas. She was tied to the bedpost.

The audacious monster concluded his torture by repeatedly kicking my head and face, before he plunged his hand on the table, snatched his cap, bellowed out for Boy and left slamming the door behind him. The kitchen and all its contents shook. I passed out.

When I had aroused from unconsciousness, I felt cold compresses on my face which Olga was administering. I was completely unaware of how long I was lying there on the floor, but relieved at the sight of Alex and Olga.

"What happened, Vitya?" Alex was sitting on the bed beside me. I gathered that they had placed me there.

"That bandit, Alex. That immortal bandit!"

"What bandit, Vitya? We have nothing here to tempt any bandits?"

"That stranger, Father's friend. The one who left his dog Boy."

I tried to sit up, but the pain was overwhelming. Somehow I managed to recite the entire episode to them, be it in pain.

A week I spent in bed. When I got up to wash my face at the kitchen sink, I stirred, in front of the mirror we had above it, actually startling myself. My face was a painter's palette, numerous colours were displayed on my face. My eyes were swollen, but less now and I had pains in my ribs. Thus poor

Olga had two patients on her hands now, Mother and me.

Alex's endeavours were twofold, he had to work on my behalf as well. When Alex returned in the evenings, he would describe all occurrences to me, with vivid details. I suppose he sympathized with my situation and thought to be more amiable.

One of his stories included a lady who resided on Franko Panovo Street. He informed me that he visited her daily. I asked why. He disclosed that he was earning a profit. The lady had a job for him, in her basement, where she once had coal, was now coal dust in its replacement. Alex started...

"From that dust, I combine water and old newspapers. When it's thick enough, I roll them into balls and place them in a row to dry. The lady then uses these balls for her stove as a source of heat. She hasn't much to pay me, but she provides us with this cornmeal that Olga's cooking for us now, which reminds me...

"You know, Vitya, the government declared they would provide cornbread to the needy at the local bakery. I stood twice in line, but each time as I approached the counter, the cornbread was gone."

After listening to Alex's description of this cornbread line, I was determined to go and stand in line myself and receive this gift. Therefore, I was up at three in the morning, certain I would be the first in line. When I came close to the bakery, unfortunately I noticed ten people already waiting in there.

It was a frosty morning. The streets were dimly lit, not all bulbs were in place and working. Desolate streets, save for us impoverished, expected recipients of charity. As we stood there resolutely, we jumped upon hearing loud yells, "Stop! Stop!"

Consequently, gun shots rang in the chilly, stark, stillness of the morning. We all ran for cover. I tried to enter a backyard of one house, but the gate was locked. I ran home and waited half an hour, before returning to the bakery.

Now the line for alms extended nearly to the next street. I had no option. I waited, too. An hour lapsed. Then another. I asked this elderly woman standing ahead of me, "What time will the bakery open, ma'am?"

"I believe at six, son."

Eventually six arrived. We heard some noise ahead of us. Within ten minutes the crowd began dissolving as the dawn turned to day. I asked the lady, who had a black handkerchief tied on her head, "What is going on, ma'am?"

"Can't you see, son? The people are returning home!"

"But, but the cornbread?"

"What cornbread, son! No more! It's gone!"

"How can that be, ma'am?" I had tears forming in my eyes as I stated, "They were only open for ten minutes, ma'am!"

"I know, I know, son, but you and I are not related to the baker. The cornbread goes out through the back door of the bakery as well. You and I can wait here until tomorrow, line or no line, we won't get cornbread!" She hung her head low and limped away.

I approached the bakery door, which greeted me with a large sign dangling on its window: *Everything gone.*

That evening Alex and I discussed our day's events. I asked him whether he was still involved in the task of producing coal balls.

"No. She had no more dust. I went to the third, but had no luck there either. Although, I did meet that fellow that shewed us away before, remember him? He is not as menacing as he formerly conveyed himself to be."

"Are you sure, Alex?" I repudiated.

"Listen, Vitya, first and then offer your criticism, understood!

"His name is Poule. He even offered me a cigarette! He recited his life story to me. Poule's father kicked him out of the house. His mother passed away in this village...I can't remember the name of it now. Anyhow, we walked around the corner of Great Milosh and Nemanya streets and he pointed out a house to me, stating that two Catholic nuns reside there. In a few steps we were across the street and within the yard of their home.

"It was modest, but very tidy. We went around the side, where the kitchen door was and Poule rapped on the door.

Instantly a nun opened the door with a smile. She was clad in this black dress and veil and wore a large cross around her neck. She already had a bowl in her hands and handed it to Poule. Once she had realized that Poule was not alone, she briskly turned and came back with another bowl. It was the most delicious barley soup I had ever eaten. I expected a second helping, but I observed Poule, who placed his empty bowl on the step in front of the kitchen door, therefore I copied Poule, who was evidently a regular here. The nun's abode, though very modest, was extremely clean and spotless. They were such pleasant and serene ladies and I was very grateful for their charity.

"Poule and I returned to the third hoping to find employment. We were just in time; a streetcar arrived. Poule found a customer, whereas I hadn't. I stood there wondering where to go now. While I was deliberating, this gentleman approached me. He sported a fine suit, hat and cane in one hand, while a briefcase in the other.

"'Young man! Do you want to work? Do you want to sell something for me?'

"I flushed in embarrassment, thinking how could I possibly solicit the way I appear? I was surprised that he even considered me. I must have thought out loud, for the gentleman replied, 'Regardless, young man, if you are willing, I have a job for you. Do you want to work or not?'

"'Why, yes, sir! Of course I do!' I managed to become vocal, after the initial shock.

"'Very well then. Follow me.'

"I followed him right into a waiting fiacre! Vitya, I was a passenger now in the fiacre and not a magnet! I was deliriously proud! Can you relish that, Vitya?! This gentleman instructed the coachman of our intended destination, the whip fell on the horse and we departed.

"We headed toward the train station, meanwhile I observed the pedestrians on the street and smiled as we passed each one. We then proceeded in the direction toward Kalemegdan, turning on Dushanova Street and arriving at Baylonova Piazza. As we stepped out of the fiacre, the gentleman turned to me as if he forgot something and inquired if I am hungry.

"'Yes, sir, indeed! I am famished.'

"'Good!' and he immediately went into a butcher shop.

"I waited patiently. My mouth watered at the thought of the meal I would receive. When he returned with a package in his hand, I broached to inquire, 'How is it, sir, that you were able to purchase meat there, when I am aware that the city is practically meatless?'

"He smiled and pointed his cane toward the butcher shop, which I observed displayed a sign with an illustration of a horse that stated: *fresh horse meat available.* How did I miss that sign? I must have been to engulfed in my own thoughts of a tantalizing dinner. Agh, I wasn't that pleased to eat horse meat. I had no option. If that man can eat it, then so can I.

"We crossed the street together and I admit, we must have been an eyeful. This noble gentleman walking alongside a beggar! We did cause a few heads to turn, Vitya!"

Alex laughed now, while I, fully absorbed in his story, urged him to continue.

"Yes, where was I...Oh yes! We reached a door of this building. This door bore a plentitude of graffiti. Why? I don't know?"

"Go on, Alex, go on!"

"I am stating this, Vitya, because this door would enable me to return to this gentleman easily. The graffiti served as a signal. Now, don't interrupt me again, Vitya!

"Now...We entered this door and walked through a long corridor. We passed by several other doors to the left and to the right, before we reached his apartment."

"Really, Alex! I don't care about that!"

"Mind you, the building was in dire need of a janitor's touch. There was trash scattered about and it was overall, dirty."

Was Alex deliberately prolonging the story to annoy me, or simply enjoying his thorough detailing. Alex noticed my vexation and cleared his throat and proceeded.

"The gentleman's apartment was the last one on the right. He unlocked the door and we entered. Aaahhhh, Vitya! If only you were there! The splendour! The magnificence! I simply can't describe..."

I thought he was masterful at his descriptions. "Go on, Alex! Further, further!"

"The gentleman hung his overcoat and hat on the coat stand and I stood as if cemented. He turned around and motioned me an offer to sit on the divan. He asked me, 'What are you afraid of?'

"You know, Vitya, it's not that I was afraid, but it was the first time I had visualized such luxury in my life. It struck me. It also struck me that I stood out like a sore thumb, out of place and not in unison with the rest of the abode.

"Large portraits hung on the walls, of important people I assume. One was of a beautiful lady in a golden dress bedecked in jewels and a tiara upon her head. Yet another was of a colonel in full dress, with medals and ribbons decorated on his chest. He had white hair and a fluffy white moustache. Eerily, it seemed as though these portraits were spying on us and observing us, particularly me.

"In the far lefthand corner stood a marvellous, shiny black piano, with crystal vases ornamenting it on top. My eyes were ricocheting and surveying all these lavish, opulent items, unable to decide where to fix my stare on, since there was much to stare at!"

"Listen, Alex. Is it possible that you spare me of these minute details? I really am not concerned with his possessions you know."

"Is it not interesting to you, Vitya?"

"No. Well, yes, but get to the main part already."

"On the wall were two large bookcases, filled with elegantly bound books, all in alphabetical order. You, Vitya, know how much I admire books!

"The large, elongated vertical windows were decorated with crimson drapery, complimenting the Persian rug he had on the floor. His home was impeccable, unimaginable to you and I. Refinement, in all its measures. The ceiling was twice the height of ours. A glorious, polished mahogany desk shone beneath another window, displaying collectibles and priceless trinkets, while the gentleman sat delicately on the matching gilded chair. On the divan were sprinkles of velvet and satin cushions neatly arranged.

"I was stupefied, rather awkward of being in such a fancy and elaborately decorated salon. Ironically, Vitya, in the belligerent state outside of this hedonistic apartment one would marvel of such flamboyance in these current circumstances!

"Realizing that magnificence does exist, but when actually witnessing and visualizing such accommodations in comparison to our destitution leaves me if not angry, then indignant to the injustice you, I and our family are daily encountering. I wasn't there to judge, Vitya, but these unavoidable thoughts did cross my mind as I observed the divinity of his home."

"Alex. Listen. You are thoroughly describing to me this man's entire living quarters, whereas, I am curious as to the reason why you were there in the first place. Can you continue, Alex?"

"You are so impatient, Vitya! I accepted his offer and sat on the divan. Now I had a better opportunity to discreetly scrutinize this enigmatic personage.

"Mr. Vassily was his name. He was bald and fashioned a groomed, short beard and moustache beneath his aquiline nose. He was extremely courteous, civil and cultivated. His movements were rather too graceful for my liking, over exaggerated, but perhaps it was his natural habit. He had crystal, emerald green eyes that allowed entry into his warm soul as he would mind me and my lack of courtliness.

"In his serene manner, he began, 'Dear boy of mine, I would like you to work for me and if you have some moments to spare, I will tell you of my proposition and of my background.

"'I am an instructor of art. I am a painter. Due to my advanced age, I no longer am fit to solicit my work. Therefore, young man, I am engaging you in this task.'

"He placed a pile of handpainted and drawn postcards into my hands. Look, Vitya, what do you think? Are they worth selling?"

I took the cards from Alex. Some of the drawings were of

those pathetic and rueful luggage carriers, pulling luggage on their homemade carts. I started berating. Another was of a man chopping wood, and the rest a series of dismal insignias pertaining to the infamous state of war.

"They're not bad. He is an artist, no doubt. Although, it doesn't provide with an exorbitant incentive, Alex. I am unable to determine to who we would market these to?"

"To people!"

"I know, Alex, but nowadays, everyone's foremost concern is survival and not attempts of forming collections of painted postcards, be as it may, of their quality. I believe that the populace strives for food and other necessary provisions not readily available."

"Good thing you reminded me, Vitya…I forgot to mention the dinner we had. I sat there with Mr.Vassily, who was explaining each and every postcard to me, when a light knocking was heard at the door of the salon where we sat.

"'Enter,' Mr. Vassily uttered, slightly disturbed at the interruption.

"A middle-aged woman floated in, ever so gently and graciously, lest she disturbs her employer. Mr. Vassily lifted up his head to acknowledge Masha (that was her name), and instructed her to prepare cutlets from the package he had purchased sitting on the table. Masha nodded several times and quietly picked up the package and floated out, the same way she had entered. In an hour, Masha summoned us to the dining room. I followed Mr.Vassily who seemed to be relieved at the summons.

"I won't elaborate much to you now, Vitya, but I must briefly describe this ornate dining room. An extensively long, dark and shiny table captured my attention. It was laden with brilliant servingware; the silver sparkled as did the crystal goblets beneath the light of a multi-tiered chandelier. Aahh, Vitya, amazing, simply unfathomable!"

A paroxysm of contemptuous words escaped me. "Alex. Enough already! I have sufficient descriptions of this man's home! Enough to embark on a novel!"

Alex startled, nevertheless continued to orchestrate. "An

overwhelming credenza was to the immediate left side of the dining room. This credenza was embellished with the finest samovar and other notables. Mr.Vassily and I ate the cutlets and mashed potatoes that Masha earlier arranged on the table. I was not privy to horse meat, but in accordance to my growling stomach, I devoured the cutlets as did Mr.Vassily.

"Mr.Vassily, now pleased with appeasing his hunger, began a recital of his past obligations and works. He had informed me proudly that he was once the instructor of art to the Grand Duchess and began detailing his lectures to them and so forth. I paid no mind to his elaborations, for I, content now, was eager to return home.

"Before I left Mr. Vassily, he had advised me to return upon the completion of sales of his postcards, in order to replenish my supply."

I looked at Alex. I had no intentions of interrogating him further. I only suggested that we should call at the Russian Tsar tavern and commit to our endeavours there. I relented.

"Vitya, let's go!" Alex appealed.

Chapter 9

It was nearly dark when we left to embark on our mission as salesmen. Unlike other salesmen, we hooked onto a passing streetcar to reach our point of sales. The curfew no longer posed an hindrance to us, since it was no longer in effect. People were seen in larger proportions on the street, although rushing unhappily, with bowed heads, seemingly uncomfortable of being out in the dark. For some reason, Alex was fixed on visiting the hotel Serbia (formerly known as Moskva). He reasoned that the transportation was more accommodating toward the hotel, rather than the tavern, Russian Tsar. Normally, I abided by Alex's rule of thumb. I really had no option, nor say, for that matter.

We peered through the glass of the hotel's bar and observed the many guests within. Alex pushed me ahead of him and sanctioned me. "Hmm, Vitya, now you go inside to the bar and I am directly going to the Russian Tsar Tavern."

Very good, I thought. Again, I am the unwilling sacrifice, the indisposed volunteer. I entered through the double doors with the help of Alex's shove. I stood there gawking and standing upon a luxuriously thick carpet.

Well...At least it's warm in there, I decided. In a matter of seconds, a sagacious porter stood hovering above me. He had some kind of uniform on and he immediately penetrated an unforgiving aura about him. His eyes were fiercely black and his teeth, banana yellow, certainly because of the pipe he held in his hand. He thundered, "You! What do you want here?"

I stood as if I were struck by lightening. "You see, sir...I would very much appreciate if I could sell these postcards here to your distinguished guests?"

I deliberately and resolutely stood without flinching, intending to complete my desired intentions and, partly, because I was overcome with a sudden fear, which my shiny, wet forehead displayed.

"What cards?" he growled as he snatched the pile of postcards from my hands.

"We do not permit any soliciting here. Particularly by you! Look at you! Do you honestly believe we would permit such a preposterous being as yourself to interlope in our prestigious establishment? What the devil were you thinking? Are you slightly acquainted with, or aware of the distinguished patrons of our hotel?" he curtly demanded.

"No. No, sir, I am not. I meant no harm. I only wanted to sell those postcards which you are holding, sir," I humbly replied.

"High officials, nobles and people of a higher class occasion here. Not even a regular soldier may enter through those doors! And here you are! You want to sell postcards, with that splendid attire upon your person! Ha! Out! At once! I am warning you...I do not want to see you here again! Understood! I will have you arrested by the police! Scum!"

I trembled. As this obnoxious porter was cursing and hollering, a group of patrons exited the bar and went to the desk of the hotel's lobby, requesting their keys to their luxurious suites. Two of the group were officers, while the other two were ladies in fashionable dress.

Upon noticing them, I immediately recalled the wretched officer I catered to without any payment from him. To my surprise, one of those officers overheard the porter's threats and began toward us. I did not need a second invitation to exit, lest that officer be the revolver-happy acquaintance of mine. I fled.

I ran so fast and breezed by other patrons, nearly knocking them down and nearly crashing into Alex, who was outside, directly in front of the door.

"What's with you? Why are you running wild? Where are you going?"

I kept running, while informing Alex, who was now running behind me.

"You would run, too!"

Alex caught up to me and nearly jumped on me. We almost fell, but balanced ourselves. Breathlessly Alex inquired further, "Vitya, stop. Tell me what happened in there? Did you make any sales? Where's the money?"

Naturally, I poured out all the nasty words, the insulting threats of the porter and so forth.

"Where are the postcards?" Alex persisted.

"Alex, are you deaf? I just finished explaining to you. I have no postcards. I have no money."

We both breathed heavily and were still shaken.

"Vitya...What will I do now? What am I going to do? I have no postcards! Mr. Vassily! Oh no!"

"Alex....calm down, I am certain that Mr.Vassily is an understandable human being. He will surely sympathize with us."

Alex, with a fixed gaze at the ground before us, was thinking. "Fine. How will I possibly confront Mr.Vassily. How can I face him? You, Vitya, have done me in! Yes...you have fixed me now!"

"Right. I fixed you," I angrily answered.

We walked the rest of the way home, passing by Vuk's Monument, not even thinking to catch a ride on the streetcar, we were absorbed in our worries.

"Alex, don't worry. Tell me, what should I do?"

"Tomorrow, Vitya, you will return to the hotel and ask that porter to surrender the postcards to you. That's all."

"What! Alex! I refuse to go! Do you realize that if I even considered returning to that hotel, you would be visiting me in prison? Do you not recall what just occurred to me there? If those cards are so precious to you, Alex, you are more than welcome to retrieve them yourself!"

"Agh, I'm going to get you!" Alex was fuming of anger.

"Wait. Alex, the porter warned me and besides, I can't return. He grabbed the cards from my hands. I didn't offer them to him."

"Vitya, the porter must have had construed that your presence there was solely for theft and not otherwise."

"He might have, Alex. I was too frightened to understand much, except for the threat of the officer that would arrest me if I didn't leave the building at once. Since when are you so knowledgeable? Are you a professor, Alex? By the way, what happened to your visiting the Russian Tsar Tavern to make sales there?"

"Nicely he fixed me," Alex mumbled to himself, avoiding my question.

"Good. I have a plan. I decided I will take you tomorrow to Mr.Vassily and you can explain the entire matter to him," Alex said.

What a sly fox! He wants me to explain.

"How can I go, Alex? I don't know him."

"No. We will go together," Alex quickly responded.

A stone lifted off my chest with these last words of Alex's. Little did I know how misconceiving Alex's plan really was.

Dawn broke. The day after our unsuccessful work. My day darkened as I contemplated the task set before me by my brother. Mr.Vassily.... I must confess all. The thoughts whirled in my mind and made me not notice that Alex stood directly above me as I lay there, staring at the ceiling and mumbling. Once I noticed him...He needn't say a word. I knew.

We walked on the damp leaves scattered about on the sidewalk. Some pedestrians were quickly walking while holding up their umbrellas. We had no umbrellas, nor did we mind becoming wet. We had more important and impeding matters to tend to. We both were content with our silence. I assumed that Alex was devising a theory, a plan to bring to Mr.Vassily, thereby explaining our empty-handed return to him. Alex was extremely silent. Regardless, I was more at ease now, since I was not to face this man alone. Besides, I speculated that Alex is the one who took on the responsibility of the postcards, not I. This time Alex can carry the torch, not me. I rushed to keep up with Alex, who was briskly walking bearing the countenance of a person determined of resolving a problem.

Shortly, we stood before the building, before the graffitied door. Alex was correct, it was dirty. We walked through the long corridor and in moments, Alex was knocking on the door. Suddenly, he shoved me ahead of him. I heard a distant voice on the opposite side of the door announcing, "Just a minute."

I turned to look at Alex and to my astonishment and disgrace, I was standing now alone in front of the man Alex so vividly described.

True to his description, I observed the serenity and undisguised candour of the gentleman.

"Good morning." He smiled.

I returned the salute and stated, "I am Alex's brother, Vitya. Mr.Vassily, forgive me, I believe that is your name?"

"Yes, yes, son, it is," he kindly responded.

"My brother sent me, the one who you gave your postcards to for selling?"

"Yes, indeed I know."

"Sir, well...You see....We had a little difficulty with the selling and we encountered some problems."

"Yes," is all he replied and I assume he waited for me to continue from the beginning of the story.

I was shuffling myself from one side to the other, in desperation.

"Sir, I am sorry. We have no postcards. We have no money either." I nearly began to cry, but withheld and regained my composure.

"Sir, I have a few dinars." I extended my hand to him, hoping it would suffice for the loss of his cards.

He looked at my hand and the money I held and commented, "Good, tell me, son, what happened?"

There I stood in the hallway, wondering why he hesitated inviting me in, nevertheless, I retold him the story and all I had encountered at the Hotel Serbia. He quietly and attentively listened without blinking. He didn't seem to be disturbed and I was slightly relieved.

He inquired of my family name, then my parents' names

individually. I complied, but was confused. I was under the impression that Alex and Mr.Vassily had already discussed the inevitable and now he repeats it with me.

"Vitya, son, we have lost a lot more in life than those cards. It is fine," and with that he finally offered me to enter.

I followed Mr.Vassily into the (pre-described) dining room, (courtesy of Alex). The table was set for tea. All linens, samovar and zakuska (snacks) were set out, though for a setting for one, but Masha was immediately informed of my visit and laid out another setting. She did float as Alex described and I smiled recalling Alex's words as I studied her movements. I was invited to sit at the table and Mr.Vassily sat right next to me.

He poured out the hot water from the samovar into our cups, followed by the concentrated tea from a kettle. I was fascinated by the elegance and more so by his refined manner. I agreed with Alex now, I felt awkward, almost clumsy. My attire was not suitable for this atmosphere, even less for the tea. I was embarrassed, not only due to my presentation, but the whole matter regarding his postcards.

Not only did he disregard the entire incident, but invited me to tea with him! It was such a paradox of my expectations. I was not lectured, but treated as a long awaited guest, with such formal hospitality! Only a true gentleman could behave in such a manner. I was so touched by all that, I was forced to bow my head, lest my teardrops were to be noticed. I wiped them with my sleeve quickly, hoping that I didn't look obvious.

"What is the matter, son?" Mr.Vassily gently inquired, with his sincere, emerald green eyes emitting warmth and concern.

"Oh, nothing, sir. Everything is wonderful. Too wonderful! I have never been in such a beautiful home and sat at such a table laden with all these divine things before me! Mr.Vassily, you are a very kind man, a very generous man!"

"No, Vitya, my dear child. Don't say that. My home is not as you say. Why it is not even close to the homes I resided in back home," he noted, wiping a tear that ran the side of his nose, with his napkin, then offered me the plate with zakuska. I accepted and was actually very glad and even thankful to Alex for abandoning me at the door.

"Vitya, I believe that you and your brother suffer the most. You children are especially subjected to the ironies, injustices and miseries of the war." He patted my head.

"Child, I am an old man now. I haven't much company these days. You would do me an honour of listening to this old man's stories?"

"I would be happy to, Mr.Vassily." It was the least I could do for poor old Mr.Vassily.

"When I was a younger lad, approximately twenty-five years ago, the representatives in St. Petersburg summoned me to instruct art and painting to the Grand Duchesses. Only one of the Grand Duchesses portrayed an earnest interest and desire toward the arts and painting. I spent all my days in the winter palace. I was generously rewarded of course and I honestly enjoyed my position there and my residence. After some time, I was directed to instruct elsewhere, the family being satisfied with my work no longer found my tutoring necessary, thus I was recommended with many honours to the hometown of your mother."

I wondered why he mentioned my mother. Instantly I recalled my father's teasing and harassing of my mother's artistic abilities and her award. Should I interrupt Mr.Vassily?

"Ahem, excuse me, Mr.Vassily, if I may ask, what does your story have to do with my mother's hometown?"

"Patience, son, slow down and soon enough you will know.

"When I arrived at my destination, I was accommodated at this charming hotel, courtesy of the court, allowing me to briefly rest after my very long trip. The following day, I was to visit the governor of the town and receive further instructions, pertaining to my employment.

"Upon my arrival at the governor's building, I was welcomed by these two guards who were scrupulously observing any trespassers and hindering their entrance to the edifice by locking swords as I was soon to find out. I was ordered to disclose my intentions, which was followed by an examination of my papers, and that had immediately engendered my admission.

"Once inside, two clerks had kindly ushered me to the

governor's office. They left me in a waiting area, returned within seconds and escorted me into the office. My eyes surveyed the entirety within moments and finally rested on the governor himself. He assumingly noticed my surveillance and void of any objections, politely offered me a seat.

"I had such a pleasant discourse with the governor. Apparently, he was notified and aware of my arrival and my duties, thus I did not need to recount my mission. He supplied me with the address of my new employment and had a comfortable fiacre prepared and waiting to take me to the home of my new employer.

"As we rode to my destination, I admired the scenic route we had taken. Fairytale houses, complete with groomed gardens, titanic trees and merry people strolling leisurely. Lovely ladies, escorted by handsome gentlemen sauntering along those streets, each would bid good-day by the tip of the hat and a nod of the lady, on that special, sunny day.

"We stopped in front of a beautiful snowy white, house. Four columns majestically, stood guard at the front. The lavishly, manicured green lawn, sprinkled with clusters of colourful flowers assembled in such a fashion that begged for a restful and tranquil walk and admiration. It was a picturesque setting and it motivated me to paint that magnificence one day. There were numerous windows, too many to count, which beamed reflections of the awakening sun. During my investigation, the coachman and fastidious lackey had already taken my possessions to the front door, meanwhile, I noticed a curtain quiver in one of the upstairs windows. I fancied I was spied on.

"Once inside the mansion, I observed that the vestibule screamed of luxury. In the centre a large, marbled table displayed an enormous bouquet of fresh flowers, presumably from the garden itself. An exceptionally large chandelier with multitudes of crystal droplets hung low, showering light from the elevated ceiling. To the left and the right, wings of wide staircases ascending to the second level foyer, bridged by a gilded palisade. The butler returned and I was asked to enter the drawing room, where the Mrs. was awaiting me.

"Vitya, the entire room was fragranced by the aromas of

more fresh flowers, I realized that the lady of the house was fond of them, hence the beautifully landscaped gardens. Golden framed paintings and portraits decorated the walls. The furnishings were in vogue with the times. What can I say, Vitya, simply elaborate!

"I admired the lady whose visage portrayed fundamental authority in the absence of her spouse. I humbly introduced myself and the same was returned. We chatted awhile and before I knew it, it was time to rest, freshen up and dine. My room was equally sublime, in harmony with the rest of the household.

"The interior of the house was splashed with a vast assortment of priceless collectibles. Exotic vases from the Far East held, naturally, fresh flowers. Mini statuettes were portrayed along the long corridors. Not to mention all of the oversized paintings that made one feel as if they were in a museum. This mansion, though large and at times dimly lit, did not produce timidity, rather an understood luxury that coolness adheres to.

"As the days became weeks, I had come to know the three daughters of Nikolai Vladimirovich well. Each of them were refined, pretty and genteel in their own significant way. They enjoyed the art lessons, I might add, particularly Zoya. She did exceptionally well in her paintings. Her ease with the canvas and paintbrush were apparent in her notable drawings, she was a natural of course. She did not need much encouragement as her other two sisters. She was enthusiastic and diligent in her studies and maintained all her tools to perfection. She modestly welcomed praise and honours for her work. She had a natural talent. It was a pleasure teaching her, I profoundly enjoyed.

"Within a few years we had decided to hold an exhibit of her works. At these exhibits were celebrated critics and Zoya gleefully accepted their expertise critique.

"Yes, yes…I did enjoy my years there, Vitya. The girls offered no difficulties. They were well mannered and obedient.

"I must tell you of the balls, Vitya! Why that would be a crime not to mention…"

I was elated by Mr. Vassily's ebullient commentaries. I forgot where I was, why I was there and almost of who I was, a near utopia. Mr.Vassily delighted in my undivided attention, decided to retell the magnificence of the balls.

He began, "The ballroom was supremely decorated for the upcoming and raved about ball. Needless to mention, flowers, everywhere! The lackeys were dressed to perfection and stood erect in expectation of the arrival of the aristocratic guests, the elite and the well-to-do. Chandeliers sparkled, bespeckling multitudes of crystalline colours upon the tiaras of the ladies that arrived early. The candle's flickering flames danced, while the servants rushed to light the remaining un-lit candles and replace the melted ones with fresh ones, which provided an incandescent atmosphere throughout. Soon the ballroom was illuminated. The ball was to commence. Hors d'oeuvre were prepared and displayed on dumbwaiters, while servants, who also held silver trays of delectables stood in line by the walls waiting to serve the high society. Carriages arrived at every moment and with each arrival, an announcement followed, lest they insult the guests without a formal introduction.

"It was a spectacular scene. The ladies and gents, their attire, their jewels and gems, one would stand in awe.

"Well, my dear child Vitya, I must shorten my story. I strongly believe your mother, Vitya, is my former student, the daughter of Nikolai Vladimirovich."

I almost choked upon hearing Mr. Vassily's last comment. He noticed and began tapping me on my back. What is this man saying?

"Mr.Vassily, how do you say so? I am sorry, I do not understand?"

"Vitya, according to your name, your mother's name and your grandfather's name, including your grandmother, I am entirely convinced that your mother is my former student. The portrait you and Alex described of your grandfather reassured me.

"I had planned to shorten my story for today, but I see that I must continue to elaborate further."

I was lost and most definitely needed accurate elaboration. I urged Mr. Vassily to continue...

"The revolution began, Vitya. A most horrible and terrible thing. The family, your family had been given prior instructions to evacuate, with nine wagons at their disposal for their possessions and precious items and depart to France immediately. They declined, the female members of the family, unfortunately and to the dismay of your grandfather, Nikolai. They were determined to remain with him. When the situation thickened, Nikolai Vladimirovich demanded they leave and avoid the pogrom.

"I, on the other hand, heeded the advice of the officials and departed for Greece. I found employment readily, owed to my credentials.

"Now, Vitya, I am here, for as you know Greece is occupied as well. In fact the Greek princess is here in Belgrade also. I would like to ask you for a favour, Vitya? I have a note for the Greek princess and would be obliged if you would take it to her. She is residing at the mansion of the former president, Tsvetkovich.

"And...Vitya, I regret to inform you that I had heard of the fate of my former kind and noble employer. Your grandfather was killed. I knew that his wife and three daughters were in Constantinople and had become nurses for the Red Cross. Any information succeeding that time I had not.

"Now, to my delight, I met you. One more thing, Vitya, I would appreciate if you would come visit me again in three days, for I will be having guests soon. Upon visiting me, I would be grateful if you brought the portrait of your grandfather."

"Mr. Vassily, I would like to, but the portrait is quite large."

"I am certain you will master it."

"Well...I can wrap it in some paper and bring it like that?"

"Yes...yes, Vitya, do as you please."

I walked out of the home of Mr. Vassily in a daze. A plethora of thoughts waltzed in my head. He's right. Our stories do correspond. I found Mr. Vassily quite affable. His expertise at reciting all that he had told me was enticing.

Poor Mama, it wasn't enough that she had foregone drastic

transitions, but was condemned to listen and yield to the incessant berating and ridiculing of Father's. On numerous occasions, I listened to Father's demonstrative implications and mockery which he hurled at Mother. She, nodding and without admonishing, would repeat her famous words, "The day will come."

Father's actions were puzzling to me. He, though not of noble lineage, had, nevertheless, a significant background. His surname "Ahtirski" was a well known name. Often it was spelt in different manners from Akhtyrsky, to Ahktyrsky and so forth, but Father retained the spelling "Ahtirski." Near the city Kharkov was another town bearing the same name as my father's surname "Akhtirsk," where a very famous, miracle performing icon originated. It is the only icon in the Orthodox denomination that bears the image of Holy Mary and baby Jesus as black.

Father, as he stated, was the eldest of nine siblings. His family owned a fairly sizeable estate. He did possess some degree of education, for he illustrated that by his exquisite penmanship and skill at calligraphy.

Another interesting and notable factor was that the Grand Duchess Olga's own regiment, which she was a colonel of, was the "Akhtyrsky Hussars." Father being an officer of the White Army and not a simple soldier, should have been appeased, but he was not satisfied, thus Mother was the victim. Mother was of a noble lineage, unlike Father, and perhaps that is where his jealousy stemmed.

I spent the entirety of the that day at Mr. Vassily's. I did not work at all that day. I wondered what that sly fox Alex accomplished? Perhaps he earned for the day's needs? In any event, he needn't expect any adulation from my part, regardless of my exemplary day spent with Mr.Vassily. I prepared questions to shower Alex with upon my arrival home regarding his miraculous disappearance at the door of Mr. Vassily's.

I admit it wasn't of paramount importance to me, not when compared with the mesmerizing information I received unexpectedly, of my family's nobility. I was jubilant and ecstatic and redoubled my pace as I headed home, eager to promulgate our heritage to all.

When I arrived home, I had much to see. Everything was in shambles. The table was overturned and our meagre possessions strewn about. On Father's bed sat Alex and Olga in tears.

"What is it? What happened?! Who did this?" I accidentally kicked a pot which was upside down on the floor near the table and all of its contents had carpeted a section of the floor, which was already drying and staining Mother's impeccable floor.

Chapter 10

"Where is Mother?" I looked in the bedroom. It was empty. "Where is she?"

"Stop shouting, Vitya. She's not here. Somehow, she became untied and did all this you see before you. Olga was outside in the courtyard and when she heard the clamour within our kitchen, it was too late.

"Inevitably, Olga had to lock the door behind her and run for help. By a stroke of luck, she bumped into a policeman on the street. Shortly thereafter, two men in white overcoats, again, Vitya. Mother is back in the hospital," Alex revealed.

Olga further declared that she had decided to go and stay with Katarina Petrovna (an emigre also, from the town of Baku in Russia). Mrs. Katarina was a seamstress and invited Olga to stay with her for the time being.

"You and I will remain here," Alex stated sadly.

"Let's light the kandilo (a votive containing oil, water and a floating wick. Usually hung before an icon and lit on holidays, or at times of necessity, such as this one), Alex, and beseech God for help," I softly implied.

The three of us, down on our knees, prayed zealously, imitating our mother, who we had witnessed do the same many times before. Each of us prayed in our own way.

I began, "Lord, why? Why now? Now when I had some encouraging news regarding Mother and her past? Is there anyone, Lord, that can hear us? That can help us?" I sobbed as I earnestly importuned.

"If I could only give you a brief relief, a crumb of joy, I would gladly do so," I whispered out to Mother as if she were standing there listening to me.

Overwhelmed with the events and the conclusion of the day, we retired, teary eyed, exhausted and morosely bitter.

Just a few days of autumn were left. It became colder, windier and sadder. The usual and expected greyness of the skies significantly corresponded with our disposition. Monotonously, Alex and I pursued the feasibility of the third for our possible menu for the day. Alex devised a new plan. He told me, "When you carry the peasant woman's basket, Vitya, remain behind her and allow her to walk ahead of you."

"I do anyhow, Alex, for the baskets are not that light to permit me to spring forward in front of her. Regardless, why do you insist on that?"

"Because, it would provide you with an opportunity to take some bread, or other food from her basket and place it in the inner pocket of your jacket."

"Oh," and realizing that Alex's word was law, I had to comply. Alex's ignominious scheme of exploiting these basket-ridden women did provoke repudiation on my part, though it was instantly suppressed by Alex's justifications.

At the third I found a customer in need of assistance. My unsuspecting employer handed me her weighty basket and as usual I walked behind, intentionally or not, I followed. I, nevertheless slowed my pace, allowing a substantial distance between the two of us. She would intermittently turn her head to verify whether I was still behind her, with her basket.

Recalling Alex's new theory, I attempted to slide my hand in the basket, between the verifications of the woman's. It wasn't easy. In fact, I couldn't. She had ingeniously sewn the basket at the top with this heavy rope. Was it due to her mistrust, or due to the prevention of any of her goods from falling out? In any case, it proved an obstacle for my intentions. Perhaps if I attempted to undo her clever sewing, I might make a hole large enough, enabling a sampling of her goods? I did.

Beneath my fingertips I touched upon some eggs. Good! One by one, I pulled out the eggs and coyly hid them in my pocket as per Alex's instructions. My entire work was completed in half hour, the entire mission, including my payment directly and indirectly from my oblivious customer.

At one moment during the exchange following my completed work, I trembled at her inquiry regarding the payment for my services. My bulging bosom, thankfully did not betray me, though I quivered and sanctimoniously replied to her question.

I turned the corner leaving the peasant woman behind me where she dutifully began hollering to the passing shoppers, announcing her sale of fresh goods. I munched on my payment, the cornbread she gave me and began arranging the fresh eggs on the handkerchief I had in my pocket, now placed on the ground. Ten eggs in all, were aligned on the ground evenly in front of me. Seconds later I had none. I was satisfied of my sale of the eggs and settled on returning to the third.

Alex was standing at third, awaiting for customers I assumed. I handed him my earnings and was praised for my achievement.

"Alex? I realize that your new method does benefit us, but I am still not comfortable with this new arrangement," I professed.

"Look. Do you not understand? We have made an entire day's profit in an hour. That's good! Do you think there is justice when you and I return home empty handed? And when we are unable to placate the hunger of those awaiting us at home? Is that justice? We are working, and eagerly at that, but we cannot earn enough to pay the rent and sufficiently support ourselves."

I listened to Alex. Did he forget that it is only the two of us now? Although, his judgement did have merit. My thoughts turned to our family: George, in the orphanage, did receive meagre contributions from us (which I will later explain).

Olga, now at Mrs. Katarina's expected assistance from us, too. Mother, in the hospital, at times would require our benevolence. Vechislav did not bother with us anymore. He had his own difficulties. Father was gone.

"You are right, Alex. I am sorry." I shook out of my daze and answered to Alex's meaningful stare.

"How did you do today, Alex?"

"Not bad. But I do have something I want to tell you. Today I noticed some wood in the yard of a house. I decided that tonight, you and I will go there and take this wood, or at least some of it home."

"What? Wood? Are you insane? How can we do that? We have no means to take it home with us, Alex. No horse, no cart, no wagon, nothing!"

"Silence! You will find out."

As usual I silenced.

The evening arrived faster than usual, though not surprisingly, the days were much shorter now. Alex and I prepared to leave for our new mission. The streets were nearly bare void of pedestrians or traffic. Alex and I sauntered along, near the fences of houses as if we were about to engage in some mysterious and important endeavour.

Below Krunska Street, Alex had opened a gate to one of the yards of the houses. He peered inside. Assured that no one was in the yard, he turned to me and exclaimed, "There's no one! Go inside and take some wood!"

"Right. And do you not see, Alex, that there are lights on in that house? In the lower and the upper windows?"

"Of course I do! Precisely why I bid you to enter their yard! While their lights are on, silly, they cannot see into their yard outside. Understand?"

"Fine. Except…Why is it that I must go and fetch this wood? Why?"

"Because, I found it. Therefore you will fetch it. I will stand guard here at the gate."

"Right," I understood his system.

He always managed to trick me. I stood there speculating, but finally relented. I ventured in. Suddenly, I heard footsteps on the opposite side of the fence. I'm too far from the gate to make a run for it, thus I hopped into a little, prickly bush.

A man walked out of the house and passed right by me. He

headed toward the gate. As soon as I heard the clicking of the gate, I sped to the pile of wood and grabbed a large, heavy piece on top of the pile. I balanced it on my shoulder and rushed toward the gate. It swung open, though not by my doing. To my shock, a younger man stood there and announced, "Come on, little guy. I'll hold the gate open for you!" My legs nearly gave out. My heart was beating rapidly and I'm certain I was either flushed red, or pale white, either or. I slowly proceeded to walk by this stranger and accidentally brushed his arm with the piece of wood I carried on my shoulder.

"Forgive me, please forgive me!"

"Nothing, nothing," he replied as he entered the yard himself and headed for the house.

I swayed in bewilderment, turned the corner and found Alex standing there.

"Are you ever a splendid guard! Why on earth didn't you signal me?"

"I became afraid and ran. Sorry."

We both carried this heavy piece of wood home and discussed the fact that the young man who held the door open for me had not prevented me from taking the wood, nor did he question my trespassing. I believe we were lucky, very lucky!

During the course of our conversation, I began to feel itchy and needed to stop walking in order to scratch my back and relieve the itch, which reminded me...

"Alex? When did you last bathe?"

Alex reflected for a minute and remarked, "It has been a while I believe. You know yourself that we ran out of soap. Now that you mention it, I had heard of a public bath house on Misharska Street, below Tsvetni Trg! I suggest we visit that bath house tomorrow!"

A single level structured bath house appeared as we walked toward it. We neared the foggy windows and observed silhouettes prancing around nonchalantly. Upon our entry, we stood in line, in front of a man dressed entirely in white, resembling a hospital orderly. He was sitting at a desk in the centre of this antechamber. I noticed a wooden box on the table half filled with money.

The legal tender now had an illustration of a Serbian peasant on it. I remembered the money the two angels gave me, the five hundred dinars, which the occupiers minted. Once, that legal tender shadowed the image of King Alexander (who is now deceased since his assassination in Marseilles, France) when held up to the light. Presently this note stated *Serbia* and no longer *Kingdoms of Serbia, Croatia and Slovenia*, I discovered.

If King Peter II were older when he was enthroned before the war, the circumstances would be diverse. The regents of King Peter II, his uncle Prince Paul and his mother Queen Maria had signed a pact on the 27th of March with Germany. Students vandalized the German library and protested, "Bolje rat nego pact," meaning, "Better war than a pact," and had caused chaos with the authorities, thus the Germans on the 6th of April bombed the capital city of Belgrade.

Damned pikes (as we called those diving, hissing planes) that dove toward their targets and blasted out bombs. Their bombs fell on the undeserving civilians, who in a panic stricken method fled the city to the presumed safety of the outskirts. I was unable to perceive what the Nazis found so alluring in bombarding these parts of the city where the poorer class citizens resided.

Another interesting, notable and curious fact is that it was also in the areas where the Ottoman empire once ruled and had left traces of their occupation with the houses they built. The houses were constructed of mud and clay and had orange-red shingles for a roof. Lacking any foundation, it disabled further additions by the new owners of the dwelling.

Whenever I walked through the very narrow streets, where two cars parallelled deemed unpassable, I envisaged how these ruins and debacle once resembled pretty, modest and tidy homes for their occupants. Now...bombed, had fallen like a structure built of playing cards. The once inhabitants of these ashy ruins had the dishonour of having their scanty possessions, from the slanted, rusted iron bed to the three legged wooden table, gaping under the sky. A partial wall could be discerned, which seemed to signify that perhaps it is still sheltering a soul. The cherished prized possession, the stove, also stood lonely, with its cylinder protruding into the air. It had once warmed the tired, weather beaten and calloused hands of the very tired worker, who provided shelter and bread, by the very hands which the stove was warming.

Ironically the Dedinye district was more often than not untouched, unscathed and left to be. The palaces, mansions and villas who the ministers and other elite were the owners of, were nearly oblivious to state of war and were occupied with the constant competition as to whose dwelling is more magnificent, more manicured, more opulent. The Dedinye also boasted of housing the second king's palace in its neighbourhood. These high societies would be burdened with their indecisiveness as to their vacation destination, while resting and sipping fine wines. Commonly, they frequented the French Riviera. Such were the troubles that badgered the elite.

In the destitute locations of the bombed city, at one time, laughter, song and merriment prevailed. From a distance one could discern and hum along with the joyous songs spilling out into the open air, in tune with the melodies of the talented and renown, playing Gypsies.

On nearly every street corner cafés were bursting with patrons, where the workers would meet, after a long, hard day of toiling, to rest and mingle over a siphon and Turkish coffee. Near the early hours of the morn, the matron would gently escort his inebriated customer, flicking off the lights and shutting the door behind them. While the jolly customer, who now swayed from left to right, was singing the tune, "Tsrven Fesich Mama," as the band of Gypsies followed him closely behind with their famous violins.

When the merry man's wife would sternly be welcoming his eventual return home with a frying pan in hand, the Gypsies would immediately disperse, not wishing to become a part of the quarrels that surely were to ensue and knowing very well that they would greet their humble and jolly singer the very next evening. With violins under their arms, they scurried off, leaving only the dust behind them. Tomorrow, they are certain that the same jolly man would again oblige, when the talented Gypsies would harken to hit the right note by stringing the melodies by his ear assuring generous tips. For the Gypsies knew how to provoke the right emotions with their soft, hypnotic melodies for such men, who relied on them.

The more common middle-class citizens would usually mimic and strive to accomplish the quasi-high class status and were often found chatting with their equally determined neighbours, usually referring to their spouse's employment. One would boast of her husband being a banker, another would claim that hers is a distinguished clerk and so forth. At times and at the risk of their husbands' outrage, they would indulge in purchasing fine and expensive items. This action would enable them to portray their flamboyancy and frolic intentionally to the irritation of their spying neighbours, who would thereby gain additional worries, to surpass the other's achievements. The competition was nearly as bad as in the provinces.

The vexed husband, upon noticing his fine, new articles, would inadvertently clench his teeth and, avoiding the neighbours' prying ears and his wife's abominations, would pick up his hat from where he left it upon returning from work and place it on his head. His teeth still clenching, mumbling still audible, he would direct himself to the nearest café. At once he would be welcomed by the host and patrons alike, sit at his favourite table, sip on his brandy and listen to the Gypsies. With their fine music, he nearly forgets his wife's competitiveness and spendthrift habits that would cost him many more days of hard work, just to be in sync with the neighbours! Thus, this poor, middle-class, involuntarily high-class imposter, would mend his troubles in such a fashion, at such a location.

Another very important concern for the bourgeois society

was the education of their offsprings. They diligently educated their young with hopes of securing them a prominent, substantial position in the future, which equals to a possible elegant manor in the Dedinye district. The provincial populous equally maintained diverse burdens of their own. Chiefly, agricultural reasons prevented their young from proper education. Lacking in hired manpower, they needed extra hands for the cultivation and management of their crops, cattle and so forth. Female obligations entailed rigorous schedules, from housekeeping to gardening to helping with the crops, orchards and fields.

Such responsibilities thus prevented the young generation of peasants from a thorough and complete education. Despite the excessive, burdensome chores, the country folk knew how to enjoy the simple life, celebrations were regularly practised. And when a country man were to swear upon his word, such were the agreements bound upon and fiercely honoured.

In front of me stood Alex. He was third in line and I fourth. Rousing from my rumination, I began to survey the equally desperate bath seekers amongst us. Just ahead of us, stood this scrawny, smeared man with his pants clinging to his twiggy legs, who was consumed in a dispute with the appointed attendant over the temperature of the water. Few minutes later, after resolving that issue, the man snappily exited through a corridor and entered the first door on the right.

Once Alex paid our admission, we, too, followed the scrawny man's example and entered the first door on the right. Greeted by a dingy, rough sandpaper towel offered by an old man, who was expressionless and impartial to all of the denizens. This zombie man walked us to the shower stalls through a thick, heavy and hot fog. Many men were dressed in white foam and some whistling as they washed away the grime and worries, one would think as they sang in the steam and puddles of water beneath them.

We placed our belongings after disrobing, on an old, withered, wooden bench and gleefully stood beneath a shower head.

"Alex? How are we supposed to wash, when we have no soap?"

"I do," Alex smartly snapped.

"Where did you get it?"

"Look around you! Must I tell you everything? That man beside you. Do you see him?"

"Yes."

"After he lathers himself and places his soap on the ground, you pick it up and lather. That man will be too preoccupied rinsing the soap off him and out of his eyes to notice you."

When the man beside me finished lathering, I proceeded as Alex instructed. How convenient, I thought. I felt a push. "Hey you! You took my soap!"

"I did. And what of it? You are closest to me, therefore I took yours."

The man was irritated, but not enough to cause a scandal. I returned the soap, after I finished using it and rinsed myself thoroughly. We finished our showers and sprang forth out of there as light as feathers, in a state of utopia!

I couldn't help but notice that Alex looked rather well after his shower. Alex had green eyes as I do, but today, after this shower, they seemed greener. Alex was somewhat taller than I and we didn't resemble each other very much. In fact, many would argue that we were brothers.

We walked in our mended clothes: Alex who stitched his with a thin wire, yet I with a thicker one, for he had seniority. We strutted along in this manner, though fresher and lighter, much lighter. Even our dark blonde hair seemed lighter. We noticed others of our age in the city—some in vogue and in tune with the times—yet Alex and I, aside from our pitiful fashion faux pas, had fashioned haircuts courtesy of our kitchen scissors.

During these years and particularly this one of 1943, we worried ourselves not, over our appearance, especially in these turbulent times. We had much more important things to concern ourselves with, such as: fulfilling the basic human necessities, rent and providing for our family.

"Alex...what are our plans now?" I inquired as I observed Alex tighten his pride of possession—a leather belt, which he found somewhere and wouldn't tell me. I found it rather feminine, but I dared not tell Alex. The hurdles of his disappointment would bruise me. He was especially pleased with this belt, since it was leather.

I tightened my belt, mimicking Alex. My belt was a rope (actually a piece of a laundry line that I noticed hanging on the side while someone's laundry was drying. I cut off the hanging piece and, alas, a new belt!). I didn't have to resort to Mother's stocking as a belt anymore. The rope was a step up and good enough for me.

Alex ignored my initial question, but began telling me... "Vitya, today I visited some acquaintances of mine. They reside in the same building as the president of Serbia does. You know, General Nedic."

"Hah! I'm sure you did, Alex. I'm sure you know everyone and everything!"

"Seriously, I did. In that building, where I was, was not more than twenty apartments. The general lives on the second floor, whereas my acquaintances live on the third floor. I worked in their home, Vitya. I cleaned their floors and their balcony and, Vitya...from those earnings, you and I had become cleaner—this shower today!"

Now that Alex and I were alone in our home, we still had some of the cheese, left over from our previous earnings at the third and some cornbread for our dinner.

"Alex? I don't want the cornbread. This morning I attempted to break off a piece, but it was stretchy and gummy."

"All right. We will make porridge from the cornmeal flour instead."

"Thanks, Alex."

"Enough, enough. Let's hurry home, I want to read tonight. I obtained some books."

"Really? What books, Alex? Tell me!"

"*War and Peace*," Alex stated proudly.

"You have that book? That's Tolstoy's book!"

"Now how do you know that's Tolstoy's book?"

"Alex, do you think I didn't learn anything in the school we went to?"

I fell silent and began to reflect on my school days. Sometimes, I missed school, like at that moment.

We had no further obligations to end that day and Alex wasted no time to cuddle into a corner with his book and jubilantly commence reading. I, on the other hand, was forced to observe him reading. Alex was very protective of his books and jealous, lest I read something before him. Thus, he would place his cherished books beneath his pillow, secure it by placing his arm on top of the pillow and read, preventing me from accidentally grabbing a book of my own to read.

I barely managed a glimpse of one of the books he had. It was *Les Miserables*, by Victor Hugo. How tempted I was to sneak under the pillow to grab one book. For now...I had to remain content watching him read. I knew when he finished a book, he would generously permit me to read it.

The following morning was not that welcomed by Alex and I. The first snowflakes of the season began to fall. Normally, children would become ecstatic, eagerly awaiting snowball fights, tobogganing and so forth, but Alex and I had larger worries now.

We ran out of coal, wood, or any other material capable of providing heat. We had already burnt our wooden furniture, save for the last kitchen chair, which we took turns sitting on. We had taken the wooden board beneath the hay mattress long ago, thus we were pressed for material. The dust beneath the bed from the hay mattress was not excluded from the flames of the stove. Alex and I looked at each other sadly and sighed heavily.

For some reason, I thought of the large portrait of our grandfather. I ventured to ask Alex about it. "Where is the portrait of grandfather, Alex?"

Alex was staring out the window silently, without blinking. Was he ignoring me, or was he about to tell me something regarding the portrait and was attempting to figure out a way?

"Why do you need it, Vitya? If you are thinking of burning it, you are too late."

"What!"

"You heard me. You are too late. That was consumed in the fire long ago, which heated you and me alike."

"How could you?! You know that's Mother's only portrait of him! Oh no! Grandfather!"

"Relax, Vitya. It's not like I took pleasure and enjoyed doing that, but as you can see yourself, we have no more wood to burn. And that means no heat."

The dummy! How could he do it? I was steaming with anger. In a delirious combination of vexation, contempt and sorrow, I related the entire discussion between Mr. Vassily and myself. Alex was dumbfounded, silent and regretful. In one instant I was overcome with pity for him and myself and our dreaded misfortune.

"Vitya, is it possible? Is it really true?"

"Yes, Alex. It is."

"Let us find some documents in here, Vitya. Perhaps we might be lucky?"

"We can try. Let's!"

We began scrimmaging in haste in our nearly empty abode. Our frantic search was concluded with a finding of one document. We searched outside in the courtyard, behind the loose bricks of the wall, where Father hid our documents, or rather their documents. Our find consisted of one paper. A baptismal certificate.

As Alex pored over my baptismal, he excitedly proclaimed, "Do you not see, Vitya, who your godparents are?"

"What of it?"

"Your godparents are the General Major Nikolai Hrisanovich Redkin and the Countess Nadezda O'brien!"

Again I repeated to Alex, "What of it, Alex? What good is that to us now?"

"Vitya, aren't you aware that these nobles do not simply favour being witnesses to just anyone? It is known that these personages usually are inclined to become godparents to their own kind and not of a lower class."

For a long time after that, Alex and I continued our search, but to no avail. Alex reasoned and decided that we take Mother's photograph to Mr.Vassily, in addition to my baptismal certificate, and perhaps that would suffice. Satisfied of his decision, Alex began dressing, and so did I, too.

"Wait for me, Alex, wait!" No use. He was already out the door. In my haste, I slipped on the big shoes on the wrong feet and clumsily chased Alex through the courtyard and onto the street.

"Agh, must you do that to me, Alex?"

"What?"

"Could you not have waited for a moment."

Alex looked down at my shoes and remarked, "It would work better, Vitya, if you had the right shoe on the right foot."

I corrected my error and we continued to Mr. Vassily's.

When we had arrived at Mr. Vassily's apartment, we found a large red notice attached to the door. It was also barricaded.

"What's that, Alex?"

"Read it yourself."

I began to read, "*By the order of the Commandant and the Occupational Forces, these premises have been confiscated.*" There was a stamp of an eagle, a swastika and someone's signature.

"Alex? What now?"

"Vitya, it seems that the poor Mr.Vassily was apprehended. It means that everything is on hold."

Alex considered as he bowed his head and let a tear drop fall from his face. There was no further reason for our presence there and we began to return home.

"Wait! Alex, I have something. Mr.Vassily gave me a note, a letter of some sort, to give to the Greek princess. She is residing at the former president's mansion."

"Well, why didn't you say so! What kind of note did he give you?"

"I didn't open it, Alex. I wouldn't do that."

"Just the same, let us go and deliver the note to the princess, Vitya. That should be an eyeful!"

It was a gloomily heavy day, just the kind that produces major snow falls. It was well suited to our situation, but not to our intentions. We scrunched along the packed snow as we walked by the botanical gardens, which now housed a variety of dry and withered twigs and branches unshielded from the winter's scorn. Alex put his arm around my shoulder as we walked through the nasty winds, I assume to keep us warm and not blow away.

The wind bit right through our torn rags and onto our skin, but we braved the cold and proceeded forward.

"What luck we have, Vitya!" Alex sarcastically remarked.

"What is luck, Alex?"

"Right. What is luck, Vitya." He ended his statement.

The mansion was beautiful. Secluded and hidden by enormous trees and evergreens. Not to speak of the iron gates, which when opened led to the large, double doors of this exquisite mansion by a paved pathway. Though now, covered in snow, but clearly visible that it was shovelled by some maintenance crew. Alex shook the iron gate. It didn't open, nor did I expect it to. I wondered why Alex bothered to attempt this silly task. I looked at the stone wall attached to the iron gates and observed a device of some sort with buttons on it.

I pushed the button. No answer. I pushed again and again. Finally, I just kept my finger there on the button, pressing it incessantly. Alex became frustrated, at me or at the rejection, I didn't know. He pushed me away from the stone wall and button and pointed me in the direction of a waving lady. She stood outside in the winter garden, waving a handkerchief, revealing her acknowledgement of the two of us. Immediately she came to the gate.

She was a middle aged lady, most likely the maid. She inquired of our calling. Alex informed her and showed her the wrinkled, crumpled note we had for the princess. I looked at the note and couldn't place a time frame on its inhabitancy in my pocket. The maid gently took the wrinkled note and left the two of us standing there in front of the gate.

We waited approximately half an hour. By now the snow had accumulated and we looked like two white snowmen when she finally returned. She regretfully informed us that the princess apologizes, but she is unable to receive us due to some reasons unknown, though she sends us some money and thanks us for the note, with a message of precaution: We are never to appear before her mansion again, lest some unknown, dangerous persons arrest us.

We were truly surprised at her refusal. We turned around and treaded home. The lights of the mansion twinkled in my eyes full of tears as I turned back to get a second glimpse. Alex pulled me and bid me to walk faster. We were very cold, nearly frostbitten. As we trekked through the packed snow, it stuck to our heels, forcing us to stop every so often and shake off the excess snow. People were rushing to and fro, also shaking off their heels now white. Children (the few that could be seen) were jumping and throwing snow balls.

Our arrival home was welcomed by darkness. We were relieved that we had come home without hindrance. It was known and customary for the authorities to randomly stop and detain pedestrians and demand their identification papers. In view of our lack of identification papers, we were assuaged at our non-confrontation with these authorities, at least not with the ones that had time to spare. For supper, Alex and I ate some dry crackers that we had. In such a manner our day ended.

Many days had gone by. Alex worked alone; I, too. Somehow, without any prior agreement, we had come to this arrangement. Usually, when Alex returned from his work, he would tease and taunt me, upon displaying his earnings on the kitchen table. I thought he did so to instigate my working ambitions, but he needn't to, for my hunger was the foremost basis of my motivation.

One particular day, I was alone in the house. Alex had left for work. I, whether out of boredom, or simply because I needed to make myself useful, settled on rummaging through our meagre possessions. I stumbled upon a box full of an assortment of various buttons. Mother had accumulated this special possession of hers over the years, by ripping them off of unusable and worn out garments which were in the garbage. Thus she procured a feasible quantity.

I had conceived a plan. I searched about for a needle and with much difficulty, I managed to locate one. I now needed thread. Not readily available in our home! I sat looking around me and my gaze fell upon our torn, mended and re-mended sheets on the bed. Well...I un-mended Mother's mending and did so until I had a sufficient supply of thread! My materials were ready now.

I had sewn on the buttons, according to colour, size and shape onto small pieces of paper I had earlier found. This procedure pervaded the entire day. Near Alex's accustomed return home, I neatly collected my items and carefully hid my production. I needn't Alex's objections, or teases to discourage me. Besides, he does not need to know all I do!

The following morning, after Alex's departure, I took off to the Stari Djeram Piazza. I mingled in between the other merchants and was busily searching for a good location to place my merchandise for sale. I chanced upon a free spot on the ground. I began to do my work. I pulled out a black cloth I had in my rucksack (left over from school days) and whipped it in the air, then placed it on the ground. This was followed by gentle arrangements of my precious buttons, which I worked hard at, to make them very attractive to the customer's eye. A nearby peasant woman was observing me through the corner of her eye as I did my work.

Suddenly she remarked, "Hah! Now gentlemen of the city are trying to sell, too!" I did glance at her, but was not bothered, nor discouraged and I continued to do my work, in complete ignorance of her presence. Ironically, she was my first customer! She purchased ten packets of buttons from me in exchange for some potatoes. I nearly had no more buttons left to sell and those I had left, were also sold quickly. This quick sale was a Godsend for me, for the piazza attendant began browsing around and speaking to each of the merchants. I had no licence to sell there, thus I was already packed and on my way in an instant and satisfied at that, too.

Alex was sincerely pleased with my earnings and my methods, which I decidedly informed him, now that I had succeeded as an entrepreneur.

Alex commented, "Vitya, you have done well! Although, we still have the preponderance of our lack of heating materials," he added.

"I know, Alex, I know," I answered sadly, and my high descended rapidly into a low.

"Vitya, I have a plan!"

"What is it?"

"Never mind now, it's late. Tomorrow you and I must go out and find ourselves some wood and I believe I know where we can find some."

We dressed quickly the next morning, not because of our intended plan, but because of the biting cold. We crawled out of our mountain of rags and hit by the sharp, bitter air we quickly threw rags on, piled them on top of each other. Some we had to borrow from our mountainous stack on the bed and later return them for our sleep.

Everything outside was white, shocking white and one had to adjust their vision to this blast of whiteness. The air was crisp and fresh smelling. We walked a while, noting that all the streets were covered in snow, the streetcar tracks, too. Thus no streetcars were to be seen. We chanced upon a coachman with a horse and sleigh. We humbly beseeched him to accept us onto his sleigh, on the rear and onto a board attached to the sleigh. He agreed. Soon we were off to the church, St. Mark's, for this was the coachman's destination and his final stop, which suited us, because it was our destination as well. Happily we jumped off and walked toward the church and a large church indeed.

Alex began, "Look, Vitya!"

"Where?"

"Look by the church, on that open field."

All I had seen was a lot of white snow.

"What is it, Alex?"

"Follow me. Follow me!"

We came onto this open field of white snow. Some sort of ruins, wood and other unknown materials protruded slightly from the snow, possibly because the wind had blown some of the lighter snow off of the protruded items.

"Dig!" Alex promptly ordered.

"Dig? Dig what? With what?"

"Dig! With your feet! What else! Do you see any shovels around us, Vitya? No! Then dig!"

I began digging with my feet. In the process I tossed the shoe off my foot. It was two sizes larger than my foot and now filled with snow. Agh! I reached for my shoe, tapped out the snow and placed it back on my frozen foot. I continued digging as per Alex's orders. I had dug enough to reach a wooden board, a plank of some kind. I looked over to Alex who was also was heavily involved in digging.

"Vitya!"

"What?"

"Look at this!"

"What, Alex, can't you see I'm digging now?"

"Come here, Vitya!"

I went over to where Alex stood, sweaty and out of air.

"Do you see that?"

"What's that?"

"You mean to tell me you don't know?"

"No."

"It's a skull! A human skull!"

"What! Are you serious?! What is a skull doing here?"

"Vitya, do you realize where we are?"

"Where are we?" I innocently importuned.

"I believe we are standing in a cemetery," Alex eerily realized. "The old cemetery. I think, Vitya, that when the bombs fell, it blew up the cemetery and all its inhabitants!"

"Alex! I don't think I want that wood I came across. It must be the lid of a coffin. I won't take it! Even if it means I have to freeze this winter!"

"Yes, Vitya, I feel the same way. I don't want it either."

What made Alex bring us there is beyond me. He must have seen some wood before and thought it was blown there onto that open field. Whatever the case, we hurriedly left the cemetery.

As we left, sullen after our encounter with the skull. I noticed some withered, dry shrubs at the sides of the cemetery. I told Alex to follow me. We broke off some branches and some twigs and entirely unconcerned whether anyone was watching us, or not, for after our incident, we deserved these twigs, no matter how scruffy they are!

Our return home was presented with some more wood! We walked along Hilandarska Street and there was an abundance of ruins to be seen. Alex began walking upon a broken wall of this structure that had its stairs plastered against it, descending into a basement. He walked freely and I shivered with each step he took. I begged him to come down off those ruins. Finally Alex jumped down and we proceeded. We came across a wooden gate.

"Alex! Wood!"

"So it is! Good! Vitya, start taking the wood apart!"

"Absolutely not!"

"Why do you say that, Vitya?"

"Well, my brother...This time I found the wood and now you can disassemble it!"

"Very well," and Alex began to bang on the wood.

I realized that he couldn't do it alone, therefore I joined in. He smiled when he noticed my help. We broke off approximately four boards each. With all our new materials for heating, we skipped home and were gratified, for now we will be warm.

Soon enough, a crackling and warming fire was hissing in our stove. Alex prepared a kettle to boil some water for tea. He informed me that he had learnt of a new recipe for tea. It was to burn a tablespoon, or teaspoon (depending on how much we had) of sugar, thereby caramelizing it. Once the water boiled, we were to add the caramelized sugar to the water, thus forming a tea and this tea was called sherbet.

We rested before the hot stove, sipped on our tea and Alex stated, "You know, Vitya, it would be wise to call upon that lady you received cans of food from before. Remember her…Mrs. Helen? I think that was her name?"

"Yes, Alex, Mrs. Helen."

"I think you should visit her and perhaps she might give you some more food."

"Alex, what would I give her in return?"

"This," and he yanked out a pack of Camel cigarettes he had hidden in his pocket.

"You have Camel cigarettes! And to think all this time I have been smoking dirty cigarette butts! Really, Alex!"

"Vitya, first of all, they are not for our smoking pleasure, but rather in the case of desperation, we could easily exchange them!"

I now regretted my sanctimonious display and knew he was right.

Alex continued, "I earned them carrying some officer's luggage the other day and decided to save them. Do you suppose I am not smoking cigarette butts also? Look…" and he shoved his hand into his front pocket and threw several cigarette butts on the table.

I felt more awkward now, upon his confession. Nevertheless, we remained in front of our warm stove, finished off our tea and sherbet and puffed on the cigarette butts that Alex had produced.

"Tomorrow, Vitya, you will go to Mrs. Helen's home and exchange this pack of Camels for some cans of food." I agreed.

For some reason, Alex decided to accompany me to Mrs. Helen's. I didn't oppose, in fact I was happy to have his company. It was a frosty day, the snow lightly fell, hesitatingly. By the looks of outside, no wonder it hesitated. We were now barricaded in our home. The snow piled high against the door. With much struggle and difficulty, did we manage to shovel the snow aside.

Alex found a shovel in the yard and began forming a path to

the gate of the courtyard. We reached the sidewalk, which was heavily treaded and formed a convenient path, which we merged into. I walked behind Alex, following his footsteps and without looking up and I bumped into his back, for he had stopped abruptly. I looked up.

A colony of people were crossing, some joining our treaded path. No pedestrian was eager to begin forming a new, fresh path in the nearly metre deep snow. Naturally, we were obliged to accept these new trekkers and permit them to mingle in between us and onto our path.

I admired the whiteness of the city. Not only was the ground white, but everything else was blanketed with this soft, white solidified liquid and the buildings (at least the ones that remained) were white also, not cement grey. I wondered, perhaps this is where the city derived its name from? "Beograd," meaning "White City." This historical city was a wedding gift from Hungary to the reigning monarch at that time. Later on, the Turkish Ottoman Empire occupied it. Now, it was the Nazis' turn.

We had an opportunity to ride upon a sleigh again. We watched the traffic (which was scarce) as we went past them. Prior to the war, I could recall a traffic warden directing the on coming traffic with his white gloves and whistle at the semaphore. Today, he was not to be seen. Mainly in part of the snow and then the realization of that automobiles were generally driven by the occupiers, thus there was not much traffic to be encountered.

We had dismantled off the sleigh and crossed Beogradska Street, headed toward Mrs. Helen's home. As we neared her home, we were shocked to find ruins where her once meagre home stood.

"Where is she now?" Alex asked me.

"How would I know? I am not that familiar with her that she would report to me of her whereabouts, Alex."

"When did they bomb here?" Alex considered.

"Alex, I don't know that either."

"Maybe the city decided to clean up the ruins and partial ruins and anything that resembled ruins?" Alex uttered, with a puzzled look to his face.

"So much for our meal, Alex!"

"Right. So much for that. One would wonder of the fate of Mrs. Helen as well. Poor woman," he remarked.

"Agh! Let's just go to the third, Alex."

"Where? Where?"

"The third, Alex. The third!"

The snow declined to fall, gratefully. I observed some Italian prisoners of war shovelling the snow as the Germans stood above them with shotguns ready, scrutinizing their every move. This encounter reminded me of an incident I had with an Italian soldier for whom I once carried his rucksack. In response to my question, he took off his feathered hat and hit me hard, causing me to fall to the ground. I simply had asked him, "Signore, poko pane prego?" I had my hands outstretched and cupped together, with my palms outward. That blow was unexpected. I was truly hurt.

Trucks loaded with wood and coal were seen climbing along Nemanya Street. Certainly in the direction of Banyitsa. In Banyitsa there was a prison camp and in front of this building one could envision women laden with heavy baskets and parcels of cherished items and lovingly prepared breads. They stood before the doors of the prison camp, with their little children, awaiting visitations with their loved ones, or for news of them.

Alex had yet another plan. How he quickly conjured up these plans was a marvel to me. After he explained his scheme to me, he jumped onto the slowly ascending truck and climbed on top of it. He began to fling heavy logs down the street behind the truck and I, of course had to chase them and capture them. His tossing included three logs in all. After he finished tossing, he jumped down and proceeded to help me.

"Did you have to choose such heavy logs, Alex?"

"Do you think I was up there tossing roses at you, Vitya?"

Quietly, we picked up our logs and left. The passers-by did

watch us, but said nothing. I believe the driver of the truck had known as well, but continued driving nonetheless.

We sold the two logs very quickly. The last log we took home for our own use. We now had money to pay the landlord for the rent, at least partially. The log we brought home, offered us a deal of trouble. We had no saw, nor axe to chop it. Alex had found some carpenter's saw, not very sharp and most of the teeth were gone from the blade. Somehow we managed to break the log into uneven pieces, good enough to keep us warm.

Seldom did Alex inform me of his destinations when he left in the mornings and this was one of those days. It angered me, but I had no use of arguing with him. I was left to my own devices.

I went to the third. I stood there awhile, awaiting the usual streetcar. A plump woman exited the streetcar. She had in her hands some baskets and some parcels. I offered to help her and inquired of her destination. "Banyitsa," she replied.

Agh, that's far. Now that I had already offered her my help, I couldn't back down. I suggested the route....Slaviya district, then we could take the streetcar number #10 to Vozhdovatc. Finally, to walk across the field.

"I believe you want to go to the prison camp, ma'am?"

"Yes, dear, the prison camp. My son is there."

"All right," I mumbled and I picked up her baskets, threw them over my shoulder and we commenced our journey.

When we travelled by streetcar, the woman had paid my fare. She sat on an empty seat and I beside her, on her luggage. The car was packed like a can of sardines. People were also hanging off the sides of the car. The front of the car was reserved exclusively for the occupiers.

While we rode, I had the opportunity to gaze at this woman who was about to visit her son. She fashioned a men's black overcoat and a black handkerchief tied on her head. Her face had traces of her age. Apparent and most probable the added pain did not benefit her complexion. Interestingly as I thought that, tears were forming in her eyes and some fell quickly down her worn face.

"What is wrong, ma'am?" I softly inquired.

"Oh, my dear child. They took my son."

"How old is your son, ma'am?"

"Young, dear child, very young. Twenty years old, my child."

He is not that young I reflected as I was fourteen and he twenty. In consideration to my age, I did not think of him as young. Though his mother did.

The streetcar was nearly empty when we arrived. As we stepped down, out of the car, the prison camp was clearly visible across the barren field. A brick fence approximately fifteen metres high, surrounded the camp. Guards posts were visible on top of these fences. Barbed wire was included in these protective measures of enclosure.

The woman and I walked across the field to the prison camp. I, for some reason was before her, thus I was obliged to turn several times to see if she were behind me and all right. We arrived before the massive structure. A gathering of people stood before the doors, some crying, some talking and some quietly waiting, with suspense exhibited in their composure.

I was glad to drop the baggage to the ground. I had to rest three times when crossing that field. I wondered what she had in them. I examined the luggage. Maybe, at one time, it was used for much happier occasions for this young man and now it most likely carries knit socks, cornbread and other items carefully and gently packed by his mother.

She interrupted my guessing by asking, "How much do I owe you, son?"

"Owe me? Oh, yes...right. I don't know."

I watched her expressions that were so sad, I felt twice as sorry for her now. Then I remembered my own destitution, complimented by my scrawny and torn appearance, but I just could not bring myself to ask her for money. I thought, if only I were rich, I would offer her some money, at least to minimize her load of sadness a little. My stomach began its usual tune. I was hungry.

I answered her, "Whatever you give, ma'am, I will be happy."

She pulled out a handkerchief with a stack of papers in it. I looked upon it and it reminded me of the stacks the peasant women had at the piazza when they were selling in the black market. By the looks of her stack, she might have thousands of dinars.

Finally she unravelled the handkerchief. It was full of letters from her son. They seemed to be all wrinkled as if they were wet and dried in such a state.

"What are those, ma'am?"

"They are words from my son, my dear child," and the tears poured out of her eyes, onto the letters, thus confirming my thoughts of as to how they became crumpled so. She took a hundred dinars from between this stack of letters and handed it to me. I refused it. I nearly cried myself, for her, for her son and for my state of despair. I turned and thanked her and bid her a good day, with regard to her son.

Even if I had accepted her money, it wouldn't have sufficed for a streetcar fare. Regardless of that, I was not about to take whatever little money she had. I would have preferred some cornbread, though my stomach did not cease to grumble and growl. Should I ask her? No. I won't. It would be sinful. She had probably prepared that for her son. It was worse for him. I am out here. Though, alone. Utterly alone.

I continued to walk across the field again and I heard the woman yell after me, "Child, please wait! Child, stop! Take this please!" She had cornbread in her hand, I noticed when I turned around to her calls, but I had politely declined her offer and walked away.

How many more mothers like these were there? I wouldn't know. How many of them cried for their children, their husbands, their fathers and brothers? The heavy tolls of war was unselfish in distributing suffering, poverty and pain unbiasedly, to all those caught in the era.

Chapter 11

Back at the third, Alex was nowhere to be seen. I leaned against the ruins of the old Academy of the Army. It seemed to me that either the ruins were shorter, or I taller. I chewed on an old piece of cornbread I had saved from earlier work, in attempts to appease the mad, growling stomach of mine. I thought of the poor woman back at Banyitsa and of how I would explain to Alex of my work without any pay. The small piece of cornbread I chewed on didn't quiet my stomach and I was still hungry. I know! I'll go visit those nuns Alex and Poule went to! My mouth began to water as I thought of the barley soup.

In a matter of seconds, I stood before their door. I memorized the description and directions according to Alex's detailed story (this time his love of detail proved to be beneficial to me). I knocked on their door. I remembered to remove my cap off my head. Although that did not comfort me, for I prayed that the darned lice would not crawl out of my hair and embarrass me, thus I would automatically lose my bowl of barley soup. I stood there and waited impatiently. Sure enough the door opened. An older, sophisticated woman answered. She, too, was dressed in black, with a black veil upon her head and these two white, starched flaps on the sides. To me it resembled the wings of an aeroplane. I don't recall Alex mentioning that and I am most certain he would, for he is very detail oriented. Anyhow, she inquired, "What do you want?"

"A bowl of barley soup please?"

"Beggars again! I had told Sister Maria to lock the front gate, but do they listen? No!"

She sighed and shut the door in my face. With no luck there, I accepted my fate and turned to walk away, when all of a sudden a melody of a soft, angelic voice was heard.

"Young boy! Young boy, please, please come back!"

I did, I went back. She had in her hands a bowl of steaming, hot barley soup and gave it to me smilingly.

"Here, young man, take this. It is mine. Please have it."

"But what about you?"

"Don't you worry about me. Please eat and also do forgive Mother Superior's harshness, she is not herself today."

In a few gulps, I had finished the soup and gave back the empty bowl to the kind young nun. I thanked her profusely, placed the cap back on my head and bowed nearly to the ground, leaving her waving behind me.

I spotted Poule back at the third.

"Poule, did you see my brother Alex?" He appeared to be ignoring me for some reason. Perhaps he became deaf and no wonder with all the sirens we listened to daily, warning the occupiers, not the citizens of enemy aeroplanes. The buildings that housed the occupiers had a sign written in German on their door that read: *In the event of enemy bombing, entry for army only!* Again, I asked Poule the same question as I did earlier. Again he ignored me. For the third time, I hollered out to him and finally he acknowledged me.

"What! You act as if you don't know of your brother's whereabouts!"

"I don't!"

"In that case, you should know that your brother was arrested and put in the Maritsa. I saw you leave with that woman earlier. Moments later your brother Alex appeared and not long after that we were surrounded by gendarmes. I, being tall, had no trouble leaping over this wall here before you. Alex did not have such luck, thus he was taken away," Poule adduced and smartly puffed away on his Camel cigarette.

What under this heaven is he telling me? Maritsa? What's that?

"Poule? What is a Maritsa?"

"You don't know?!"

"Really, I don't."

"Well, that is the vehicle used by the police, to put persons who are apprehended into. It has iron bars on it."

"Aa-ha, why didn't you say that, Poule? You meant a police car."

"Whatever, kid. We call it Maritsa. Alex asked me whether I had seen you and I told him I did, but I didn't know where you went."

"Banyitsa," I answered.

"Kid, I don't have a crystal ball, nor a tea cup to know where you were going!"

Tea cup? What is wrong with Poule?

"What would you do with a tea cup, Poule?"

"Are you ever dumb, or are you just pretending to be, to annoy me?"

"I'm serious. What's the tea cup of use for knowing of a person's whereabouts?"

"Silly kid. Black coffee, not tea, is drunk from this tea cup. When the coffee is finished, there remains a thick sauce at the bottom of the tea cup. Whoever had drunk the coffee would then swoosh the sauce around in the tea cup, then turn it upside down on a paper to dry. When it becomes dry, a qualified reader, which there seems to be many, would proceed to read the fortune to the owner of the cup. Now do you understand? And why must you waste my time with this nonsense? I am not your teacher!"

"Sorry. But...tell me, Poule, how may I find my brother Alex?"

"Can't tell you, kid. I have no knowledge regarding this and am unable to give you advice."

"Would you know then of who I might be able to ask for help?"

"Sorry, no. I must be off now. I spent too much time here as it is."

Poule drifted off and I remained alone, in bewilderment. Who can help me? Where is my Alex? What kind of quagmire had befallen upon him? Was Poule's story plausible? I arrogantly studied the tall and skinny, phlegmatic Poule, who nonchalantly wandered away.

I decided to discreetly pursue Poule. Coyly, I followed, snuck behind posts and other convenient objects suitable for hiding. Luckily, he hadn't an inkling of his tail. He came to an abrupt halt before this delicatessen. He quickly found a customer there, who was just as glad to see him as he was to see her, loaded with numerous bags and packages.

Uh huh, now I understand Poule's disdain. He sneakily tried to rid me, lest I discover his gestation. Since I now uncovered this new "hot spot" for earning. I, too, will wait for an over burdened lady with bags.

Just as I presumed, I had a customer. A plump and robust lady sweating of her labourious task of carrying packages and bags had nearly summoned me, if I hadn't jumped to her aid quickly. Thus I also earned, thanks be to the ignorant Poule.

I found Poule back at the third. He was entirely oblivious of my actions. I crept up to him and noticed him munching on something that he was picking up from a brown paper he held. The closer I came, the more he recoiled. Nevertheless, he remained, for he had no more room behind him, the walls of the ruins prevented him from further recluse. Poule was eating salami! I was shocked and amazed of his snack. How could he possibly have obtained such a splendid treat that is so hard to come by? I ventured closer as a bird of prey, but he, noticing my proximity covered his food with the brown paper. I casually turned around. I realized he had no intention of discoursing, and least of all sharing his meal. I had to find out where and how Poule acquired this treat! Once again, I became a detective.

We found ourselves back at the delicatessen. Naturally, Poule thought he was alone. I was but a few steps behind him, a large tree helped my purpose and shielded me. This time Poule ventured to the back of the delicatessen. I slowly followed, but cautioned myself and several times I had to crouch, or fall back a few steps. To my joy Poule's back was turned and he was too busy rummaging through this medium-sized, greasy, brown box. He pulled out something and continued down the alley, contrary to my direction. I, of course, had to determine what was in that box.

With Poule safely out of sight, it was my turn to go through this box. What treasure I beheld! A box full of salami beginnings and ends. I assumed the owner didn't need it, thus he threw it out here as I was about to find out, when the back door of the delicatessen suddenly opened. The owner who sported a greasy apron had flung some more of salami and other delicatessen items into this box. He did not mind my presence, in fact he even offered some of the ends, which I gladly accepted. This new found treasure, thanks again to the ignorance of Poule, enabled us to send George mini parcels to the orphanage and Mother, too, had a share of it.

The stinging reality of independence in a big city, left one not only to accept responsibilities, endure the circumstances of the city's occupied state and forced to survive by one's own methods and devices. All this would ultimately cause and induce a phlegmatic state of composure by repetitive tragedies, which overshadowed a normal and innocent childhood. Paradoxically, in our, and other unfortunates', childhood, one was expected to survive and maintain a naive existence.

People were preoccupied with their own worries and survival. Not often, mostly never, realizing the revolting conditions and traumas of the children in their own neighbourhood. The unremitting dilemma of procuring provisions, diverted our attention from the ignorance of our neighbours. Was it due to inconsideration, selfishness, or lack of concern, which simultaneously occurred during that time in history, during the second world war.

Of all human ironies, nothing is more satirical than by the actions of near orphans in a state of destitution, reading about orphans in destitution as was the case of ours and Victor Hugo's book, *Les Miserables*.

Such common and irrelevant items deemed a fortune to us,

who, again ironically, were descendants from an aristocratic family that once relished unheard of luxuries! The extreme diversities, now a fact, were only left to be marvelled at.

Witnessing other children absorbed in play, eating, because of the scorn of their mothers' perpetually unconcerned of their own being and survival was astonishing to us. We were aware of such a lifestyle, but verisimilar would have been obscure and awkward to have fallen into such a standard of living, at that time. Our forced creativity and imagination was not of the usual childish nature, but rather a useful tool, to provide us with basic needs, such as food and shelter. Children as scavengers were seen throughout the city and we were a part of their domain.

Clothing and shoes were a most-difficult-to-obtain necessity, and in addition to winter's unforgiveness we had systematically learnt a lifestyle granted to us by the revolution, war, inconsideration of our neighbours and, pathetically and foremostly, the inconsideration of our father.

Methodically insulted by all in existence, the populace, the city and fate. Possibly, because of the naiveness most natural of children, the cruelty and injustice whether realized or not, was accepted and dealt with in ways that adults would ponder at and worse, would have dealt in terms of atrocities, or self inflicted injuries, perhaps even suicide.

An opportune was never missed by the overpowering desire for food and shelter. It must have been a miracle that had sustained us throughout those turbulent and traumatic years.

It was dark when I reached home. I decided to light the candle before the icon we had and used to pray in front of. "Dear God, why do you take all from me? My parents, my brothers and leave me here in this home, between these bare and dirty walls. Who do I cry to?" I shouted at the top of my lungs, "Aleexsss...Alex," and bitterly wept. I knew I had to be strong. I had no option. It was cold, dark and lonely and my soul felt likewise. I hopelessly watched the candle light's shadow dance on the wall and I fell asleep.

The next day I visited Mother in the hospital, with much difficulty I might add. I didn't know whether she was still alive or not. The last time I attempted to visit her, I was thrown out. They (the administrators) informed me that I smelt too much and was unfit to visit. Whether that was true or not, I wasn't aware of, perhaps I had become accustomed to my own scent? I did scratch myself a lot though, the lice and fleas were persistently bothering me. If I were cold, they wouldn't bite as much. I didn't know which of the two misfortunes were better—to be cold and unbitten, or warm and eaten. I deeply longed for Alex. I cried for many days and nights.

I often caught myself daydreaming of how it would be if I were born again and resided in the mansion of my grandfather Nikolai's. He would escort me to school and wave good bye. I would have plenty of food, clothes and other necessities. Food. No. I musn't think of food right now. I made it my habit to daydream these perfect episodes, which helped me attain the much needed slumber.

In the hospital where Mother was, nothing new was to be envisioned. Prior to the occupation, it was the government's hospital, now who knows? It stretched for a block in width. There were numerous benches beneath large welcoming trees to shade the patients and visitors during their outings. Colourful flowers were displayed in splashes throughout the grounds and the lawn was a lush green carpeting, in the spring and summer.

I walked toward the entrance. I observed a lady clad in a white uniform. No one prevented me from entering this time. I ventured to ask the lady in white, "Exccccuuuse me, ma'am? I am looking for my mother."

"I have no time to help you. I must be off to the next building immediately."

"Please, ma'am, I need to find my mother."

"What is her name and what is her illness?"

"Well, her name is Zoya and I don't know the name of her illness. All I know is that these two men in white came to our home and tied up Mother and then took her away and brought her here."

"How do you expect me to help you if you don't know the name of her illness? The hospital is divided by the categories of illnesses. Now scurry along."

Agh! I don't understand anything now.

"You know, ma'am, my mother…"

"Son, I told you, I have no time. I am not the information desk. I have my obligations. Go to the chief, or to the director of the hospital, he might be able to help you. He has a list of all the patients."

"Please, ma'am, wait!" I was skipping alongside her.

"Are you ever annoying!" the lady snapped.

I devised a plan of manipulating her into helping me find my mother…

"Ma'am, you know, you do resemble a doctor, precisely why I was determined to inquire from you. You also have a charming stance!"

"Son, are you flirting with me? Of all things, I have little time for such trivial advances, particularly from you."

What! She thinks I am making advances on her? Of all the ridiculous…

"Ma'am, I am not flirting with you. Please help me out. I told you, they tied my mother and brought her here and I don't know where to look for her!"

"Look for her in the psychiatric ward!" With that she doubled her pace and fled from my sight.

Psychiatric ward. What and where is that? I looked around. No one. Wait, there's a janitor! I ran up to him. He stood beside a trash can and was leaning on his broom. I bowed to him and began, "Good day, sir. Please tell me where is the psychiatric ward?"

"Young man. First of all, you needn't bow in front of a trash can and secondly, the ward you are looking for is right over there," and he pointed in the direction I was to take with his still fragrant, smoking pipe.

I left him, thanked him (this time without bowing) and he followed me with his eyes, I noticed as I turned back to wave at him.

This section of the building frightened me. There were iron bars upon the windows. Regardless, I was settled on finding Mother. I tried to open the door and nearly fell back, unaware that it was locked. I pounded on the heavy door three times, which was answered by a distant rumbling voice, "Who is it?"

"I'm looking for my mother, Zoya."

"What mother?"

"My mother. Zoya!"

"Wait!"

I heard the clinking and clanking noise of keys and a loud unlocking of the door. Before me stood a mountain of a man, with milky eyes and an austere expression. He motioned me in, "Enter, enter."

He locked the door behind me and then walked ahead of me. We went down this dark, scary corridor. He looked back to see if I was still following him.

"Where are you, kid?"

"Right here, sir!" I quickened my pace.

He unlocked a door we had come to and then another unexpected door was before us. He unlocked that, too.

"Go in. Look for her in there," and he left me.

Locking me in with all these patients. Hundreds of eyes were upon me. I felt completely awkward and didn't move. The large room housed many patients, too numerous to count. There were six windows, barred windows that is. The patients were singing, dancing, crying, flying and some were yelling around me. I was lost. One patient came up to me dressed in the hospital gown, "Oh, you are Prince Charming!" If she thought I was Prince Charming, sadly, she must be in the right place. Yet another patient this time twirled up to me. "Do you dance ballet?" A third approached. "And I am a fairy you know!" Agh, where am I? Why did that man leave me in here? Who do I ask for my mother? Is it possible that they put my mother in here? I felt a pinch on my arm. "You are too thin, lad. I prefer bulkier men!" I snatched my arm back, away from her, and squirmed through the crowd of singers, dancers and musicians playing their invisible instruments. I neared the windows at the back of the room and in one of the corners I observed something familiar to me. I went closer to this person. She was dressed in a hospital gown and her head rested on her knees as she sat there crouched on the floor, in the corner. When I came closer, she raised her head.

"Mama! Is that you?" I cried.

"My son, Vitya! You are here, my child!"

I bent down to her and we hugged and cried for a long time.

"Look, Vitya, where they put me! I wanted to look out the window, but that old witch over there pushed me into this corner and told me that this is her mansion."

I looked over at the older woman, who did look frightening and her eyes were ablaze with fury. I noticed when she felt my gaze and returned the look.

"You know, Son, these people here, they are not well, they are not normal. Why did they put me in here?"

"I don't know, Mother, I really don't."

"Vitya, I must tell you something, but promise me that you won't tell anyone? Please!"

"All right, Mother."

"Look at me, Vitya. Look at my arms and at my legs. Under my gown, too, there are bruises."

I saw large circular bruises on Mother's arms and legs. Some were dark, some were still fresh.

"Mama! What happened? Who did this to you?" I shockingly inquired.

"You see, Son, sometimes I like to pray to God and when the attendant spies me praying, he uses his broom handle to beat me so."

I was crying and stroking the poor, thin, loving and bruised arms of Mother's.

"Mother, I will directly go to the chief and ask him why they do this to you!"

"No! Please, child, don't! If you do that, I will be beaten even more!"

Why must my poor mother suffer so? At least I could go and tell that monster of a woman who forbid Mother from looking out the window, to leave her alone. I realized it was of no consequence. The old hag was now dancing around with the other ballerinas.

"How are they feeding you, Mother?" I sighed heavily.

"They feed us like livestock. They usher us into a hall and feed us cornmeal soup and sauerkraut stew."

Agh, why did she have to mention that?

I instantly recalled my visits with Alex to the Russian centre for emigres. In the basement of this edifice was a smelly kitchen, which handed out charity to the poor. Often Alex and I would call upon their charity.

Their sauerkraut stew stunk so bad that it made my stomach turn. Even though I was hungry, the smell of the stew caused me to feel nauseous. When we would sit there on the benches eating our meal, rats would run between our feet on the floor and this fact added to my grief. I often wondered whether the dirty and smelly chefs would add those rats to the stew. Such thoughts my mother provoked with the mention of the sauerkraut stew.

"Where do you sleep, Mother?" I uttered in desperation of changing the subject.

"Every night we are taken for cold showers, followed by the disgusting dinner, which usually consists of the same menu we had for lunch. We are then flocked into these rooms for sleeping, twenty per room and two to a bed. I sleep with that one over there that's flying," Mother pointed out to me.

"She states that she is a hibernating bird. It suits me well. She tires herself sufficiently well during the course of the day with her flying, thus providing me with a peaceful and quiet sleep. I know them all, Son. Some of them are good, but some are awfully strange."

"I know, Mother. I see that."

"Tell me, Vitya, where is Alex, Olga and George? Who is taking care of you all?" she quietly and contentedly inquired of me, expecting a comforting answer.

What do I tell her? I have no idea? God help me. Give me words to tell her and comfort her, please!

"Everyone is well, Mother, and they all send you their regards."

She looked at me. "But only you came, Vitya. Where are the

rest of the children?"

"They are working, Mother."

"George is too little to work."

"Of course, Mother, I know that. Auntie Katya is watching him."

"What! No! I don't want that! Oh dear, oh my...My day will come. My day will come!"

"Please, Mother, not that! Not your day, not now!"

"You are right, Vitya. I must be strong." She gazed at me with her glossy eyes and repeated, "I must be strong!"

"I must go now, Mother."

"No, Vitya, stay. Don't leave me here, please!"

"I have to, Mother, but I will go to talk to the director and ask him to let you out."

"Good, Vitya, do that."

She let go of my legs and I went to the door from whence I came in. I knocked on it, but had no response. Mother was soon by my side and told me to pound on the door three times, for that was the signal the guards used. Shivers ran down my spine at the thought of being locked up in there.

Soon enough, the door opened and the growling words of the guard commanded me to exit. Hearing the thunderous words of the guard, the patients drew back from me and from the exit. Before I left the room, I turned to hug Mother one more time and she softly whispered, "Don't forget me, child."

"I won't, Mother. I won't," and I felt her warm tear wet my cheek. "I will never forget you."

The fresh, crisp air hit me as I exited the building. It was much better out there, even though I was alone and hungry.

Many lonely days were before me. During my visit with Mother, she informed me regarding my Auntie Nina. She told me that she, too, was struggling, came to visit when she could, whenever she gathered enough little items to bring to Mother. Mother also informed me that Auntie Nina attempted to visit us at home, but never found anyone there. Thus, our connection with Auntie Nina was nearly lost. I was too preoccupied with survival and by the sounds of it, I couldn't expect much from my aunt, for she, too, was in dire need of charity herself.

I did go to the director of the hospital and implored him for the release of Mother. Unfortunately, I was not of legal age to accept such a responsibility, he told me. In a sense, I surmised it was better, for if Mother had a fit, I wouldn't be of much aid to her and she would need to be alone most of the time, for I had to work.

The following days I found myself eavesdropping and more often, unintentionally overhearing the people I carried the baskets for when they recounted the war updates, while I munched on the food I acquired via Alex's methods. They were talking about the German's withdraw from Russia. Perhaps the situation was changing?

Of my earnings, I had paid the landlord every week, little by little. I often would sit alone in the kitchen and muse, reflect, cry and wonder, especially about my brother Alex.

Alex's fate was of a terrible nature. The German forces that arrested him had sent him to Germany to work. He had managed to escape and return to Belgrade, but only to be caught between two warring factors. Being captured by both intermittently, he experienced forced labour, pillaging of villages and forced apprehensions of young males, who were soon to join him. Later, after he escaped by hiding in a rain barrel, he was caught by the opposing party. There he was put to reside in a barn, under constant surveillance and awaited execution as the others did in his company. Fortunately, he was released and not executed. His trauma was apparent, once I beheld him, which I will later retell.

Unusually, I was offered a job. Distributing newspapers for an old man. I was to rise every morning at two and set off to deliver the newspapers on the old man's route. I did this for a while and the old man would collect his pay. I would summon the old man to pay me my share and he refused to. I implored him politely and again he declined. He ultimately informed me that he had complaints from his customers. They complained of not receiving their newspapers. Was the old man lying or not,

I wasn't certain. I knew I had delivered them, but whether somebody stole them before the recipient had the chance to take it inside, I didn't know and couldn't verify.

Again, I attempted to collect my pay from the old man, who was so withered and wrinkled that he resembled a raisin. He threw me out of his apartment, located in the district of Pashina Brda, meaning "Pasha's hill." This term stuck since the Ottoman Empire's rule.

I was outraged at this incidence and thus this old man had evoked an insurgence upon himself. I did rise at two in the morning again, but not to work, rather to claim my revenge upon this mean, selfish, old man. I found a sufficiently large rock that would do its purpose of breaking the window of the man's apartment. I decided that if he wouldn't pay me for my work rendered, he would then pay for a new window instead. I was satisfied. For that week, since I had no pay, I ate the smelly sauerkraut at the Russian centre, without rejoicing.

Finally spring! Not only did spring bring new blooms and fresh foliage, but also brought the holiday of "remembrance day." During these holidays it was customary for the mourners to visit the cemetery and bring plenty of food and other items and distribute it to anyone who might be present, to eat or take, in the memory of the dearly departed. Since I was alone, one bag was sufficient for the visit to the cemetery. Ironically, in poverty, even sorrow was beneficial.

I took the side entrance to the cemetery, off of St. Nicholas Street. I hadn't observed many people. I saw one older woman naturally dressed in black and she was busy with her arrangement of the items she brought. She placed a clean, bright tablecloth over the grave and then proceeded to put all the treats upon it. I ventured closer. Without looking up she remarked, "No, I'm not giving anything out yet. The priest hasn't been her to bless it yet."

I drew back and took a few steps and was on the street. I found a cigarette butt and went back in the cemetery and hid behind a monument to smoke it. I didn't want the old woman, nor the priest, to lecture me.

If I went to the other side of the cemetery where the priest was probably praying and blessing all the food, it would be too late, for I am certain there were others like me awaiting the final amen and then politely accepting all the goods. Thus, I relented to remain calm and wait.

In no time, I saw the black-cloaked priest swiftly pass by. I took the routes of the priest and keenly observed any generous mourners as I strolled by with my bag. I was lucky. I filled my bag in no time and not only did I receive treats, I also obtained a pack of cigarettes! Great! I could barter that later and then pay the remainder of the rent I owed to the landlord.

The mourners at the cemetery were kind indeed. They offered all kinds of treats, including shots of brandy, which I declined immediately. My experience with brandy was as such:

I had bad teeth, with many cavities. My father would put some spirit onto a tablespoon and pour it directly onto my aching tooth. It would burn immensely. This also reminds me of the incident I had with the fish:

My mother had been at the piazza and brought fish home for dinner one day. I, out of eagerness to be helpful, while she tended to something outside, had decided to fry the fish in a pan I had placed on the stove. I sampled the meal I had prepared. Suddenly, I felt a sharp pain in my tooth. The little fish bone lodged itself into my cavity. I couldn't close my mouth. I screamed. I shoved my fist into my mouth to prevent it from closing.

Mother had walked into the kitchen, looked at me, then at the stove.

"What is this? What have you done, Vitya?!" She was unaware of my misery. I tried to tell her, but only mumbled out words with my mouth open. Mother turned pale, she thought I was choking. She grabbed my free hand, for the other one was still in my mouth.

We ran through the courtyard and bumped into the landlady. Mother cried and begged her to tell us where the nearest doctor was located. The landlady pointed her fingers here and there, finally instructing us to a doctor who apparently was on our street. Needless to say, we flew there.

Running into their house (the doctor practised at home) wildly and without knocking, startled the doctor, who looked at us quizzically. Mother yelled out, "Help, doctor! My son is choking!"

I began to wave my hand around frantically, in an unsuccessful attempt to explain that I was not choking, but had a bone lodged in my tooth. The doctor came to me and told me to remove my hand. I refused.

"Son, I won't hurt you. I have to look at what is causing the trouble and will help you."

I relented. He saw the cause of my trauma and took a pair of tweezers he had on a shelf and pulled out the bone.

A chorus of angels I heard, the pain was gone. Relieved, I then retold the incident to them. Near the ending of my story, Mother had interrupted me and turned to the doctor, "Doctor, would you kindly fix my son's teeth? I can clean and wash for you in return for the repair of his teeth?"

"I'm sorry, ma'am, I can't."

"Please, doctor, I will work very hard..."

"No, ma'am, I said I can't. I mean it."

"But why, doctor, do you refuse us?"

"Because, my dear lady, I am not a dentist. I am a veterinarian."

Thus, I was destined to remain with bad teeth, but luckily, no pain, at least for the time being.

Thus, the offering of brandy from the mourners at the cemetery had reminded me of my experiences. I left the cemetery and encountered other visitors, who also had their bags full, courtesy of the mourners. We hastened to depart from the area, for fear of being apprehended by the authorities and delivered to the Nazis, who would send us across the River Sava where they usually sent prisoners, amongst them Jewish people and Gypsies.

At the beginning of the occupation the Nazis had ordered

that the Jewish people wear a yellow track (ribbon) around the sleeve of their arm. During that time, a handful of Jewish people could be noticed walking outside bearing this yellow ribbon and star of David, in the neighbourhood where they predominantly lived, in the area of Kalemegdan, near Jovan's Piazza. Later on, they were not to be seen. I did not have much opportunity to learn more of their fate, nor to mingle with them, save for the family that had temporarily lived with us earlier.

One day I decided to visit the Jovan's Piazza, thinking I might find some work. Mother had a habit of frequenting this piazza before. There was a butcher there, who would offer Mother bones, which she used for soups that she made for us. When this butcher was absent, his daughter would replace him. She would more often give not only bones, but additional little chunks of meat and a few dinars, too!

I glanced around the piazza, with hopes of encountering her. I found the kiosk, but the familiar butcher and his daughter were no longer there. Now it was under new management. We hadn't been to this piazza in a long time, approximately between the years of 1941-1944.

That particular day the piazza was full of patrons, although the kiosks were not full. It was unnecessary for me to remain there, for there weren't any customers in need of my help. I began to journey home. At once I noticed a gathering of some men. They were not of a tall stature, rather my height. They seemed to be arguing, or discussing something of importance, for the slippers they had on the ground didn't seem relevant to them momentarily. I was behind them. They didn't notice me.

I crouched down on the ground and crawled between them. I managed to grab hold of a pair of slippers. A heavy burden was upon my hand in seconds. "Ouch!" The pain in my hand was caused by the foot of one of these men, who caught me taking the slippers. I raised my head to grab a glimpse of the owner of the foot upon my hand. He was Chinese! What were they doing here?

He stared at me and puzzled me. He was evidently cross-eyed, thus I wasn't sure where he was looking. Suddenly the other member of the group spoke to the torturer of mine in

Russian! In Russian? That befuddled me even more so. I immediately confessed my understanding of the language.

The cross-eyed man swore in Russian thereby confirming their understanding. One of the other men instructed the cross-eyed man to remove his foot from my hand. Whew! What a relief. They bent down to look at me and they, too, were bewildered at my knowledge of the Russian language.

"How do you know Russian?" one of them asked.

"I am Russian. My family is. My family was forced to flee during the revolution in Russia."

"We, too, young one; we, too!"

"How is it, sir? You, too?" I inquired, aghast at their revelation.

"We are Kalmitsi!"

Kalmitsi were descendants of the Mongol tribes during the times of Tsarist Russia. They were famous for being brilliantly skilled horsemen. They, too, had fled with some of the Whites during the revolution. Apparently, some of them found themselves here with the Russian emigre. In the foreign land, they usually occupied themselves in the field of horse tending. They hadn't ventured far from their known loves and amazing skills. Their wives were known to wear special hats constructed of this strong and versatile textile, which now they used to make slippers, thereby assisting their men in providing for the household.

We had a brief discussion and informed each other of our heritage and fate. They were so pleased with me that they presented me with a pair of slippers; in fact, they were the same pair of slippers I initially attempted to snatch from them. In addition to this kindness, they further informed me of a city called "Panchevo" where there was to be found an abundance of bread. Even better, white bread! To arrive to this city, one must cross the River Danube. What I had heard thrilled me! Now, I had a new dream, a new ambition: Panchevo!

It was a misty, cloudy day. I woke up early. As usual, I had no one to speak to, no one to utter a word to. My stomach growled, reminding me of hunger. I searched around the bare and foodless kitchen and naturally found nothing edible. I must go out and find some food. Right! Food....Panchevo! I said aloud, "I need to go there."

At the intersection of Dimitriyeva Tutsevicha and Djuricheva streets, a large, concrete ice box was abandoned on a lot and near a fence. The opening of the ice box faced the fence. In that ice box slept a former captain of the White guards.

Crouched inside, unshaven and wrapped in rags, when this captain exited his home, he didn't stand upright as we do, but crawled out awkwardly as he was hunched-back. Ironically, this posture enabled the entry and exit of his home with ease.

With much difficulty did he raise his head and was accustomed to turn his head to the side, to envision whoever, or whatever was near him. He pranced about in extra large shoes and wore no socks upon his feet. This poor man was usually taunted by the careless children, who would mercilessly tease him whenever he dared to exit his home, "There is Judas! Dirty Judas!" Why they chose that name is beyond me, but nevertheless, the name stuck. Poor man, "Judas," would grunt and growl at them and they would flee, screaming and laughing, when they heard him.

I questioned myself about what did this poor former captain of the Whites guard live from? I noticed a little dirty bottle of liquor peering out of his pocket. He informed me that he cleaned shoes for a living. Given the state of this man, it was not unbelievable, for his posture accommodated him. He had a meagre pay, enough for a piece of bread and obviously for liquor, and the fact that he resided in an abandoned ice box required no overhead. I was not intimidated by him. I knew him. He knew me. He knew many things. Vladimir Nikolaievich was his name.

"Mister Vlado?" I usually addressed him by his proper name, although sometimes, the name "Judas" did slip out. Luckily, he never would hear that, or pretended not to.

"Yes?" Mr. Vlado answered in a crackling, hoarse voice.

"It's me! Vitya!"

"Agh...what is it?" Mr. Vlado didn't always like company, perhaps I came to visit at the wrong time.

"I want to ask you something, Mr.Vlado," and he crawled out of his home. He sat on a large rock, conveniently located near his ice box, which served him as a foot stool, actually a chair. I knelt down beside him."Vladimir Nikolaievich, first, I am hungry!"

"Agh, agh..." he replied as he shakily pulled out a dirty and greasy handkerchief from his pocket. He unwrapped his little parcel and broke off a piece of cornbread and handed it to me.

As I ate, I noticed a tear drop escape his eye, flowing along the creases of his deep, wrinkled skin, then through his thinned-out moustache and beard. Did he regret giving me the bread? I didn't think to ask him, until I had nearly finished my piece of cornbread. "Mr.Vlado, why do you cry?"

"You know, Vitya...When I was young and strong and serving our beloved Batsusha (Tsar, a term of endearment, commonly used when referring to the Russian Tsar), I had never imagined my destiny and where it would lead me to. I never surmised the poverty I would be living in. Now when I see you, our new generation and this daunting fate of ours, I am very discouraged, indeed.

"My family was a well known noble family. We had servants. We never treated our servants severely and always remembered to provide gifts for them for all holidays.

"I had visited the rich emigre here, Vitya, and what I had encountered had embittered me much. They had stolen riches amongst their possessions, not to mention the stolen titles they granted themselves. Agh, it is terrible! One of these families, I shall not name to you, had opened a jewellery store here. I had heard of these "noble" families and sought them. I was quite interested of their nobility and of their fate. I had no intention of obtaining any alms from them, for my pride wouldn't permit it.

"Agh...Vitya, and look at the true nobles. Your mother, for example. What a devastating fate! I told you about your grandfather Nikolai?"

"Yes, you did, Vladimir Nikolaievich."

"Look at us now, Vitya, and cast your eyes upon my mansion. An ice box! I had a terrible time, yes, I did. I battled against the Reds, but had lost in the battle. The commissar had broken my back with his sword and rendered me unconscious for three days on the battlefield. I had awoke to the gentle care of some elderly village women. They decided to take me away from the danger.

"I found myself in a cart, a cart that they had thrown a pile of dung on top of me, in their bid to discreetly pass through the heavily guarded areas and deliver me to the hands of the Whites. I was disabled and still am, Vitya, as you can see yourself. When I rise, it is not the sky I see, but the ground beneath me. Soon, my dear child, my end is near," and with that final statement he took a big gulp from his bottle of liquor. "Yes...the sun warms at day and this here at night." He excused his drinking and further said, "You know, Vitya, my whole family was slaughtered.

"Vitya? Why did you wake me?"

"I have a question to ask you. I heard from some that the city of Panchevo has an amplitude of bread, and listen to this, Vladimir Nikolaievich—white bread!"

"I know, I know, son, but that is a long journey from here. You have no fare to travel to Panchevo, and even if you did, son, the guards would prove to be major obstacles. They are not pleasant to those leaving Belgrade, seeking asylum elsewhere you know. My advice to you is not to go!"

"But I must! I am hungry and they have bread!"

"Agh...I see you will not heed my advice, Vitya," and Vladimir Nikolaievich returned to the coziness of his ice box and continued his slumber.

I was determined. I quickly passed under the bridge, where German tanks could be heard rumbling by as they headed toward Karaburma. On the road ahead I didn't see many people and if there were, I hadn't noticed, for my thoughts were with Mr. Vladimir.

He, too, once a noble and honourable captain, was now an old, hunched beggar, and even the children had mocked and tormented him, by calling him "Judas." Poor Mr. Vladimir, he was absolutely correct, though, concerning the rich immigrants from Russia who were of that sort. I can recall a time when Mother had went to Beogradska Street to one of the richer Russian families. They had owned a store and offered Mother the skins of ham, but never a morsel of meat. Another family she knew was near a hotel called "London." A jewellery store, owned by a wealthy Russian family. Mother had toiled there several times, while that old miser (owner) would hover over Mother as she washed the floors and cleaned, for his fear lied in any theft of his jewels.

During my recollections, I neglected to realize that I had finally arrived at the Danube train station. My new journey was about to begin...

Chapter 12

Swarming on and around the platform were black-clad soldiers, armed to their teeth, travelling God knows where as they marched around with irrefutable authority. This was the least of my concerns, lest they arrest me, for my goal was the ultimate arrival to the town of Panchevo and for which I had no fare to accommodate me. Therefore, I strolled by the station in the direction of Karaburma (a district, yet with another vestige of the once ruling Ottoman empire by its name: Kara, meaning black and burma, meaning ring). As I was walking, I speculated as to how I might jump over the wire fence encircling the station. Certain of inaccessibility, I relinquished the thought and continued ahead. Not only was the fence an obstacle, but the perambulator soldiers who were ready and only too willing to aim at any trespasser.

Thus, in a malcontent state, I sought other methods of becoming a stowaway. Along my path was an abattoir and the offensive smell confirmed this, or was a prelude to the nastier stench ahead. Hills of trash were to the left of me as I had sufficiently distanced the train station and came to the city's dump yard, so to speak.

At the bottom of one of these hills was a middle-aged woman rummaging through the stack of trash. She had several bags around her and one in her hand as she dug and searched for any useful items. She was quite protective of her bagatelle, this I learned when I had neared her. "Good day, ma'am!"

"What good day? Why are you here?" She was agitated at my

presence and revealed a churlish temperament. "This is my
territory, sonny! I have many in my family and I am not inclined
to share with anyone. Do you hear?!"

"Listen, ma'am, I am not here to rob you of your treasures,
I am earnestly seeking some information," I sarcastically
answered.

"Ha! Look at him! He wants to discuss! Leave! Leave now!"
she repetitively proclaimed.

I left her to her trash and commenced my walk. My
perception did not fool me, there was an elderly hobo, on top of
another nearby mountain of trash. What's the difference? I
might as well be hollered by him, too, and I approached the
large hill. Although, I did manage to grab onto a stick I had
found along the way through the dump, to serve as some kind
of protection against these poor, unfortunate vultures.

"Sir. If you permit, I would like to ask you something?"

He calmly acknowledged me, by tilting his dirty, holey hat
and a quick spit on the trash beside him as he said, "You
should know and be very observant of these piles and of its
owners! You went by quite well with that one," and he directed
me with his gaze toward the distrusting woman. "She's known
to be rather violent when any attempts are made on her pile!"

I unintentionally exhibited a sarcastic expression upon
hearing these words from the hobo, but retained my
composure and further asked, "Mister, I am looking for the
train that goes to Panchevo. Would you know which one that
is?" I pointed over to the sets of tracks right behind the dump yard.

"Yes. I do. It's the fourth set of tracks over there and the train
is on them. That train will take you to Panchevo," the old hobo
declared.

"Thank you, I am very grateful for your help, sir!"

I merrily leapt over some mini piles of trash and found
myself at the tracks, since the wire fence was not an obstacle,
it only enclosed a small area surrounding the station. I looked
around me, for fear of any authorities nearby. I was relieved at
their absence. I jumped over the sets of tracks and came to the
train wagons. Great! But how do I get in now? The doors are all

sealed. I walked by ten wagons, until I reached one that had no roof on it.

I climbed upon the joint of these railway freight cars and in no time, I swung myself into the wagon. It was empty, save for a large, cardboard box in the corner. I looked into the box, it was also empty and came in good use for me. I went into the box, just in case someone decided to check out these freight cars and also, to shelter myself from the slight drizzle of rain which showered me lightly, beneath the light grey cloud. I didn't expect an outpour of rain, which didn't deem threatening, for but a hundred metres away, the sun's rays were penetrating through the greyish, white clouds.

I heard a loud pang and some more squeaking noise, then a jerking of the train and the screeching wheels upon the tracks signalled our departure, of course in accompaniment with the train's noisy whistle. Now I felt safe. I crawled out of my box, to get a better glimpse of my transporting vehicle. It owned a musty, dingy and rusty smell. Nevertheless, it was my tool of achievement to my destination—Panchevo!

The walls of the car had cracks on them, some large enough to permit me to gaze out and observe the course we were taking and the greenery that fled past by us. Suddenly the train slowed down and I squinted to observe through the crack of a window to see what's the cause of our slowing halt. As the train curved, I was able to envision a preceding bridge ahead of us and not only a bridge, but a collection of those black-clad soldiers. As the train approached the bridge and the soldiers, that annoying loud whistle was heard again. "How annoying! Must you do that? Stupid whistle!" I soliloquized.

Judas, I mean Mr.Vlado, had warned me and now I remembered what he said, his precautions. Those black-clad soldiers: that assembly was known as the fifth colony. They were Germans born in Serbia who had joined the forces and called themselves "Folks Deutchery," and the other occupying forces from Germany called themselves "Reich Deutchery." I shivered in a cold sweat, fearful of their demeanor and more so of my apprehension.

At once... *Thump, bang, thump.* I jumped in my box, but not audibly enough to cause a search of the car.

"Empty! Move on!" I heard the soldiers speak amongst themselves. Then, I keenly observed the fading sounds of their footsteps as they passed me. We must have been detained at this bridge for nearly an hour or so, it seems. My relief and sighs came when the train jerked again, the screeching rusty wheels began turning again on their tracks. I wiped the cold sweat off my forehead with my sleeve. For a while, I sat there in the box, realizing the proximity of capture and possible imprisonment. Agh, when will we reach the paradise town of Panchevo? I decided to leave my box for some fresh air. Once I was full of this fresh air, I returned to my box, to rest and fell asleep.

I stood upon a terrace. A tranquil pond with large lily pads were before me. I turned around in that beautifully warm night and right behind me, I beheld a glorious mansion. Its brilliant illumination reflected and danced upon the pond, which had induced my turn to observe it. Spectacular! All of its numerous windows were ablaze with lustrous rays emitting from them. A faint melody could be discerned in the distance, if listened to carefully, and amongst the faint, soft melodies was a chorus of voices, laughter and gaiety. Through the large, glass double doors, couples danced, waltzing away merrily. The enormous elegant chandeliers hung above the dancers and permitted them to accentuate their bejewelled gowns and tiaras. I pinched myself as I stood there in bewilderment. "Ouch! That smarts!" I sat up, crawled out of my box and the pain on my leg assured me that I was dreaming and I was not near a mansion, but rather in this box car.

The monotonous rumbling of the train distracted my sadness and reminded me that we are soon to arrive to Panchevo, the town of paradise and the town of bread! Daylight broke, I yawned and stretched and went to spy out from my window, the crack. Yes. We are arriving, I noted some houses as our speed slowly declined and soon reached a halt. Excellent! I'm here! How do I get out now? I looked about me.

There was a spike, adjoined to the wagon which was protruding from the top. I flung my pillowcase (the one I brought with me to carry all the bread back home) in attempt to climb out. No such luck; the pillowcase, or I, was too short. I took off my belt, the rope. I tied the rope to the pillowcase and now flung it with all my might. Aha! I did it. The pillowcase caught onto the spike. I quickly climbed up; luckily, I was not heavy, for the pillowcase would have torn and given way. I jumped over the wagon and landed onto the ground.

I unwrapped my pants around my neck, (I was compelled to tie them around my neck, because once I had removed my belt, my pants hit the floor), I dressed and then surveyed the area around me. The train I was on was not sitting on the main tracks, but was pulled off to the side tracks. When that happened I wouldn't know, for I was at the mansion and didn't hear anything.

I fell to the ground and stealthily crawled across the sets of tracks in front of me. After all, the soldiers might be here, too? I crawled like a snake until I reached an open field. There I was free to stand amongst the large waving crops of wheat. No wonder they had much bread! I treaded through the field and reached a road.

It must have been very early in the morning, since I hadn't encountered any souls. "Whew! I am in a foreign land!" I announced to myself and actually believed that I reached a foreign country. I reasoned that, because I had crossed the River Danube, this automatically became a new foreign land.

The road I was on was the one leading to the train station. I walked by it and headed I presumed, toward the centre of the town. To the left and right of me were houses, very different from those found in Belgrade. They actually were, two houses abridged and right between them was an adjoining gate, with a large yard in front of it. Beneath the bridge was a loggia and entry to either of the houses, one door to the left and the other to the right. The houses were commonly whitewashed and very pleasant to the eye. The roads were, to my amazement very wide, perhaps, approximately thirty metres and by the roads were these canals and no sidewalks, nor paths to walk on.

I walked aimlessly, looking for the corner store, or a bakery that produced the famous white bread. I passed by many houses, but no stores. I reached a parallel street and continued along a new path. Still, no store and yet another parallel street and no store. What now? Where are their stores, their bakeries? I stopped to think and decide what to do next, when I heard the screeching noise of the opening of gates.

Out came two short, but husky, Bavarian horses that were pulling a cart behind them. The coachman yelled out, "Whoa," ordering the horses to halt. He dismantled and went to close the gates from which he exited. I humbly approached this man thinking that he must surely know where I could find the white bread.

"Eexcccuse me, sir? I came from Belgrade and I heard that there is much bread to be found here in Panchevo. Would you please direct me to the nearest bakery?"

The man, unsurprised at my presence, nor my question, had pulled out his pipe and began to light it. In between his puffs, attempting to get his pipe smoking, he twisted his mouth and remarked, "We don't sell, nor purchase bread here, young man."

How could that be? Those Kalmitsi told me that I could find much white bread here. "But...sir..." I wanted to explain to him of what I had learned from the Kalmitsi, but he interrupted me with, "Come with me, lad," and he led me through the door beside the gates, meant for pedestrians.

We reached the yard of his home and at once he bellowed out, "Wife, come out here!" A brightly-dressed woman appeared in an instant, she fashioned a handkerchief on her head of the same design as her dress, in a rainbow of bright colours.

"Listen, go and bring a half loaf of bread to this boy here!" authoritatively he remarked.

"Of course," she answered and she went to carry out the request of her husband, without giving me a second look as if it was most natural and common that lads dressed as I come to take bread from them.

Once she returned, I was overwhelmed. She had a large, round loaf of bread. She cut half of it and gave it to me, after she had wrapped it in a paper of some sort. I was beside myself. I didn't know what to say, but mumbled, "Ahem, mister...How much for this bread? I do not think I can afford all of it, sir." I tried to seem business-like.

"Good! I didn't ask you for payment! Now, tell me, child, are you hungry right now?"

"Yes, sir, I am...I really am."

"Good."

Now he ordered his wife to bring some gibanica (cheese pita) and a glass of fresh milk. When I heard that, I nearly fainted. I had trouble to keep my composure, I was dumbfounded. Before long, she returned and she brought me a large plate with a huge slice of gibanica, the size of a slice of watermelon. I accepted it, my hands shaking, which embarrassed me. I gobbled it up and it was absolutely splendid! I drank the delicious, cold milk and proceeded to thank them immensely. I thought, dear Lord, here in this wonderful land, this paradise, the people are so hospitable, so generous! I am grateful to be here in this paradise: Panchevo. As I was taking leave of my courteous providers, I had once again inquired, "Where is the bakery? I need to bring some of this delicious bread home to my family, to the poor."

"Son, there is no bakery here and, if so, then it's too far into town, but I can advise you to go to these houses along the road you came from and I am most certain they will provide you with enough bread to take back home."

"Thank you, sir. Thank you, ma'am. You are too kind!"

With a song in my heart, I skipped along the road and began to house call. If only those in Belgrade could see me now! I was delighted, I was ecstatic! I found paradise. Heavenly people live here! I lugged my pillowcase, which was now half full, and decided to carry my precious cargo over my shoulder. A few more houses to go and I would have plenty to give to Mother, Olga and of course, some left for me. One more house to visit...

I skipped to the door and was about to knock, when the door had opened. A heavy set woman appeared. Through her foggy eyes, she measured me from head to toe. "What do you want? Do you know that begging is not permitted?!"

A cold, tragic, foreboding aura came over me. I bowed my head and said, "Ma'am, I am asking if I may purchase some bread? In Belgrade...That's where I come from, there is no bread, thus I came here to your lovely town, after the advice of some friends."

Insultingly she gawked at me and thundered, "Wait!"

I waited what seemed to be an eternity to me. Was she making the bread? Or was she gathering some flour for me? I momentarily began to calculate as to how and to who I would sell the flour to and finally pay the rent.

She returned with an air of an aggressive judge. She stormed up to me and following her was her husband, who was equally as implacable as his spouse. The man advanced, with a conclusive look about him, determined to deliver me. They exchanged a few words between each other, in a foreign dialect. She nodded her head and left, while he took hold of my collar and dragged me down the road.

During our brief trip, I had managed to construct a minimal description of my captor. He was not of a tall stature, very plump, almost like a ball and his mien was loathsome. His immutable convictions were obvious as I pled with this deliverer of mine, "What did I do, mister? Please let me go! Where are you taking me? Please, mister, let go of me!" I sobbed as I was still holding tight to my pillowcase, which was dragging behind us.

"Quiet!" the old, ruthless and unrelenting gaoler declared.

With numerous, unsuccessful attempts, I had tried to break free from his vicious grasp. The entire way to the jail, I begged, pleaded and cried for my release, continuously stating, "But, sir...I only wanted to buy bread!"

"I'll teach you, you urchin, that begging is not permitted!" he growled and spat on the ground.

A three-story-high edifice was his (our) destination. On this ominous building were windows bearing iron bars. We whizzed by the iron gates and my deliverer began to discourse with the soldier on guard, in German. Above the doors was a large sign stating, *Police*, with an eagle and swastika above it. Here is my end, I decided. What will become of me now?

That pig! What harm had I done to deserve this? In a flash, my ear became a handle to the guard, who nearly carried me through a muddy yard to another awaiting soldier. My ear was thus, handed over to the next soldier and we leapt through a hallway and fled down a set of concrete stairs, all the while my head was bent, lest my ear be torn off as I skipped alongside the tormentor.

We went through this brightly lit corridor, past many iron doors set approximately fifteen metres apart. By now my ear was burning with pain as the soldier pinched harder, with each step. We came to the last iron door, a soldier stood there as well. He told him something in German and suddenly the soldier unlocked the loud lock, which rang through the corridor, causing me to quail. He pushed the door open and I was thrown inside. "Ouch!" I screamed as I fell in and hit the ground. I immediately cupped my burning ear with my hand. My cherished pillowcase was gone. The soldiers tugged it out of my firm grasp and, because of that, I had an additional pinching of my ear.

It took me a few moments to gather my composure, but my ear was continuously stinging with pain. It was a dark, sombre jail cell. The air was heavy, stale and wreaked of urine. I regained my sight after the adjustment from the corridor to the dark cell. I lay there on the cement floor.

In this cell were wide benches against the walls, meant for the prisoners to sleep on and it was in use at the time. Three men were sprawled on the benches. One of them called over to me, "Hey, you there. Come and lie down on the bench."

I sat up and still cupping my ear, walked over to the bench. Though still timid, I felt a little more at ease now. The man who called me looked not much better than I. He, too, being scrawny and being older than I, was unshaven, which gave him a dark and gloomy appearance, but he lacked a grudging comportment. I sat beside him, for now he sat up when he noticed I obliged to his request. One of the other prisoners simply turned around and faced the wall and the other was lying on his back staring into the abyss through the barred window.

Our two other cohorts were slightly better attired than us. The initiator of my approach to the benches inquired, "Why are you here, kid?"

"I really don't know," I confessed while shrugging my shoulders.

I began to retell my fortune and misfortune to this stranger, my new acquaintance, and felt comfortable enough to ask him, "And why are you here?"

"Shush!" and he placed his finger on his lips, signalling me with his eyes toward the other two on the bench.

If he wants to be secretive, it is his decision. I quieted down and brooded. I had a dilemma entirely my own. What will become of me now? Here I am sitting in a jail cell with these men, criminals! What will be? Who will visit Mother? What will Olga think when she realizes that I am not visiting her and delivering her little gifts? And George? Alex, oh Alex, where is he? If he only knew where I am!

My gaze fell on the other prisoners. I studied them and speculated on their infractions. My offence was hunger. Poverty, anguish and despair were now complimented with the insult of injustice and prejudice toward the poor and needy. How naive of me to fall into this trap. Paradise...Huh! I turned to the wall and fell asleep.

I awoke to confusion. "Where am I?" I mumbled. No one answered, for I think they were all dazed themselves and didn't want to confirm our location. Oh, yes...I know now. My ear, oh how sore it is and swollen. That dirty pig! The pain evoked an outpour of perfervid curses running amok in my mind as my painful ear reminded me of the soldier, the jail and the loss of my pillowcase, my bread. I rubbed my eyes and began to violently scratch myself, for the things the cell didn't lack were bedbugs, fleas and other annoying pests.

My companions were already awake. My new acquaintance was standing by the window, observing something of interest to him. The other two sat squatted in the corner and were watching my acquaintance as he completely ignored them.

"Hey, kid, come here." My acquaintance summoned me

again. "Look out the window."

"I can't. It's too high."

"Do you expect me to lift you? Go over there and grab that bucket with the lid on it and bring it over here, but watch you don't spill it. It contains urine."

I did as he asked and I stepped on top of the bucket. I saw a soldier standing in the yard amidst large pigs and the pigs were eating something off the ground.

"Sir, what is so interesting about that, that I had to come and see?"

"Take a better look, kid!"

"What! Look at him! He has my pillowcase! He's feeding the pigs with the bread I had much trouble to acquire! How did you know that was my pillowcase?" I shakily inquired.

"When you were thrown in last night, I saw the soldier grab your pillowcase from your hands."

Bitterly I wept and sobbed, almost into a delirium I fell. How could they do it? What kind of cruel and vindictive people were they? I turned to look at the other two prisoners, who seemed maimed and reticent as they apathetically witnessed my wretchedness.

I came down off the bucket and returned it to the corner where it was before. "The pigs are feeding pigs," I whispered dismally. I returned to the bench and crouched, resting my head on my knees.

Hours lapsed. I was starving. They fed us nothing! They simply ignored us and fed the pigs instead. Suddenly the door opened and the same ear-tugging monster appeared. He motioned the other two insipid inmates to follow him. They left. I turned to look at the expression of my acquaintance, who hasn't left the window the entire morning. I stood up and planned to approach him, but he waved me down with his arm, telling me to remain where I am. Several minutes went by in this solitude. The door swung open again and again, the same soldier appeared and now ordered my acquaintance to leave the cell. My acquaintance turned to look at me and with a foreshadowing deportment upon his weary, unshaven face, he waved once with his hand good-bye to me. I never saw this man again.

I sat there alone now. Now it's my turn. My last hour! I crossed myself and prayed fervently, "God, save me!" The door opened as I uttered the last words of my prayer. This time, unusually, another soldier was standing at the door and motioned me to come as was done with the previous three prisoners. I followed him down the corridor. This time, my ear was left alone, thank God.

We arrived to the first floor hallway and were met by another soldier. Probably the executioner I considered. His daunting eyes emitted a scornful gaze as he took me over from the first soldier and directed me to follow him. With no prior elucidation he announced, "Come now, hurry! You have been ordered to return to Belgrade."

The unexplainable, unimaginable rush of joy I felt upon hearing his final command nearly provoked me to embrace him, and with great effort I controlled my anxiousness. I was showered with glory. God answered my prayers! I will never return to Panchevo for the white bread anymore! The persecution I endured for this white bread is much too costly!

I was now at the train station with this quasi-executioner. There was a train awaiting, I assumed departing for Belgrade. The quasi-executioner, now considered an endearing saviour of mine, slid a door open to one of the freight cars which was not sealed. He pulled me up by my pants and tossed me in and slid the door shut behind me. Regardless, I was thrilled at the thought of returning home, to my empty home, but safe home.

It was dark—which was to be expected in these freight cars—for it was not meant for passengers and the fact that night fell didn't help. The annoying sound of silence cast a tremor to my being. The comfort I found was in my exhaustion, which led me to sleep.

The early rays of the sun were poking through the tiny cracks of the car and overall, though dim, the interior of the car was more visible. I had sensed a very familiar smell last night, too, but I was too tired to investigate, especially in the dark. Now I had better circumstances: the daylight, to help me determine where that horrid scent was derived from. There were many large, brown, half-dampened barrels sporadically placed in the car. I went closer to discover the disturbing and offensive odour. I knew it! That smell, of course! There were heads of pickled cabbages in those barrels and, naturally, this scent I detested due to the horrendous meals I ate at the Russian centre's basement. The disgusting sauerkraut stew! I reflected, did they know how much I loathed this smell and threw me in here as additional punishment?

Thanks be to the despicable aroma of the car that transported me into another daydream and recalling the Russian centre, once again. This Russian centre was located on Queen Natalia Street and possessed an underground tunnel, which led to another building on the street of Knez Mihailova. Above this tunnel was a picturesque parkette, with fragrant flower gardens and large protective oak trees that shaded the parkette's visitors from the sun's rays on hot days. The deep, green grass served as a lush, playground for their children, who would run to and fro, to the delight of their parents. The richer Russians who brought a stash of money with them, amongst other valuables, used this parkette for their relaxation. Yet the true nobles, the aristocrats, defamed and robbed of their possessions and titles, just as Mr.Vlado had discussed were found underground in the dark, damp and cold basement of the Russian centre, waiting in line for and eating the smelly sauerkraut stew out of desperation.

An incredible metamorphosis, such as this turn of events that portrayed itself. The tawdry were sitting on velvet chairs, sipping wine out of crystal glasses. They ate scrumptious meals prepared especially for them, while below, the floor they stood upon and by means of circular stone stairs built in an unknown previous era was a large soup kitchen.

An enormous, army-sized pot sat upon a foot stool in the centre of the room, with a large dingy ladle within it. We stood in line with our tin bowls they provided us, in order to receive a ladle full of this wretched concoction. A miserable middle-aged woman, without a smile upon her face, nor a comforting word to the poor, would blob a spoonful of stew into our bowls mechanically and routinely. In addition to our stew, we were given each a piece of rock hard cornbread, which the woman grabbed out of a sack on the floor beside her. We washed our tin bowls at the end of our meals as we were obliged to and which wasn't difficult for us to do, since water washes water well.

Yes...the terrible necessity of this kitchen was a reality. At times we were compelled to visit this kitchen two to three times a day, depending on our earnings for the day. I recall, we once sat beside some Gypsies who were earnestly attempting to disguise themselves, for fear of capture by the Nazis. Alex...as usual, would strike up a conversation. He conversed with an elderly man within their company. Alex curiously inquired whether they frequented this kitchen often and the sad, wrinkled old man informed Alex that they actually slept there in a corridor's corner beneath some boxes. Alex further interviewed them, "Aren't you cold when you sleep here? If it is as cold as it is here now, I can imagine how cold it becomes at night."

"True, my son, but here we are safe. We would rather be cold here, then sent to the prison camp."

"What do you eat?" Alex continued.

"Pork roast," the elder replied cynically.

Alex, aware of his blunder, blushed.

"Do you see that large pot of stew over there? Don't be astonished if you were to find chunks of meat in it. That meat might very well consist of these rats you see roaming around us."

As soon as I heard that remark, I nearly vomited. I pulled Alex's sleeve and begged him to leave, for I just couldn't stomach this conversation any longer.

"Vitya, why are you so weak?" Alex chuckled.

I could not comprehend Alex's calmness, after hearing the last statement of this elder. He further shocked me when he stated, "Well you know, Vitya, the man does live here, he does see what goes on."

"Agh, uck, I've had it!" Alex laughed wholeheartedly at my queasiness.

We left the basement and as soon as we reached the first floor we were overcome with the delightful aroma of fried potatoes and buckwheat, prepared for the guests.

"Look!" Alex ordered and I looked. There was a trash can full of potato peels.

"Quick, take off your shirt." I had to comply with Alex's demands. I knew what he was about to do. My shirt now wrapped the discarded potato peels.

"Let's go. Now! If the chef notices us, we are in for it. He feeds the pigs with this. Run, Vitya, run!"

If only but for a day I could have been shielded from the unremitting tensions of hunger, I would have been grateful. If it were eradicated and vanquished from my worries, I might have, along with my siblings, have had a childhood. Often I pondered, what is the limit of human endurance?

Innumerable occasions of condescending pleas to anyone who would listen, who would harken to our miserable entreaties and perhaps mercifully appease our hunger and our destitution. Enervated not only by starvation and the overladen responsibilities imposed on us, we were luckily infused by willpower and the eagerness to survive, which in turn was the main factor, the foundation of our motivation. Interestingly enough, we harbored no resentment toward others, thankfully so, which duly enabled us to to continue and eventually acquire and sustain a normal living standard.

The train kept chucking and rumbling along the tracks slowly, I leaned against the wall of the car and piteously recalled the information I received from the Kalmitsi and the heedful warnings of Mr.Vlado. It is but a marvel, the undenied confidence children possess, multitudinously deceived, yet not depreciative.

We approached the same bridge I passed when I was travelling in the opposite direction. The same procedure ensued. Now, without my pillowcase of bread and amidst the smelly cabbage, I was returning empty-handed back home.

Finally, the arrival at the Belgrade station. I chanced to open the sliding door and to my delight, the door easily opened. The first view I had was of the tracks and weeds. No platform to disembark the train, for this again was not a passenger train. No problem, I jumped down, hopped over the sets of tracks and found myself at the same garbage dump I had left behind when I had started my journey.

Tsvicheva Street seemed ostensibly longer than usual, thus I redoubled my pace in a hurried attempt to arrive home. At the intersection where Tsvicheva turns into Djuricheva and intersects Dimitriya Tustevicha, I came across a crowd of people that were gathered around the old, familiar ice box. The home of my dear friend Judas, that is, Mr.Vlado. I quickly advanced to protect my friend from these intruders and gawkers.

"What are you all doing here? Leave my friend alone!" I hollered.

Unintentionally, I shoved one of the observers who immediately retorted, "Hey, kid! Watch it!"

Without any apologies, I snaked through the crowd, which curiously resembled a black mass, or rather, a murder of crows, since their attire was nearly all black, or other faded dark colours.

I was at the forefront now. What I had seen didn't please me. Two men were pulling out my friend from his ice box. I knew. Tears trickled down my face as I kept wiping them away with my sleeves.

"Where are you taking my friend?" I begged for answers, but no one answered me. They were all absorbed in their own discussions and observations, "Yes, yes, I heard that he was a captain of the guards," then another, "He was a very noble man." The last and most significant culminating statement flowed out from one ignoble observer was, "Indeed...What can one do? He had no one, his family was butchered I heard!"

"Enough! Stop that! It's not true, he had me! Me I tell you! I was his friend! No one ever bothered to talk to this poor, old man while he was alive and now you are all gathered here like some kind of commentators!" I sobbed as I emotively stated.

The spectators just stared at me.

My poor friend Vladimir Nikolaievich, a.k.a. "Judas," was gone. The only friend I had at the time. I crossed myself and continued home, realizing that there was nothing I could assist them with. As soon as I reached my piles of rags on the bed, I crawled beneath them and cried myself to sleep. I had slept for the night, the entirety of the next day and night and rose the day after. I was tired, famished and lonely. How terrible it is when there is no one to talk to.

The day was cool and grey, but I had to leave for the sake of eating...The Russian centre, what else? I settled on eating the rock hard cornbread, which I moistened with a glass of water, bypassing the sauerkraut stew. Amidst my surroundings were the familiar faces I usually encountered when visiting, although I did notice a few new faces amongst us. Eating in this awkward room, with these people who I shared much in common with, I disdainfully stared at the same woman, who was completely phlegmatic, seemingly satisfied of her demeanor as she served the hungry, the wretched souls awaiting a tin bowl of stew. I stirred when I felt someone had sat near me.

"What are you doing?" a snow-white haired and moustached, elderly man inquired.

Does he not see that I am eating? "I am eating," I mumbled without looking at him.

"Yes, I know."

"Why do you ask then?"

"I meant, young man, what do you do in general?"

"Nothing."

I began to feel suspicious of this man who was interrogating me for no apparent reason.

"Good, then," he replied, satisfied of my answer.

Is this man normal? I avoided looking at him, thus to prevent him from further disturbing me and inconspicuously slid a few centimetres away, careful not to insult him.

"Young man. I have a job for you if you are interested?"

Realizing that the man was not insane after all, I turned to him and joyfully remarked, "Of course I am interested!" I beamed a smile.

"Excellent! Come with me!"

Together, we left the basement of this establishment and now were at the main floor. "Son, first I would like for us to have lunch, before we begin discussions regarding work."

Now that's what I call an employer! I nodded in complete agreement and satisfaction. We entered a room where a dozen tables where covered with sparkling clean, white tablecloths. We sat at the first table we came across and I was very careful not to place my hands on the white tablecloth, for fear of getting it soiled.

A snobbish waitress came to take our order. As she neared our table, she stopped a few steps farther from us, gawking at me all the while. Obviously insulted at my presence in their restaurant and inwardly thinking that I belonged in the basement downstairs and not up here with the distinguished.

Realistically and most unfortunately, I was a patron of the basement's soup kitchen and her supposed observations were not entirely incorrect. Nevertheless, she announced the special of the day in a monotone voice, "We have sausages and mashed potatoes today," she was now only referring to the white haired man beside me. I thought if he orders that, it would truly be a celebration!

"Two orders!" He proclaimed and a celebration it was indeed! I was so excited, I believe that I glowed in anticipation of this fabulous meal.

The waitress came and as before, stopped a few steps short of our table, nearly leaning forward as if there were an invisible obstacle preventing her from approaching our table. I found her rather haughty, but mused, perhaps I had an offensive odour? Come to think of it, it has been a while since I bathed. In fact, the last time was with Alex at the bath house. I shrunk in my seat, attempting to prevent any disagreeable fumes from emitting any further.

She carefully and methodically began placing all the necessary and unnecessary cutlery, napkins and glasses before us, on the table. She briefly left and returned with two tall glasses of ice, cold water. I attentively observed all her systematic movements and unusually, found it entertaining.

At once, my stomach growled. When will she finally deliver our meal? I looked around me in embarrassment, imagining that my growling stomach, in addition to my impoverished appearance, which boldly announced impecuniosity, had correctly confirmed my estimation. The well-dressed, pretentious and condescending patrons, heavily decorated with costume jewellery, were nonchalantly scrutinizing me and didn't bother to conceal their indiscretion by turning their piercing and judgmental stares, upon my recognition of them.

I looked to my companion for comfort, but diverted my attention as soon as I sensed the tantalizing aroma of our meal. The waitress placed one dish in front of my benefactor and nearly dropped the plate of mine before me, fearing that she ventured too close. She hadn't moved but a few steps away and nearly half my plate was already consumed.

My benefactor, spying on me from the corner of his eye, who was slowly chewing and tumbling his food in his mouth, from one side to the other, noted, "Oh dear...I do not believe I can finish my meal."

"I'm here! I can finish it...That is, if you can't?"

Within minutes, my benefactor's plate was sparkling clean, exactly as my own plate was. Without breathing, I devoured the scrumptious food. The man took a napkin from the table, shook it in the air and wiped the corners of his mouth. He looked at me and smiled. I returned the gesture, completely appeased and gratified that my stomach was now full. Upon his payment of our bill, we happily departed from this restaurant.

I admired my benefactor, who was though modestly, but cleanly dressed in a faded suit and very tidy in his appearance and his manner. I reflected how detached this man was from the obvious glares in the restaurant, purportedly insulting to the guests that a gentleman was in the company of a pauper and had the audacity to bring one to such an establishment.

With the burden of eating out of the way, we finally introduced ourselves to each other.

"My name is Sergei Sergeievich. What is your name?"

"I am Victor Andreievich, but everyone calls me Vitya!"

"All right then Vitya, this is how the situation is at hand...

I am a distributor of the local newspapers. I bring them to my home at four every morning. If you could be at my home at approximately five and take the papers to be delivered to a route, which I will supply you with..."

Oh no! Not another paper route! I certainly do not need another incident like the one I had previously with that old miser! I studied my new friend, he was very kind and generous to invite me for lunch, thus he was not a shrewd. I do think I could trust him.

"Mr.Sergei, I accept your offer!"

As we continued to discuss the trivialities of the matters at hand and walking slowly, immersed in discussions, we arrived at the district of Slaviya on Tsar Dushan Street. We continued until reaching the district of Naymar where Sergei Sergeievich resided.

As soon as we entered his home, we were welcomed by Sergei's wife, Irina Petrovna. She looked at us wide-eyed and quizzically, first at her husband, at me, then back at him. I nearly read her expression, but had become quite accustomed to this apparent disbelief of the combination of the two of us, the gentleman and the pauper. He mumbled a few words to her and we proceeded through the short and narrow corridor.

In the salon was a beautiful, but old, piano, a fancy settee, a few chairs and a desk. On the windows were white, sheer curtains with flowers embroidered on them. The room's scent was fresh and clean. On the impeccably dirt-free and shiny floor was a red rug and on the walls of the room, portraits of Tsar Nicholas and his family were hung.

They asked me to sit and I chose to sit on a chair, for fear of any louse or flea jumping off of me onto the fine, beige satin settee. Irina Petrovna left us in this room and her black dress shuffled behind her as she closed the door after herself. She, too, was meticulously clean as was her husband as was their home. She was a genteel woman, one would easily determine so. Her silver-grey hair was very shiny and combed into a tight bun at the nape of her neck. When Irina had left the room and shut the door, an amazing spectacle was to be seen. A gorgeous Cossack's uniform, with epaulettes on the shoulders, bearing the rank of a colonel. Angularly sewn bullet casings were threaded with golden thread on the chest of the uniform and around the sleeves as well. It seemed to me that the uniform was a brilliant decor of the door. The light grey colour of the uniform nearly emitted a light all its own and hung there proudly as is if signifying that the owner of this uniform was noble and obviously high ranking.

As I was in awe of all the items in the room, I hadn't realized that the two hosts were standing in front of me. Irina Petrovna had asked, "Young man, would you kindly honour us by joining us at the table?"

I felt like someone had poured cold water over me. I was addressed very courteously and in an extremely refined manner. I stood up and immediately revered by bowing low and declaring, "It is a great honour of mine to be invited to such a grand table and by two very noble and generous hosts."

I recalled when my grandmother had taught me how a gentleman was to offer and accept invitations and other basic noble etiquette. As I bowed low, I observed my dingy attire, my dirtiness, my odour and was, therefore, flushed with embarrassment and nearly cried.

The dining room was a modest room, but also immaculately clean and tidy. It was a smidgen darker than the salon. There was a medium sized table in the room, a dainty crystal chandelier hung directly above the table. More pictures hung on the walls and of course icons. It was a custom to have icons in the eastern corner of the room, with a hanging votive before it.

We sat at the table and the delicious scent of hot soup at once penetrated my nostrils. I didn't observe my hosts very much, but rather the food, for we had lunch hours ago. I ate the meal with much appreciation and savoured every sip and bite. After our dinner, the samovar appeared on the table and we had tea.

I was instantly reminded of Mother who adored having her tea and would beg for tea whenever I would visit her. This samovar initiated more than a recollection for me, it reminded Sergei Sergeievich of his past and the story behind the acquirement of this very beautifully etched samovar.

The old man, Sergei did most of the talking, actually, all of the talking as he fell back into nostalgia. He softly and convincingly spoke as he sipped his hot tea and bit onto little pastries, which were set on the table alongside the tea. Amusingly I had watched Irina Petrovna set the table for tea. Twelve small silver spoons and twelve porcelain dessert dishes, also richly decorated were placed beside a tray of delicacies. Why she had placed the setting for twelve, I didn't know, perhaps she had a habit of doing so?

Sergei testified that the samovar was a gift to him from the governor, "A type of reward for the achievements I attained during my duty as colonel of the Tsar's honourable guards," he proudly stated, then proceeded to explain the origin of the samovar. It was crafted in St. Petersburg, by renown artists and professionally gilded with the utmost of care and prestige. Sergei was now admiring his samovar and patted it several times while stating, "Indeed, I had very good days with the governor."

"Why don't you write about it?" I advised.

"Umph, to who, Vitya?" The monarchy is gone, obliterated. There's no return," he implied and continued...

"Oh, how wonderful it was at the governor's balls! Because of my designated assignment, given to me by the Tsar to assist the governor, I had easily befriended the amiable governor, who, naturally, invited me and included me in all his balls and soirees!

"Ahhh! The balls, Vitya...I, I just am speechless when it comes to properly describing the magnificence! The chivalry I've witnessed and the statute of the aristocrats and nobility, who needn't to display their distinction, for even if they were dressed in the shabbiest of clothes, their demeanor and carriage would betray them as to their non-subordinate values.

"The master of ceremonies, with his staff, stood at the entry of the ballroom and formally announced the arrival of 'so and so' by tapping his staff on the floor, followed by the notification of their names. As they marched in one by one, an exhibition of manhood and chivalry, in all its splendour. Tall, muscular men who carried themselves in their uniforms to such a degree, that one was immediately inclined to honour and bow upon encountering them. Whereas the beautiful women, who floated in like swans, gowns swaying behind them, demanded the attention and admiration of all those present. Their diamond diadems, upon their heads glistened and shined as did their glamorous, bright smiles. Entirely and utterly proud of their significance, enhanced by their gentlemen escorts, were warmly welcomed and received in the most cordial ways, successfully achieving reverence from their hosts and other guests present.

"An enchanting scenery, Vitya! One would be sufficiently entertained just admiring the guests as they arrived and not long after, begin to dance. Upon the glossy floor were pairs of these personages that glided swiftly across the ballroom as if they were skating on ice. The gowns twirled in such a fashion that one would imagine that the gentleman leading the dance was displaying an exquisite piece of artwork. A marvellous spectacle! Ahhh...the colours, the vibrancy of their gowns and their moods set the atmosphere ablaze with jubilation and celebratory performances, which were eagerly applauded upon their completion.

"These balls were the talk, rave and envy of the town. For days, nearly weeks, the events of the ball were still on the lips of the guests that attended and the envious who didn't, alike. Indeed...the balls were majestic. The soirees, too—don't misunderstand me—were glamorous in their own right, but the balls were the glory and pride of the host, who had taken great measures to decorate and accommodate his anxiously awaited guests, and then was profusely proud when complimented on the success of his mission."

Sergei Sergeievich was so enthralled with his story and his proclamations that he nearly choked when he sipped his tea, but he coughed a few times, followed by a sneeze, a clearing of his throat and then commenced.

I was sweating, all that talk of glamour and glitz was making me dizzy. I felt as if I were there in the ballroom with all those nobles and aristocrats. Quite similar to that strange dream I had in the train.

Sergei Sergeievich began to recite all the notable guests of the ball and I nearly faded into daydreaming when I suddenly heard, "And of course, there was Nikolai Vladimirovich Krasicki and his family and then there was..."

"What? Wait, Sergei Sergeievich...Wait!"

"What's wrong, Vitya? Did I say something to offend you?"

"No, no of course not, sir, but you just said the name of my grandfather, sir. My grandfather... You said his name!"

"Your grandfather? Who was your grandfather? Was it..."

Sergei Sergeievich began reciting again, until I stopped him at the mention of my grandfather's name.

"Vitya? Do you mean to say that Nikolai Vladimirovich was your grandfather?"

"Yes. That is if you're speaking about the right person."

"Nikolai Vladimirovich had a wife named Alexandra and three daughters named Tamara, Nina and Zoya."

"Sergei Sergeievich...Zoya is my mother."

"What are you telling me, Vitya? Is it possible? Could it be?"

"Sir, it is possible and true, for those are the names of my family."

Upon Sergei Sergeievich's discovery of my family, he had obligingly informed me of the many things of which I already heard of and some not.

Thus Sergei Sergeievich stated, "And there you have it, Vitya. The stories I know of your family. You know, Vitya, whenever I have tea, I usually am thrown back into my past and begin to recall certain incidents, which my precious samovar compels me to do. When my dear wife Irina Petrovna is not present to listen to my tales and my recollections of times past, my new guest, willingly or unwillingly, such as you are today, Vitya, becomes the sacrificial victim of my nostalgia. This shortcoming of mine I can't control and I feel as if I were to attempt to, it would cause me to go mad."

I felt that my benefactor's implications were truly genuine and that his expatriation was not ostentatious. I knew that he had more to say, thus I turned my attention back to him and away from my contemplation, with hopes that he would finally provide an elucidation to the topics we were discussing.

Irina Petrovna sat with us, too; she quickly had cleared all the dishes and loyally sat to listen to her husband's reverberations, so I believe, for her lip-synching demonstrated this. I tried to picture Irina Petrovna in a ball gown and tiara, but my thoughts were interrupted by a tap on my shoulder.

"Vitya? Are you becoming tired? I will end my story for today and continue another time, over tea of course! Perhaps you are tired now, Vitya, and should go home to rest, but remember to be here early in the morning to deliver the papers!"

"Yes, of course, Sergei Sergeievich!"

"Vitya, before you leave us, I do want to describe your grandfather briefly, if you'll permit and later I will elaborate, upon your next visit with us."

"Yes, certainly, sir!"

"Your grandfather, Nikolai Vladimirovich, was a very noble and honourable man. He was of tall stature and equally impressive in his uniform. When one would meet him, an immediate and absolute obedience, loyalty and veneration would overcome oneself. Indeed, he was a serious man.

"He had attended the governor's ball, which I described to you, for he was a close friend of the governor. When he and his family arrived, well...It was memorable. His daughters were beauties and the gentlemen who were inclined to pursue them were many. I recall one of his daughters, Zoya that is, was pursued by this handsome and notable captain. After this ball, Nikolai had held his own ball, yet another divine event, which I will not summarize momentarily, Zoya and the captain were betrothed following that particular ball."

"Excuse me? Sergei Sergeievich, you are speaking of my mother! My mother is wed to my father, Andrei Alexeievich! You, sir, must be mistaken!"

"No. Vitya, I am not. I know Zoya is your mother. I am sorry if my story offends you, but, Vitya, it's the truth."

"Well, sir, I suppose I will be inclined to hear many things."

"Vitya, I see that you are tired. Go home now and we will talk more later, but do remember to come in the morning!"

"Yes, sir, and I thank you humbly for all that you and your wonderful wife, Irina Petrovna, have done for me. I will see you in the morning."

I was escorted to the front door and left them with a small package in my hand, which Irina Petrovna had earlier prepared for me to take home. How kind they were! I waltzed home, with a glistening mirage before my eyes of the ball, its guests and of my family.

All that I had heard coincided with the other stories I had heard before, from my family, from the artist at Baylonova Piazza and of course, from Judas, that is, Mr.Vlado. The stories matched, all of them, by whomever I encountered and knew my family. My decision was to remain silent for the present time and acquire more information from my new friend.

As I heard it, it was quite common practise for women of nobility to assist the injured, by becoming nurses for the Red Cross. I recall when my own family...My mother, aunt and grandmother would drift off into their own nostalgic moments and begin reminiscing of their trip aboard the ship, on which some royal family members were also passengers of.

Yes, many things are not comprehensible to me in regard to my mother. My mother suffered immensely, not just physically and mentally, but by the fate that was handed to her. All that must have attributed to her illness and, if not, then certainly added to it.

Each of us children had our own misfortunes and tragedies handed to us. We all suffered at the hands of our father and mother's inability to care for us, the condition and the state the city was in and, in general, by unconcerned citizens. Though there were a handful of compassionate and sympathetic people who did offer some food, money, or a kind comforting word, we were basically street urchins, our target was survival. We had no political interest. We were simply tossed around as I will describe later.

What possible words could be utilized to describe the unimaginable ironies, vexation and hopelessness a destitute and hungry pauper feels when informed of an unreachable era, a time when his family had provisions and beyond that...luxuries! These moments of mine remained with me forever, but I knew I had more important matters to tend to...survival. I was also obliged to provide, though meagrely, to Olga and George. Alex...I prayed for fervently, for I missed him beyond words. Vechislav, whether out of necessity, or a simple decision to walk in our father's footsteps, had abandoned us as well. We were left to our own devices and to the whips of fate. My family nobles....Yet we are the noble's pauper children!

Chapter 13

I neared Aunt Katarina's home, I had to see Olga. I knocked on the door's window, which had lace curtains within, preventing onlookers from a thorough view inside this modest home. It did permit the obstructive view of the oncoming person about to answer the door though.

Both were home, Olga and Aunt Katarina. They greeted me with hugs and kisses. Soon I was retelling them my stories as we sipped on the tea, Aunt Katarina provided for us. As I had expected and waited for, the reprimands and lectures followed the ending of my story. I was told that I should have heeded the advice of Mr. Vlado and of how ridiculously naive I was.

The worried look on their faces and the sighs and general expressions by them, for me, were suddenly comical. I knew they were right, but I couldn't help myself, they were like two hens, continuously warning me and remonstrating.

Eventually, after promises of being more cautious and prudent, I managed to leave the scorn of my two well-wishers and return home. Satisfied of Olga's well being, I now pondered on the task ahead, not only of my new job, but the parcel I must obtain (the salami ends) to give to Auntie Katya (our neighbour, the one Mother detests) to take to George in the orphanage. Exhausted and spent of the days events, I retired to my bed of rags and set my old alarm clock (a gift from Aunt Nina from the past), for an early awakening.

Dddrrrrrrring...ddrrrrrrrrring. I slammed down on the alarm clock's button. It was fresh and cool inside, thus I could imagine how cool it was outside. Autumn has set in. The trees were now like pieces of art, proudly showering their red, yellow and orange leaves, providing a colourful crunchy, at times soggy and quiet carpeting for the pedestrians.

I had slipped on 'somebody's' pants, perhaps Father's, perhaps Vechislav's old pants, who knows? I knew they were there, good reason enough to wear them. Speaking of Vechislav, I nearly forgot of him. There were occasions we met on the street, but now, I believe he was sent away by the army. Where? I wouldn't know. Will he come back? No...I can't think of that now, I have work to do.

Thank God for the rope-belt I had, for I would not be able to keep my pants from falling, which were at least three sizes larger than I. I also devised a wise system for the bottom of my pants. I folded it over several times and then pinned them, thus I could walk without hindrance. The rags I had to wrap around my feet serving me as socks, I hated. Lucky were those who had the privilege of owning "real" socks! Nevertheless, they were accommodating in a sense, preventing my feet from swimming in the shoes I wore, which were also too large by two sizes.

The moon was still visible in the sky when I left home. The morning sun has not yet begun to shine. I was walking toward the home of Sergei Sergeievich, on the carpeted sidewalk, courtesy of the hovering trees. The streets were stark and bare. I walked briskly and cautiously, fearing the thieves, drunks and other unknown people of the night. I crossed myself, pulled my cap down and nearly skipped all the way to Sergei's home.

I found my friend outside of his home, who was involved in the preparations of the bundles of newspapers. I spotted a canvas sack, bursting with the papers within.

"Good morning, Sergei Sergeievich."

"Good morning, Vitya! Here, look, I prepared a sack for you," and he pointed to the exact sack I had observed, the one that was bursting with papers.

"Here, Vitya, here are the addresses where you should deliver the papers, and when you have completed delivering, come back here. If you are fast enough, you might even manage to deliver the afternoon papers as well!"

"Very well, sir," I answered and threw the heavy sack's shoulder strap over my shoulder and commenced to my route.

Because of my previous experience as a newspaper carrier, which I purposely hadn't informed Sergei Sergeievich of, I had easily completed my task. I was tired, though, for the climbing of all those stairs in the mini-buildings and running through the courtyards did prove to be exhausting. Luckily I did not meet any unfriendly dogs along my path, for my only pair of winter pants would have acquired new holes to them.

The sun was visibly high in the sky by now and without my realization of it. The air was still nippy, but invigorating, for with the slaps of the wind upon my face, I was prevented from drowsing as I walked back to Sergei's home.

Along the way back, I was met by people rushing off to work, children marching to school and by busy housewives who had their crocheted hand bags over their arms as they headed to the local piazza for the necessities to prepare for the day's menu.

The city was still somewhat in a ruinous state, but obvious reconstructions were under way. In some parts of the city the electricity was reconnected and the citizens, not entirely at ease, established their routines and continued to live accordingly.

But a few more steps and I will be directly at the door of my benefactor and employer. Only once I knocked and the door swung open. "Oh, it's you. Come in, do come in. My husband should be back soon, Vitya. Come with me," and I followed Irina Perovna to the kitchen.

I entered a very bright and happy white kitchen. The smell of clean and other delicious aromas immediately caught my senses. I was told to sit at the table. On the meticulously clean tablecloth, cross-stitched with little flowers and designs, were blue and gold, porcelain plates, shining cutlery and napkins. I studied the kitchen and its contents. How different it is from my kitchen, I mused. Their walls maintained shelves, which also were brightly painted. These shelves were laden with many different coloured jars, that not only decorated their walls, but were to be a part of their menu at some point. Numerous jars filled with jams of all sorts as well as sauces and pickled vegetables portrayed the skillfulness of the lady of the house.

On the centre of the neatly set table was the steaming and famous nostalgia-provoking samovar. The centrepiece of the kitchen, as we know, was the glistening stove. Simmering pots were signalling anyone present that the housewife was truly a masterful chef and the scent of the bread baking in the oven, equally enticed the awaiting devourers of the feast. I pondered...even though Irina Petrovna was a genteel woman, she certainly was handy and skilled in the tasks of housekeeping. She must have been up as early as I this morning, in order to have prepared all I see before me, not to mention the swaying laundry in the wind outdoors, which I noticed when I looked to see where the pleasant fragrance was coming from. I observed a few pots of pink and red flowers on the window sill, which delicately scented the room with each passing breeze and mingled in with the other delightful aromas within Irina Petrovna's kitchen.

Such a comforting room, I thought. The brightness, the aromas, caused even the most ill-tempered to be calmed and comfortable. Hanging from the centre of the ceiling was a decorative lantern, which of course was electrical. And on the eastern corner of the room was an icon (as with all rooms) with a hanging votive before it. This immediately reminded me of my icon at home and how the votive hasn't been lit for the longest time.

There were many decorative items and pictures in this kitchen. As I scrutinized each and every article, Irina Petrovna was pulling out of the oven the hot, steaming fresh bread that she expertly made. My mouth instantly watered. I heard the unlocking of the front door and before long, my friend, my benefactor walked in. Apparently he was tired, too, for he seemed serious. He had courteously saluted us and left the kitchen to go and wash before having breakfast.

I was now brooding and numbly staring at the floor. I don't understand anything now. He had told me to come back and deliver the afternoon papers if I finished on time with the morning delivery and I did. Now I must sit here obligingly and wait for him to wash and have his breakfast. Again, I was reminded of home and of Mother as I stared at the lemon-yellow floor, obviously scrubbed well. Since Mother had left us, there was no one to wash our floors, which have become grey and dingy. It was of no wonder that we had even more bed bugs and fleas now. When did this woman, Irina Petrovna, find the time to do all these chores?

With these thoughts, I drifted off to Mother. Yes, I must go to see her. Now, of all times she had taken up smoking and I certainly wouldn't give her the cigarette butts, which I am accustomed to smoke. I need to go to the black market and purchase her a pack (now I knew what the black market meant, for Alex had finally decided to inform me). Ha! Whenever I did bring her cigarettes, they inconspicuously vanished. Not by the means of Mother smoking them, but by thieves. Either the patients or the staff found it their right and to their convenience to snatch them away from her and poor Mother was in no position to retaliate. Oh, my dear, dear mother, if only they wouldn't beat her so. When I confronted the hospital authorities regarding this, they defended their actions by blaming Mother's wildness.

I told Mother of their version and she was fuming with anger. Her main offence was the fact that she liked to pray and they, upon encountering her doing so, would systematically abuse her. I must go, I must go to see her soon.

Our breakfast began and my daydreaming ended. Sergei Sergeievich sat at the table. We began eating the delicious food given us, which consisted of eggs, bacon, cheese and, naturally, the freshly-baked bread. What a feast! What a celebration! I impolitely forgot to ask whether the setting on the table before me was intended for my use. I was confused as to what I should eat first? I wanted everything! I ate very quickly, lest the hostess begins to clear the table. At the end of our meal, we had tea. Linden tea.

"My wife collects the linden tea, dries it, and we use it throughout the year," my host proclaimed.

Alas! A new marketing scheme! I could do that and then sell it, thus I would earn additionally! Considering how many linden trees there were in the district of "Lipova Lad," meaning the "Linden's Shade," there's no limit to the amount I could earn! I at once began to inquire of the procedure of collecting the tea.

"Well, my dear son," began Irina Petrovna, "you see these flowers here," and she pulled a jar off another shelf that escaped my attention. There were many more jars on that shelf. She showed me the flower and told me the methods of collecting them.

I decided to ask her what those other jars on the shelf were, the ones that had escaped my study earlier.

"Oh, those? Those are more jams and preserves, sauces, teas and spices, dear."

I was bemused.

"More tea?" Sergei Sergeievich offered, noticing my unusual gaze upon the lemons, as if he had read my mind. "You know, Vitya, in this business I am in, I have opportunities to meet many kinds of people. They provide us with these lemons, eggs and bacon as well as other necessities for our household.

"Now...let's forget about that and go to rest for a short time, before we commence our work. Irina Petrovna will show you where you may rest."

I followed her into a tiny room, directly beside the kitchen. This room was sort of a pantry, but had a settee within it. More shelves were to be found in there, stocked with more jams, preserves and the such. How does she do it? I looked at the settee and my eyes began to close. I could hardly keep them open and didn't notice when Irina Petrovna had shut off the lights, for I lapsed into a sweet slumber.

I felt someone tugging at my foot. "Get up. Come now, get up!"

"Already? We just lied down!"

"That's what you think, my young man. The afternoon is nearly passed, come now! We'll have lunch and then go to work."

I rose and splashed some water, which Irina had placed on a little table, along with a pitcher and basin and a little hand towel. I went to the table. It was set again, in the same manner, same carefulness, but for lunch now. Irina Petrovna placed a heaping, hot bowl of paprikash in front of us and I welcomed the appetizing aroma. Again, I asked myself, how does she do it? Anyhow, we ate very well. I certainly would enjoy a cigarette right about now, but dared not to display the butts I had in my pocket, that is if I had any left. They were most likely squashed from my sleeping on them.

"Vitya, we are now quite satisfied no? And we do have a little time to spare before we launch into work, thus I decided to continue my story to you now...

"Now, where was I? Oh yes, I remember! The balls, well...They were grand, particularly the one I attended at your grandfather's house," and Sergei Sergeievich gave a brief summary of this ball and stated, "Indeed...those were the good times before the revolution set in and ran amok, causing chaos and unavoidable dilemmas."

As Sergei was ceremoniously speaking, Irina Petrovna was tip-toeing throughout the room, careful not to interrupt the story with any noise. She had cleared the table and washed the dishes nearly in silence. My eyes followed her, but ears were perked and I absorbed all Sergei Sergeievich had to say.

"The chief of police, court counsellor, namely...Nikolai Vladimirovich (who was advised by the governor), came to see me and we had a most serious and sombre discussion, Vitya. He spoke as such:

"'Sergei Sergeievich, I have received news that Her Imperial Highness, the Dowager Empress Maria Feodorovna, along with some escorts, will be coming to our town of Kursk. As you yourself see, my friend, we are surrounded by traitors of all sorts! Between them...My friend, there are even some

Cossacks! We must be on guard, alert and scrupulous. There are many pretenders, we are to take every precaution and extreme measure to assure the safety of our most honourable and divine guest.

"'I am assigning you, therefore, to designate and appoint the most trustworthy and loyal guards to protect and accommodate the Dowager Empress. Since I had a favourable recommendation from the governor himself as to your loyalty and honour, I thus beseech you to fulfill these orders.

"'We don't know who we can trust anymore, Sergei Sergeievich, and it is in you that I trust.'

"'Indeed, Nikolai Vladimirovich, I do agree with you. Unfortunately, many nobles and gentry alike have abandoned their palaces, their homes. Chaos and pillaging is rampant within our city. I as well have heard of paramount treachery existing. I also have heard of our once prestigious guards throwing down their weapons and fleeing to the forest! Alike, I heard that the Reds are not too far off from here. Absolutely revolting, I do say!'

"'Sergei Sergeievich, I have another request to ask of you. It concerns my family. I want them to leave before it's too late. I want them and their belongings as well as some precious heirlooms and valuables to be taken to the train station, and I have already prepared a car for them. They are to depart for France and I have taken care of their accommodations and provisions, by my discussion and agreement with the authorities there. I must remain here. I am obliged and willingly determined to help the Tsar. I will do as much as I can within my power. Now, I wish to bid you a good afternoon and success on the completion of your orders.'

"'Nikolai Vladimirovich? Shall I remain in my uniform?'

"'You must! With your rank, the remaining army that we do have here will obey you.'

"We embraced each other and bid each other farewell and the honourable Nikolai Vladimirovich had uttered, just before he departed, 'May God be with you.'

"I wasn't sure if I'd meet Nikolai Vladimirovich again, but I did. I began to carry out my orders and gathered a hundred

Cossacks to escort me to the home of Nikolai Vladimirovich.

"We arrived at the palace. The spouse of Nikolai Vladimirovich received us, after a minor misunderstanding, for she was not expecting anyone and was not in the form to be having guests. I and a few of my loyal guards entered her room. We found her quite agitated, for she must have had a presentiment. I informed her of my orders and she declined. I attempted to, with great respect and reverence toward her, to inform her that it was not an option, it was an order.

"She replied, 'My daughters will not agree, Colonel. They will simply not hear of it. If you wish, I will have them come to us here and perhaps you might be able to explain things to them.'

"She summoned them. A servant appeared and left, and very shortly thereafter, the daughters came, the three of them.

"'Mother, what is the matter? Why do you call us?'

"'Children, we have orders to leave. The colonel here has informed me that your father has taken measures and precautions for our safety and we must obey.'

"At once, the three of them chimed in chorus, 'Oh no! Most definitely not! We are not leaving. What for? Why are these people here?'

"Each of them questioned their mother, intermittently turning to us, who were standing there, quite uncomfortable with the entire situation. I observed the wife of Nikolai, she was very graceful, even in those trying moments. She paced the room in her long, velvet dress coat and slippers. Her facial expression was of worry and concern. Her eyes had a meaningful and sorrowful look to them, which I noticed when she implored me with them to come to her aid.

"'Children, you must understand your mother. We have been sent here by your father. Our city, our country is in danger. Traitors and enemies are about us and they are demolishing and murdering everything and everyone in their path as they march through the country. Thus, you are obliged to heed to your father's orders and pack as quickly as you can. I, along with my army, are here to escort you to the train station, where you will be departing to another country and later will be informed of further developments.'

"The girls became anxious and noticeably upset. The questions rained on us from each of the girls and without allowing us to answer them properly, they began showering us with more questions, intermittently to us, to their mother and to us again.

"'We don't want to leave our home, our country, our people! Who is doing all this to us? What about our father? We are certainly not going to abandon Father? No!' And Zoya added, 'I am not leaving Father, nor my husband!'

"It was a difficult task, very difficult for us. I knew, by the story Nikolai told me of his previous attempts to send them to safety, after he was cautioned by his advisor and had no success. Again, the girls were firmly resolved. Their mother, with numerous attempts of explanations, implorations and attempts to calm them, had herself become irritable. I felt sympathetic to their pleas, but I knew I couldn't falter. My orders were such and it was my obligation to carry them out.

"Well, Vitya, I believe I have spoken enough for today!" Sergei Sergeievich sighed.

My ears were burning as Sergei Sergeievich recited all this to me. I was lost, in another world, so to speak. I was nearly drowning in all the data I had just heard and couldn't help keeping my mouth from hanging open as I was drinking in, all that Sergei Sergeievich was pouring. I assured him (Sergei) that, for certain, I hadn't had enough and that I wasn't tired at all. Eagerly I awaited for the story to continue, though we did have an intermission for dinner.

Irina Petrovna had prepared a delectable meal and I ate quickly, partly because I was hungry and, partly, because I wanted to hear more. Funnily, we were oblivious to Irina Petrovna's absence while she was preparing and setting the table, for our engrossment in the story was paramount.

Our meal ended delightfully and the discussion, I mean the recital, continued...

"Vitya, I'll continue now and you sit back and listen to me...

"Agh...The Tsar we heard was detained en route to St. Petersburg. It goes without saying that we were utterly shaken upon learning of this news. I relayed this information to

Alexandra Nikolaevna, who proclaimed, 'Colonel! What shall
we do? How could all this be happening? What of the
guards...the army and the loyal Hussars?'

"'I told you, Madam, pack! We do not have the luxury of time,
Madam, therefore I am insisting that you all pack, without
hesitation!

"'Alexandra Nikolaevna, look...At least prepare your
youngest daughter Tamara now and I'll take her first with some
of your things to the train station and be back for the rest of you
later.'

"'Yes, Colonel, that will do, for she doesn't have very many
possessions, she is young. I'll have her ready in no time.'

"Not long after our deliberation, I was off to the train station
with approximately fifty Cossacks, I had left the remaining
Cossacks at the home of Nikolai. On my way to the station, I
had encountered bandits running amok, pillaging and
torching houses. Anarchy had ensued. Gratefully, we managed
to gallop through the disorder and chaos and arrived at the
station in favourable timing. I had found an acquaintance of
mine and Nikolai's and had confidently left Tamara in her care,
explaining the circumstances and intentions to this noble lady.
The lady was eager to cooperate and be of assistance.

"Like a lightening bolt, I strived to complete my mission. I
was now galloping back to the mansion. Again, encountering
upheavals on my way. I had great difficulty discerning the
armies and understanding of who was coming and who was
going. Like a blur, or a cloudy vision before me and literally so,
for the clouds of smoke had made it all the more troublesome.

"I reentered the home of Nikolai and found his wife in the
study. As soon as she saw me, she fled toward me with her
arms waving about and claimed: 'Colonel, I have had no news
from my husband! I am very worried about him! I must tell
you...The servants, they have gone mad! Tell me, Colonel, how
did you arrive at the station? Did you settle Tamara on board
the train? What is the state of the city?'

"I could barely manage to answer some of her questions,
though I tried. At every instant as soon as I began to speak, she
would interrupt me with more cries and inquiries. I knew she

was grieved and so was I, thus I had patience with her.

"She continued, 'Colonel...I simply can't understand all this, nor believe it! The servants...They have tied some kind of red cloth around their arms and began to shout. It is a wise decision you had made by leaving some Cossacks here. Who knows what they (servants) would have done hadn't the Cossacks tamed them.

"'Sadly though, Colonel, I do believe that even between the Cossacks their was some abandonment, for their arguing was audible.'

"I informed Alexandra Nikolaievna that Tamara was safe on the train with our mutual friend ____.

"'Oh my, how will I ever pack all the necessities and our cherished possessions? You'll be glad to know, however, that I had sent a carriage to the station with some of the trunks I had packed earlier, Colonel.'

"'Very well, Madam, it is good. Now, leave everything else and commit yourselves to my pleas and let us depart, for I am determined to fulfill my orders.'

"'Of course, Colonel, I do understand your position indeed. We shall depart. But, Colonel, you must go to your wife first. You must find out how she is faring in all this madness and bring her here. We can then depart and flee together.

"'Flee...how terrible it sounds, Colonel, for it is the coward that flees and we are not and it is the criminals that flee and we are not, yet we flee, because we are forced to.

"'Colonel...I must be honest with you, I haven't achieved much with my two daughters. They refuse to go and haven't packed a single item! Furthermore, they have locked themselves in their room and haven't been out since. I don't know what to do. But...Let us leave that now, I shall try again and you, Colonel, do go to your home. I am most certain that your wife is very concerned, for you haven't been home for a while, I assume. We have spent too much time deliberating and fussing. Do go.'

"I knew that Alexandra Nikolaievna was right. I hadn't been home for a while and was very worried about Irina Petrovna, thus I relented and left with the intention of bringing Irina back with me to Nikolai's home. As I left the home, I realized that Alexandra's guess was correct, there was a handful of Cossacks left in front of the mansion. I took five of them to escort me home. The distance was not great between Nikolai's home and mine, therefore I arrived in minutes to my home and to my wife.

"Irina Petrovna was overcome with worry and grief. She leaped into my arms when she had recognized me. She had heard through some friends and neighbours of ours that the situation was desperate. She began to worry and nearly decided to leave in search for me! It was excellent timing that I had arrived then, for a little longer and I wouldn't have found her at home. I persuaded Irina Petrovna to go directly to the station, rather than back to Nikolai's with me. Luckily she had already packed, in the event of my orders for us to leave. I sent her with three Cossacks to the station and prayed that they arrived well.

"Vitya! You'll fall off the chair like that!"

"Forgive me, Sergei Sergeievich, I didn't realize I was that close to the edge of the chair. I'll be careful."

"Fine, just be careful. I wouldn't want you to fall down! Now, where was I?

"And...I rushed back to the house of Nikolai. Before I had left them (Alexandra and the girls), I had given the orders for the preparation of the carriages for departure, to the Cossacks on guard. I further charged the captain, 'In case of danger, immediately order the women out of the home and flee to the train station!' The captain loyally agreed and saluted me.

"I rushed, Vitya! In desperation I did. As I was galloping with my horse in the forefront, the two remaining Cossacks were slacking behind. I turned my head to shout at them and order them to hurry, but had noticed that they had turned their horses around and had proceeded in the opposite direction! I had not the time to chase them, thus I continued forward. They abandoned me.

"In the distance I had envisioned the roof of Nikolai's home. 'Ah ha! I am close!' I chastened my horse to go faster. I flew through the open gates and rushed to the entrance, expecting to find the prepared carriages, the guards, the captain. Nothing! No one was there! They were all gone!

"I ran into the home and flew up the stairs in the direction of Alexandra Nikolaievna's bedroom. Mind you, etiquette no longer was an observation, nor was it significant. I rapped on the door and alarmingly remarked, 'Alexandra Nikolaievna, it is me, the colonel! Open the door! Please, Madam, it is me!' A vague clatter was heard and the door opened.

"'Come in!' Alexandra Nikolaievna pulled me in and complained, 'Look at these two! They won't budge! They are determined to remain here, Colonel!' The girls were sitting on the bed, embracing each other, with tears of fear in their eyes, they implored me and shook their heads in disapproval of the decision.

"'Girls! What is it with you? Why are you disobeying? Do you not realize that the situation is catastrophic? You must do as you are told!'

"Nothing. Pertinaciously they stared at me while shaking their heads. I was running low on time and was becoming agitated with their contention. I was alone now, meaning no guards, no Cossacks, no captain, no servants even! I asked Alexandra Nikolaievna what had happened to the guards and the captain.

"She professed, 'Well, Colonel, I wouldn't know. We have been here in this room all the while. We had barricaded ourselves in here, with the resolve of whatever God permits.

"'But, Colonel? Tell me where is your wife? Is the poor being downstairs alone? Do bring her here, Colonel. I can't imagine why you would leave her downstairs alone?'

"'No, no, Madam. My wife is not here. I sent her directly to the train station. I did not find it feasible to have her accompany me here. Now, I must order you all to leave with me now!'

"'Indeed, Colonel, we will oblige, but...Have you heard anything from my husband?'

"It was apparent, I was not about to succeed here. I had only one option left and that was to frantically search for Nikolai. He himself would have a better chance of victory as to their submission. From the sole repetitive pleas of mine, the fact that we had only one horse now escaped my realization. Once I had realized that, or remembered, I informed Alexandra Nikolaevna that I would go to fetch her husband, bring him back and then decide from there. Naturally, she accepted my suggestion as did the girls.

"There were dark clouds looming over the town as if in accordance with the dire situation. I looked back at the palace as I galloped and couldn't help but to feel a sharp pain. Its magnificence, now stark and gloomy. The people, our people, no longer laughing, but screaming, shouting and arguing. Even the bare trees were in unison and acknowledgement of the cataclysm as their dark, crooked and gloomy branches pointed in every direction, nearly shaking in anger as the fierce winds blew. It was nearing the end of October and was very chilly.

"I felt the whistling, cold wind on my ears as I galloped toward town, toward the station. In the core of the town, vandalism, looting and depredation was ensuing. With tears, I fled by them, knowing that I was unable to prevent them, to seize them, to reprimand them and stop the de facto defacement and rampant carnage. The route I took to the station was crowded by masses of people of all sorts. Carrying their bags and the few possessions they were able to grab, they walked, limped and cried, from the burden of their belongings and the fact that they were leaving their beloved homes and town behind.

"Reminiscent of times past as when Moscow was attacked by Napoleon Bonaparte as the citizens fled the city. Hah! History repeats itself, though...Now we are not under attack by foreigners, but by our own people! As my gallop turned to a trot, then a near halt, I watched the crowd and recognized some of them, who acknowledged me by their nods. I thought, what an apathetic circumstance to meet these acquaintances on the street, at this hour and under this situation.

"The beautiful women, some of which reminded me of the delicate Anna Karenina in Tolstoy's novel, were now disgruntled, obviously tired and completely lacking interest as to their appearance. Amusingly, though, I spied on some genteel women sitting in a fiacre, made-up and powdered as they roared to the general...Yes, the general, now turned coachman, to hurry up the horses, lest they miss the train! The ladies were shrieking, 'Madness! This is inconceivable madness!'

"I was curtly approached by some soldiers, who with all their might were trying to apprehend my horse. With my sword I brushed them away as they were yelling out to me that they had orders from a general to gather up horses.

"'Move back! What general's orders?! Away, I order you!' I began to desperately search with my eyes for Nikolai, or anyone who might know his whereabouts. I heard gunshots in the distance sounding like canons. The debacle was severely near our town, indeed! I must hurry!

"You know, Vitya..." Sergei Sergeievich began to cough, a dry cough, for he was visibly exhausted of his orating, but he nevertheless had full intentions to continue after our brief intermission of tea.

Absolutely enticing! I marvelled at Sergei's reciting, retelling of the events. He thematically sketched the entire affair as he orated with profound enthusiasm, now even grimacing when the moment called for it. I almost forgot where I was and felt as if I were observing a play in an opera (which I've read about in books).

Sergei's poetic nature enabled him to depict the horrid moments of those times past and swallowed me into the era of the unfortunate juncture. And he continued...

"You know, Vitya, I arrived at the station and ran along the platform of the station, looking for Nikolai, my wife, or anyone who might help me find them.

"It was ludicrous! I barely managed to forcefully shove my way into the station, tie my horse to a post and hope it would be there upon my return. The confusion, the anxiety that overcame the crowds of people, was astounding.

"I finally came to the doors of one car of the train and shoved and pushed through to enter the car. I found my wife, shockingly. I was nearly giving up the notion of success of finding anyone! I informed her of the entire situation at hand and I had to explain to her that I was compelled to leave again and search for Nikolai Vladimirovich. She was grieved, but accepted the facts.

"I was very much grateful, Vitya, for the few remaining loyal Cossacks that did carry out their order and had brought Irina Petrovna to the station and placed her on the train.

"Anyhow, I left Irina Petrovna and now was being cursed as I was shoving to get out of the car. 'What are you doing? Can you not make up your mind! Look at him, running to and fro!' I payed no mind to their complaints and in this frantic predicament even forgot to apologize to the few that I had stepped on, on my way out of the car.

"Now...the horse...I was hoping to find the horse where I had left it. The difficulty to manoeuver through the station, on the platform, was overwhelming. Everyone was pushing and shoving and yelling. Some screams, some curses, some apologies could be heard. Regardless, I aimed now at locating my horse and with my hand on my sword, I was prepared to use it if necessary.

"I know what you are thinking, Vitya, but it was such the case and the time...

"I heard an explosion in the distance and worry had overtaken me. What was with Nikolai Vladimirovich? What of his family? Frantically I pulled through the crowds. As I was doing so, I had at once felt a strong grasp of my shoulders from behind. Impetuously I turned to confront my assailant.

"'It is you! It is really you! I have been searching for you desperately! And here you are! Oh, the burden is lifted off of me! It is you, Nikolai Vladimirovich, lest my eyes betray me!'

"I grabbed hold of his arm and pushed through the masses again, this time not alone and extremely careful of not letting the grip of my hand on Nikolai's arm loosen."

For a second I snapped to pause and come back to reality, and realized that I hadn't been very polite to Irina Petrovna when she had served us the tea and acted as if it were expected to be served and unheard of, if it wasn't. Back I went to my listening and soaking up of Sergei's nostalgia...

"Nikolai Vladimirovich shrugged and yanked his arm out of my firm grasp. With a mixture of anger and confusion he warranted. 'What the devil is wrong with you? Why are you pulling me away from the station? Is it rigged with mines? Are we under attack? Tell me!'

"His personal guards now enveloped us and as they formed a tight circle I exclaimed, 'Why this? Why the apprehension of your guards, Nikolai?

"'No, I haven't heard of the train being rigged and as of the attack, well I haven't heard of it yet, though it is possible, judging from the sounds in the near distance. But, why are your guards trapping us?'

"'Well, Colonel, I'll tell you...It is simply chaotic, the situation! The Red bandits released some prisoners and they are causing havoc and ransacking. Unfortunately, the Whites are retrieving.'

"The train cars were now locking, and because of that noise, I jumped. 'Don't leave yet! No! Wait, don't leave yet, not yet! Nikolai, forgive me, I must tell you something. I...I am sorry, but I couldn't persuade your wife and two daughters to leave your home! Oh, forgive me, I failed!'

"I continued my screaming over the heads of the masses of people, to the conductor imploring and ordering the train not to leave, not yet! Not realizing that unintentionally, I was now holding the front of Nikolai's shirt in my hand and begging him for his forgiveness, while explaining my inability to bring his wife and daughters to the station.

"Nikolai Vladimirovich, learning what my screams and gestures were about, grabbed my shoulders again and smiled to me as he stated, 'Colonel, slow down! It is not as you think.'

"'Oh my goodness, Nikolai Vladimirovich, if only you knew of my pleas, warnings and nothing...Nothing would provoke them to oblige. And...And my Cossacks, they abandoned me, but a handful remained loyal.

"'Nikolai, sir...I urge you, we must instantly return to your home and save your family. Only Tamara is on the train, sir, there in that car with one of our acquaintances. We must hurry, Nikolai Vladimirovich, and not waste time here.'

"'Now, Colonel! Grab a hold of yourself and permit me to inform you! My family is not in peril, not anymore. I went home after I had tended to some matters and was curious whether you had accomplished your task, for forgive me, Colonel, I knew how headstrong my wife and children were. Just as I assumed, I found them and respectively was informed of Tamara's departure to the station.

"'What colossal destruction I encountered along my way home, Colonel, abominable! Unspeakable and monstrous acts...Innocents murdered, homes burnt to ashes and the disgusting treachery!'

"'Yes, yes it's true, I know, Nikolai Vladimirovich, I had witnessed what you speak of myself,' I interrupted Nikolai Vladimirovich.

"'Colonel, it saddens me so, the entire town, the country is in mayhem. I caught up to a horde of bandits on my way home and was forced to stretch out my sword, causing them to disperse like disorderly bulls across the field. Ironically, I had the displeasure of recognizing some familiar faces amongst the bandits. Yes, yes...There were some of my servants' children between them. The same children I had clothed, educated and cared for and this is how they repay me!

"'Anyhow, irately I hastened to arrive to my home. My path, enigmatically speaking, was lit by the dancing flames in the sky of the poor innocents' burning homes, who with great effort had established the humble dwellings for their families, now...abandoned.

"'I arrived at my home and exactly as you stated, Colonel, found no Cossacks, no guards. I sent some of my men to the rear of the house to investigate the screams we had heard, while I dashed into my home. No one was to be seen.

"'I scurried up the stairs and suddenly heard a scream. I raced faster. It was dark and luckily I didn't trip and fall. I was now in the corridor leading to the bedroom and had envisioned a distant silhouette near the doors to the bedroom. I ran toward her and she stood there in shock, shakily holding a lit candelabra in her hands; her face was illuminated and expressed a frightful appearance, even though she was the most tenderest creature! She recognized me and I her.

"'Dunya! What on heaven's earth are you doing here? Why did you scream? Where is my wife, my family?'

"'Sir…umph, I am truly glad to see you! Glad you are home! Secondly, sir, it was not I who screamed, sir, but your wife, Alexandra Nikolaevna!'

"'Where is she?'

"'She is in the bedroom and I had knocked on her door, wanting to inform her of vandals in the yard. She began to unlock and open the door, ever so slightly, when she had heard the running footsteps and clatter from downstairs. She screamed and shut the door, without even taking a look at me.'

"'It is all right, Dunya, I'll see what I can do.'

"'I began knocking on my wife's door. No answer when I hollered out to her. Nothing. I banged on the door, again nothing. Silence. I told my men to be prepared to shoot down the door and just as they were about to aim, the door opened.

"'I saw my wife, pale as a ghost, shivering, and when she saw me, she shrieked and fainted. We had to put her on the bed and I ordered Dunya to bring the sniffing salts. At that moment, my two daughters ran up to me.'

"'Father, please don't be angry with us! We are terribly regretful for not obeying your orders! Father, we simply couldn't leave our home, our country, our people and most of all you!'

"'Children, I understand your concerns and feelings, but right now, it is such the case. The country is in ruin, people are running amok. Scandalous and unheard of misfortunes are taking place, even now as we speak. It is no longer a concept, nor a luxury of time, you must prepare now!'

"'Mother, oh our dear mother…' and they ran to their mother that was arousing back to consciousness, after the remedy of sniffing salts. Suddenly, a knock on the door, caused us all to stir and direct our stares to the door.

"'Enter,' I ordered. We all anxiously waited for the appearance of this knocker. One of my men entered. He had informed us that the Reds were headed toward us and at a quick pace. I had a serious discussion with the girls, with the help now from my wife and it was decided.

"I grabbed my wife and ordered the men to take my daughters and Dunya of course. Just as I had grabbed my wife, she swiped the portrait of me off the wall and hugged it. I thought, even at these horrible moments, she is thinking of such! I admit, I was deeply saddened.

"I felt a tremendous obligation toward my family and their safety as you yourself, Colonel, must feel toward your wife.

"We left the home, but were unable to exit through the gates; we saw the lit torches in the distance and cumulus dust. Perhaps these were the released prisoners? Without further hesitation, we decided to go through the forest, which was behind the mansion. We were met by the men I had sent to investigate the riotous bustling in the yard. We all commenced toward the forest. Gratefully, the rogues didn't follow us into the forest and the night had been our accomplice. It was an added advantage that I had knowledge of the forest's paths, for I used to hunt there with my guests. Thus, I had no difficulty finding our way in, through and out of the forest.

"There you have it, Colonel! Now you may safely and without hesitation board the train and join your wife. My family is on the train as well, safe. I wish you Godspeed and much success. I must return to my men and tend to my duties and my mission.'

"'But, Nikolai...Won't you join us on the train?'

"'No, Colonel, I will not.'

"We embraced and I glimpsed a tear sliding down his face, moistening his moustache and beard, which glistened in the night. He pushed me away and kept repeating, 'Go! Go now to your wife! There is no time, Colonel, the train has signalled its departure!'

"I looked toward the train and at the car my wife was in. I turned to say something more to Nikolai Vladimirovich, but he was gone, vanished in the crowd.

"I ran toward the train, again pushing, shoving, cursing and I couldn't reach the door. The train began to move. I was running alongside the train, alongside the window of the car my wife was in. I couldn't see within, for the trains were taller than the ones here, Vitya.

"I was hopping and running and managed to observe my wife, who now was standing and frantically waving her arms motioning me to run faster and jump. I was running at the edge of the platform and saw no possible method of entry. The whistle kept blowing and I kept running.

"'Sir! Colonel! Grab my hand!' A young soldier spotted me and my dilemma and offered me his assistance. In one hop, I was standing at the door of the car.

"The car was overloaded with passengers, packed solid. Soldiers prepared for battle and other ranking officials were aboard, all interlaced with the gentry, the bourgeois and some common folk. It was a motley assortment.

"'Don't worry, Colonel,' one very kind soldier stated and yet, another kind Hussar gave up his seat for me. I sat down, beside a captain. I couldn't get to my wife momentarily, for it was humanly impossible to shove through. We were like sardines. I decided I would try later, at least I was on the train!

"I began to study the captain seated next to me. He was rather young, or deceivingly so. Very muscular and had a rather handsome face, though his eyebrows were nearly joined. I assumed this was due to his deep contemplation. I asked him, 'Captain...Have you heard any news?'

"'Bad, very bad, Colonel. Treachery all around us!'

"The captain was now inspecting all the passengers in suspicion.

"I continued, 'Do you know, Captain, exactly where is our destination?'

"'Colonel, even if I knew, I would not be in a position to disclose this information. I can tell you that we have already stopped several times on our route and each time acquired a new conductor. Colonel, we are in desperate times,' and he looked about him at all the tired, sullen and dismal faces of the passengers, while perfervidly whispering to me and he further proclaimed, 'At every stop we were given orders to disembark the cars and stand guard. Thankfully, we had not any encumbrances to delay us. We are striving to achieve our goal.'

"I understand, Captain. I am wondering, if you might be able to assist me? I am or will be searching the train for Nikolai Vladimirovich's wife and daughters. Do you know him?'

"I have heard of him. Do describe his family to me, perhaps I had encountered them.'

"I began to describe the family and I omitted Tamara, for I knew where she was, saw her and verified that the rest of the family was not in her company.

"I do not recall such a family, Colonel, but in case I do, I will inform them of your inquiry.'

"'Sposiba, Captain,' and I sat back awaiting for the next stop with thoughts of travelling through the compartments of the train, to find the family of Nikolai.

"The howling wind whistled through the cracks of the train, for it was a commercial train and not the luxurious trains we were accustomed to use when travelling for leisure. I turned to look out through the window. The sky was of a pinkish hue and I began to ponder, was it a village burning? No...It was the break of dawn, sunrise. I was beyond exhaustion. I was so tired that I couldn't fall asleep. I wondered about the captain, and did he have a family of his own? I was not in form to continue my conversation with him, for maybe sleep would prevail.

"The train came to a screeching halt as we approached the station. I observed more new faces on the platform. I decided to disembark and try to find Nikolai's family. I began to walk a little ahead of my car and was caught by a tap on my shoulder. It was the captain.

"'Colonel, I must ask you to refrain from walking about right now on the platform; it is for your safety and, secondly, we might be leaving at any moment. I advise you to return to your car.'

"'Indeed, Captain, you are right. I shall return to the car.'

"I had no fortune of locating Alexandra and her daughters. Although, I did find my wife, who was ecstatic, crying of joy and embracing me.

"The train signalled its departure, the captain was correct. We were on our way again. I retold Irina Petrovna of all the misfortunes, difficulties and the unsuccessful search of

Alexandra and her daughters. My information evoked a paroxysm of poignant condemnation toward the brigand, succeeded by a flowing of tears and forlorn. Irina Petrovna concluded that, since I had not achieved locating them and due to the impeding circumstances and dangers, she wouldn't hear of my leaving again, in search for the family. She further lamented that they are on the train as Nikolai Vladimirovich stated and I shouldn't worry. For the time being, I relented to her pleas, which nearly turned to orders, for the sake of calming her and for the sake of my own being. I had to try to sleep, it had been a very long, long time since I slept...

"I awoke when the train stopped. Yawning and stretching I inquired, 'Where are we now?'

"Irina was sitting opposite me now and was staring at me. 'Kiev,' she answered.

"'Already?'

"'Yes, already. You, my dear husband, had slept soundly for an extended amount of time.'

"'I'm going to go out onto the platform and take a look around.'

"'Oh, no you're not! Open the window here and look as much as you wish!'

"Obviously, she was still anxious and I didn't want to contradict her, thus I opened the window and looked outside. The platform seemed very quiet and the people didn't look as apprehensive and sullen as other passengers at the other stations.

"In the distance a vague shouting could be discerned. I protruded my head farther out the window, to enable myself a better view.

"'Piroshki! Bulochki!' Aha! Street vendors! Here? What a difference between this station and the previous ones! Is it possible? There is no war here? In no time I was standing upon the platform, to the dismay of Irina.

"An officer was standing not far from me. I approached him and asked him of the situation here. 'Nothing out of the ordinary,' was his reply.

"I continued, 'Where are the Reds?'

"'They withdrew. Our army seized a sizable amount of territory.'

"We saluted each other and I returned to my car and wife. We left the station and for a considerable time we travelled, finally arriving in Odessa. There I was able to locate some of my good friends, who had informed me that the Whites were breaking, defeated and slowly withdrawing, although, the authorities in Odessa were still under the Whites. Knowing the case at hand, I had decided to pursue a means of departure from our beloved country, for something within inspired me, or intuition told me that there's no return.

"There was a ship departing for Greece. You know Vitya, I paid an exorbitant amount for our fare, thereby securing our place on the ship. During our journey we heard the discomforting news regarding the capture of Crimea by the Reds and later by the Germans."

Thus Sergei Sergeievich's exceptionally prodigious monologue ended. Needless to say, I was inebriated and swollen with all the information I had received. Time stood still. I spent the entire day, well into the night at their home. Utterly exhausted, but thoroughly amused and intrigued, I began my dazed walk back home

Chapter 14

The alarm clock rang and, of course, I slammed it. I got up and gazed around me. My home, my small, dirty and lonely home. I had great trouble falling asleep last night. I was nervous, agitated and finally depressed. Sergei's story caused many thoughts to arise many considerations. I wondered why my grandmother and aunt always spoke significantly more than my mother regarding their past. My mother would sit there, stare at whatever was in front of her, sometimes down at the floor as the two of them chirped away. The only thing she would do was nod in agreement and hug her father's portrait. Yes...The portrait, the one we no longer have...Agh!

She acted as if she wanted to forget the past; perhaps it was much too painful for her, especially when compared to the life she had here.

As if fate hadn't served me enough hardships, now this new shattering revelation—my grandfather's struggles, the nobility and heritage. I didn't have much time to ponder and dwell on these thoughts, because the harrowing fact of survival had always taken precedence. My wretchedness, my hunger and my pathetic abode always confirmed my poverty-stricken stance in life. Notwithstanding, I couldn't help to recount the recital of Sergei's, which caused an ache deep within my empty belly, remembering Mother's sufferings at home, at the hospital, entirely unwarranted.

I mused at how I might change the current situation, but lacking support, both moral and financial, resolved to commit myself to surmising new systems of attaining the most, base necessities of life. Sitting most often alone, in these recollections of tales I've heard from my encounters, I would sometimes grunt a sarcastic laugh, to be followed by bitter tears.

My painful howls at night as I screamed for Mother, Brother or even Father, granted no answers. No one to reply to my moans of loneliness, of destitution. Oh how bitter it was.

Splashing icy water on my face to recoup my presence of mind. I shivered. Aware that I had the last of the newspapers to deliver and I had to leave. I was doing this for a month now and I was genuinely grateful to Sergei, for he paid me well. In fact, they (Sergei and Irina) always made certain that I never left their home hungry. Sergei would ask me, "Are you pleased with your pay?"

"Of course I am, Sergei Sergeievich, very much so. Thank you."

In spite of their good intentions, I was informed by Sergei that I was to be off work for a week. He said he had to leave, would be back and that I should return then. Bitterly, I left Sergei Sergeievich, regardless of his promise of returning and promise of continued work for me. I couldn't help but feel an arousement of suspicion within me. Why did he have to leave suddenly? What was the urgency?

Another fascination was in regard to his abode, how well it was furnished and of all the necessities he always replenished. I realized what he had told me earlier, that he knew many people and they would pay him at times in these methods, but still it is incomprehensible to me, to support his household, on the delivery of newspapers? The more I thought, the more suspicious I grew, perhaps out of bitterness due to my unexpected unemployment.

I entered the courtyard, after I had spent the day delivering the last of the newspapers and obtaining minuscule errands, in exchange for food and went directly to the landlord to pay the rent. I waited in front of their door, after several taps on the window. The greasy, middle-aged, pot-bellied, humourless and hostile landlord (to name a few of his traits) appeared.

"What!" He insultingly looked at me as if it were such an honour for him to open his door to me.

"Here, this is yours," I apathetically stated.

His eyes suddenly glistened. Like a cobra, he began to squirm and inquired, "How much is there?"

"Enough to cover the rent and then some. Perhaps toward the future payment."

Agh, the swine! What an obvious transition, not even disguised. Disgraceful, even an urchin as I would know how to behave more civil! I left in disgust. I went to my home and straight to bed. I was mentally exhausted, disgusted, suspicious, but...I had to refrain from further contemplation, I was going to burst. Particularly, because I lacked a human being near me to talk to, to confide in. I fell asleep.

The days were shorter now and much colder. I had awoke to a recollection. I bumped into a lady a few weeks ago when I was delivering newspapers. She had asked if I could do a job for her. As soon as she explained the work, I informed her that my brother Alex had worked for her previously. She was very agreeable upon this news and all the more persistent for me to promise to come as soon as the autumn grants us its certain chill. The work, being no other than coal ball construction.

Recalling Alex's description (always so vivid), I believed I had a good grasp on the methods of producing these balls. Therefore, today, I knew what I was going to do, I was to visit the "coal ball" lady! After all, it is cold. I resolutely dressed and headed to the lady's house.

Naturally, on my way to her house, I began to think and ache, where is Alex? Where is my brother? Oh dear Lord, how I miss him! I don't know where to look for him? It's been nearly eight months since he disappeared. I never told Mother this. I hadn't seen Father either and didn't miss him, although any voice at home was better than none. I visited Olga as often as I could, but felt like an intruder and disturber of Auntie Katarina's, since she was always consumed in her work and employed Olga to assist her, thus my visits were short. Mother...I went to whenever I possibly could, always making sure that I had something to give her. She always begged me to bring tea. She was an avid tea drinker and I had no means of assuaging her pleas. Little George was in the orphanage and I had no parcels to send him, I had barely enough for myself and was in dire need. The delicatessen I frequented for the salami ends had become cruel and greedy; now they no longer had that box in the back of the shop.

I came to the "coal lady's" house on Kosovska Street. I was nearly certain and reassured that I would have definite employment, for the weather was now my ally. I boldly knocked on her door. I waited and no one answered. I knocked again. Nothing. Now I was becoming frustrated and anxious.

After several more knocks, I began to turn around and

involuntarily mumbled out, "Oh yeah, well then you can make the coal balls yourself!" As I took a step to leave, the door squeaked open. Lo and behold, the coal lady appeared!

I nearly tripped backward upon viewing her. She startled me! She had an old, red, tattered bathrobe on and these little pieces of rags on her head, which her hair was rolled onto and tied. Her eyes were bulging and she had dark circles beneath them. I thought that even the birds would have taken leave and flown off when visualizing her. Nevertheless, I needed work.

The coal lady had now leaned forward to get a better look at me. "Who are you?" As she leaned toward me, I noticed her heavily powdered and made-up face, though that didn't prevent her from looking like a raccoon. She probably had insufficient sleep.

"Coal, ma'am. Remember the coal?"

"Coal? Oh, of course, the coal! Oh my, I forgot! Did I tell you when you should come?"

"We agreed upon the autumn, ma'am. Now it's autumn and I'm here."

"Son, you know, today...Today is not such a good time. I recently woke and...Perhaps at another time. That might be better."

"Better?" Better, I thought, ha! Perhaps, but the orchestra in my stomach didn't seem to agree. "Please, ma'am," I began to humbly beseech her, "I didn't eat since yesterday and with great hopes I came to call on you," and I began fumbling my beret with both hands in front of me as I repetitively begged for work.

"Dear me, fine." Silence. "Wait here."

I do have some luck, although I nearly lost this job. I sat on the step and waited. I looked through my pockets for a cigarette butt and found one and lit it. I smoked as I waited. I thought, I must go visit my mother; it's been a while and I think I'd like to visit Olga, too. This is great, I have a job! I might be able to purchase some items for Mother and Olga.

The lady finally reappeared. "Come with me, young man! I took the key to the basement and now will show you what to do."

We descended into the damp, dark basement. The lady lit our way with a candle. In this basement were many locker stalls. We passed by many, until we reached hers. I observed the items as we passed them. Some contained old suitcases, some had dusty and forgotten boxes and other unnecessary knick-knacks that people can't seem to part with, yet throw it down there, out of view.

Anyhow, in the locker where I am to work, the lady pointed out the tools of the trade. A very large metal basin approximately 1 ½ metres by 1 metre, a pail for fetching water, an enormous pile of coal dust and a stack of old, yellow newspapers. She proceeded to instruct me as to how to make the balls. Attentively I listened to her, although I had a good inkling as to its manufacture, thanks be again to Alex's descriptive and detailed stories.

She left after she was certain that I understood the method. Now I was alone. Not only that, but she had taken the candle with her and the only light was from a tiny window, very high up on the wall, where some daylight barely managed to squeeze through.

My eyes eventually adjusted to the dimness of the basement. I poured the cold water from the tap into the basin and put the newspaper and coal dust in. Then, I began to knead this dough with my feet as instructed. It was cold, very cold, but my feet either warmed the mass of dough, or I became adjusted to its coldness, which didn't bother me after a few minutes of kneading. What a dirty, cold job! In my efforts, I began to brood...

Regarding the leitmotif stories I had heard thus far, new elements were now introduced into my life. The prospect of a bravado lifestyle, ultimately and ridiculously unattainable, and the manifested oppression, easily obtainable, in fact already achieved, was for what purpose? Why had destiny defiantly sent forth volcanic information of a "once was," when I was hungry and downtrodden to the point of depression? The only motivation and cure was the infinite starvation and need of provisions, for even savages hunted for survival. What did all those stories entail, I asked myself? To further insult the obvious fact that I live as a pauper, yet of a noble's seed? The elongated stories had imprinted in me an unwarranted, disconcerting effect, perhaps unintentional, leaving a transcendent, mystical epitome, congruent to the oppressive poverty-stricken entity.

Ironically, it is thanks to the coal dust that I earn my bread! Now I understood the phrase, very commonly used by workers: "It is black bread we earn with hardship." Soon, I had a row of coal balls on the cold, damp ground. Unaware of the time, though aware of my hunger, I nearly ate one of the coal balls I was making.

I heard a squeaking noise in the corner of the locker room and recognized it to be a mouse. "Ha! My little friend, you won't find any food here in the basement, except for these coal balls!"

Where is that lady? Why didn't she bring at least the crust of a piece of bread, I am famished! I was dizzy and nearly fainting. I forced myself to complete the last row on the ground, just one more ball. I stood up and began to totter. Why doesn't she summon me? It is becoming dark.

I had to wash my feet in the icy cold water and drag myself out of the locker and into the hallway, locking her stall behind me.

Cursed is this life filled with antipathy! The entire day I spent in the cold, dark and damp basement, with the coal dust and with mice and starving to the point of unconsciousness. I limped my way up the stairs and was rubbing my legs to regain circulation. I was very cold, bitterly hungry and to the point of ululation!

I forced myself to bang on her door as hard as possible. She didn't answer. Oh that old carcass, she has no intention of paying me! Agh! I gathered my forces and banged and hollered.

"Who is it?"

"It's me!" I was screeching now.

"Oh my goodness, it's you! I forgot about you! Oh dear me, do come in!"

The apologies flew as she opened the door quickly and pulled me in.

"Follow me to the kitchen!"

I followed her and, as we walked through her home, I sensed the fragrant scent of incense (the kind that's used in church). Immediately I thought, aha! A religious woman, yet she easily forgets me in the basement! The room began to spin in my head as we entered her kitchen and the savoury aroma of cooked potatoes slapped me.

"Sit down, sit down! Are you hungry, son?"

"Ma'am, I am so famished that I could not only swallow whatever you are cooking, but the pot along with it!"

I sat down at the table, which was covered in a frilly, white tablecloth. In seconds, I had a bowl of hot stew in front of me. I stared at the stew.

"What's the matter? Don't you like the stew?"

"Oh, ma'am, of course I do. You have no idea how much...But I can't eat with my fingers!"

"Oh my, oh dear, I am sorry!" She raced to grab a spoon for me. I breathed in the stew, nearly the bowl, too!

"Do you want more?"

What a question! Of course I do, no need to ask me twice! The bowl was in her hands instantly. Now, I literally savoured the food and truly delighted in it. I was immensely grateful to her, for I knew I was at the point of fainting.

She asked me whether I had completed the job. I informed her that there were many more coal balls to be made from the mountain of coal dust in her locker. She requested that I return and complete the task and would remit payment upon completion. While I sat there eating, we began a minutiae discussion.

"You know, son, I am a widow," she began. "My husband was a clerk in the ministry. We were happy. I do have a large family, but they are in the village. On one hand I benefit form this, for they always provide me with fresh meat and produce, but on the other hand, I am lonely."

The general course of conversation was of trivialities, which is normal when people are becoming acquainted with one another. After my dinner and our brief talk, I realized that this lady wasn't all that bad. I believe that she genuinely did forget about me and who knows...She might have difficulties of her own, thus her mind was not concentrated on me in the basement. We bid each other a good night and I departed.

Walking back in the chill of the night, I began to rehash and mentally organize all my obligations for the next day. I remembered Sergei and how he advised me to call on him in a week. Very soon that will be and I looked forward to returning to work for him. He did ask me, once to bring Mother's photograph, but I forgot to, thus he reminded me to bring it when he returns. I also thought of visiting the bath house Alex and I went to before, but I hadn't enough money and the thought of becoming dirty again tomorrow, didn't make it a tangible idea.

Dawn...I had to get up and get to work, making coal balls. It has been nearly a week that I have been working at the coal lady's home. I was finishing off the last of the coal balls today. Upon my completion, I went to receive compensation. As usual, I went directly to the kitchen and sat at my usual assigned place at the table. I debated whether she would feed me, or not, since it was my last day. Her home was filled with the scent of sweet cabbage stew.

The finale of my duties, instigated a contiguous sadness within me. I had become relatively attached to this lady, even though she was only an employer, nevertheless, a soul to talk to and the added bonus of hot, homemade dinners was another cause of my grief. I would terribly miss the dinners.

True to my assumptions, I received dinner, the delicious cabbage stew. The usual trivial discussions ensued. I promised the lady I would return when the need arose for more coal balls to be made. She thanked me for the work I did and handed me an envelope. I left the lady, happy, yet sad.

The autumn mist and fresh air escorted me home. The mist turned to a drizzle and I thrust the envelope in my inner coat pocket, pulled up my collar and nearly ran home that night.

At home, with nothing to do. I decided to rummage through the rags and whatever little I had in the apartment, in hopes of locating one photograph of Mother. I had luck, I found one. It was a family photograph. I stared at it for a long, long time. It was taken years ago and I remember when we took it. So many changes occurred since then, so many. In the photo Mother's hair was very short, but it's the only one I found and I didn't feel like looking further. I went to bed, in the silent apartment, in my rags, in my grievous state. I missed my family.

The next day was blustery, cold and didn't look promising. I began my walk toward Sergei Sergeievich's home with the photograph in my hand. The wind blew fiercely at times, thus I folded my arms, hugging myself, preventing the wind from blowing beneath my thin jacket. I confidently strode past the landlord's now, for I had paid my rent. The coal lady had sufficiently compensated me and I the landlord. It was a good feeling to walk by, in confidence, initiating a proud sense of responsibility in me.

Damned shoes! Full of holes and my feet were getting a little wet from the piles of soggy leaves on the ground. Just a little more and I'll be in front of Sergei's home. The air smelled of a combination of burning wood and soggy leaves, I felt a sullenness, a sort of premonition. As I neared Sergei's home, I noticed messiness in front of their door.

Leaves were gathered in the corners of their portico. I knew for a matter of fact that Irina Petrovna's pedantic manners wouldn't allow for such a display in front of her door. This caused me to feel uneasy. I was at the door now and the standard laced curtain on the door's window was not there and the window was bare as well. I pressed and cupped my face to the glass to permit a better view within.

It was empty! The hallway, the walls, nothing! I banged on the door, I knew that it was in vain, but I banged regardless. I had provoked only the gazes of passers-by and nothing else. How could he? How could have Sergei lied to me? He told me to come and here I am, but where is he? Where am I to look for him? I am stupid! Suddenly emasculated, I condemned myself for my naiveness and staunchness.

The insoluble situation rendered me stupefied. I began to shake uncontrollably, whether from the cold or the disappointment I wasn't certain. What of my employment now? What about this photo of Mother? Oh wretched life! Destiny again, didn't permit this union. I had no choice, I had to leave. I was extremely disappointed to the point of screaming there in the middle of the street and crying and throwing a fit. I didn't of course, but I felt I could have.

I raced back home and the blustery wind mercilessly whipped my face and bit at my cheeks sharply. I ran home and jumped into my bed of rags and slept. I slept for a long time. I had awoke the next day. I didn't even eat. I was too saddened and afraid of becoming apathetic, or worse, because of my surroundings and the environment. I was hit with hardships too many times.

Days of melancholy were spilling one into the other. Between these days I would habitually look for work, beg, visit the nuns for a bowl of charity soup and, as the last resort, the dreaded soup kitchen in the cellar of the Russian centre. Most often, in this state of mind and despair, I would lose track of the days and not know what day it was when I had left that particular morning.

On the street were a handful of pedestrians, I didn't bother to look at them, nor they at me. I came to a street sign, looked up at it: *Toplichka*. Good. I'll go visit Olga and Aunt Katarina; at least if anything, they can tell me what day it is.

The home was fashioned now with a window bearing a multi-coloured patched curtain on the door and window. I knocked numbly.

"Who is it? We are closed for the day. Come tomorrow." I then heard some mumbling, something falling down such as a pot, some cursing, then nothing.

Again I knocked, and this time I yelled out simultaneously, "Open the door, it's me, Vitya!"

Aunt Katarina peeked through the curtain by pulling it to the side a smidgen. After she was reassured that it was only me, she opened the door, but only enough for a snake to squirm into. Luckily, I was thin. I barely managed to squeeze in and, when I did, I saw the cause of obstruction. A chair. Why all the locks on the door? Why the chair beneath the door knob. I didn't know, but was about to find out.

Aunt Katarina's home consisted of one room. This multi-purpose, multi-task room was clean, though a little sloppy, but modestly up-kept. This tiny four-by-four-metre home provided a kitchen (an iron hot-plate on the table, with sets of two plates, two cups, a medium sized pot and a smaller one), a bedroom (a bed against the wall at the rear of the room) and a workplace (a singer sewing machine by the window and a chair, heavily padded with various scraps of colourful material). In the corner was an icon of Jesus Christ and a lit votive hanging in front of it. Patterns of dresses and the such were scattered about as well as loose threads and all the necessities of sewing.

Aunt Katarina never spoke of her past, only an iota of her past was mentioned by her. She would only say that she had a large family, they lived well, but now all is gone to the blazing fire. All is burned and consumed in the flames. She was bitter, she was a realist and she was headstrong. She refused to succumb to despair and found ways to manipulate destitution. She obviously couldn't provide a more spacious abode, regardless, she had a roof over her head and some food on her table. As I studied all, my surveillance was interrupted by Aunt Katarina.

"Vitya, are you hungry?"

I suddenly realized that I hadn't eaten in a while. My stomach did growl, but I had become accustomed to that and I was falling into a mild depression.

"Would you like to eat? We have eaten you know, but I believe we have some left over in the pot."

She took a small pot off the table and poured the remainder of their dinner into a bowl, the "popara" boiled stale bread. Agh! But I was hungry, now that she reminded me of eating. She gave me the bowl and began, "What brings you to us today, Vitya?"

"I missed Olga and you, of course. I also wanted to ask you what day is it today?"

Aunt Katarina didn't answer my question and Olga was sitting on the bed listening as Aunt Katarina continued, "How do you like the dinner?"

"It's fine, thank you."

"You know, Vitya, there's oil in there! Indeed, we have oil! I had repaired a jacket for a customer, who was so pleased that he gave us oil!"

She was proudly displaying the bottle of oil. I nodded and ate, without pleasure, despite the oil. I gulped the stale bread stew and chewed on the cornbread as quickly as I could, to fill my stomach and prevent any lingering aftertaste. I stared at the ground as I ate, avoiding eye contact with them. I noticed that she had no floor. It was ground, a dirt floor, thus she had a few handmade rugs scattered all over the ground.

I finished the task of eating. I asked Olga whether she had visited Mother lately.

"Yes," she replied. "They want to transfer Mother to some other destination, out of Belgrade."

"No! Absolutely not! That can't happen!" I unintentionally shouted.

"Who are you that you say it can't happen and prevent it?" Aunt Katarina cut in.

"I'm her son!"

"Yes, but you don't have the authority to determine, nor to prevent it."

"How can you say that? My mother isn't crazy you know!"

"I know. I know, dear, that she isn't. But...She is in the department of the mentally ill and they treat all the patients as such, equally, regardless of their ailment."

"What will I do now? Do you think she is still in Belgrade?"

"Yes, she is. Why, when Aunt Katarina and I visited Mother last time, we had a dreadful experience! We barely got in and were interrogated for a couple of hours. Due to Aunt Katarina's attire that day, which closely resembled those of the patients, they had assumed that Aunt Katarina was an escapee and, therefore, had given us a difficult time. By the time we had convinced them and proved them wrong, I was surprised that we saw Mother at all, for it was getting late. Unfortunately, Mother was not in good spirits; she begged us to take her out of the hospital and begged us for tea." Olga proclaimed and began to shed some tears.

Aunt Katarina stood up, draped a cape over her shoulders and announced her departure, stating she had some deliveries to make of altered goods. Olga and I were alone now. Even though I was comfortable with Aunt Katarina, I still practised caution and was reticent toward her. Especially because of her bitterness, I didn't want to remind her of the past, nor did I feel a need to inform her of my family's past. If anything, after all she was an adult, she might have known more than she portrayed.

I wanted to begin my discussion with Olga from the top, and just as I was about to begin she poured out words obliquely, unremittingly disclosing fragments of information and incoherently reiterating. I tried to stop her, she was very anxious to inform me of some kind of information. Finally, I managed to break her consistent ramblings and calmly requested her to elucidate the incident, for I didn't understand a thing she said, words were flying, names and the such.

"Vitya...Fine...It happened like this...There was a man and I was sitting here, you see, right here and, well...He began asking questions, about Mother and us...And, and..."

"Stop, Olga, slow down, you're too fast!"

"Vitya, I have to be, I'm not so sure how long Aunt Katarina will be gone, not that she forbade me to tell you, but I noticed she hadn't said anything herself to you. I must inform you, you are my brother!"

"Olga, all right, but I can't understand when you are mumbling and throwing words at me."

"Yes, Vitya, I'll slow down now.

"The man...Exquisitely dressed, a true gentleman, came here approximately a week ago. And you know how Aunt Katarina is about uninvited guests. She hesitated to open the door for this man. She was peeking at him through the corner of the window. Because of her strange attitude, I became frightened and hid underneath the blankets on the bed, after she had signalled me to be quiet with her finger on her mouth. Again, the knocking and now a deep voice was heard. Aunt Katarina tip-toed over to me and pulled the blanket off my face.

She was angry at me. 'Do you think this blanket is going to protect you? Go and take a peek through the window, perhaps you might recognize this gentleman?'

"I had no choice. I tip-toed over to the window, trying desperately not to knock anything down, for the room was in a disarray. I looked, I mean peeked, and I didn't recognize this man. He wore a top hat, a handsome suit and spats upon his lacquered, black shoes. His apparel and carriage had calmed me and I told Aunt Katarina that such a fine gentleman would probably do us no harm. She relented and we opened the door.

"The gentleman stood tall before us, cleanly shaven, with his hat now in his hand and a cane dangling from his arm. He practically walked in, without invitation, and we moved to allow him inside.

"'May I?' He pointed to the chair and, before we uttered a word, he sat down.

"'Who are you, sir? What brings you to us?' Aunt Katarina asked.

"'Oh my, forgive me! I am sorry! Allow me to introduce myself, I am Count____. I had to sit down immediately, for I have an injured leg and am usually not this impolite and unmannerly. I had spent a generous amount of time in front of your door, thus my leg began to hurt me. Yes, now I remember, I must go and release the coachman, for he, too, was waiting. I shall be back!' With that he left us.

"When this Count___ returned, he began his unusual discourse. You know, Vitya, I was unable to reach you, to tell you all this."

"Well, go on, Olga, tell me now!" I adjusted myself in a more comfortable position on the chair and waited for her to start.

"Fine...Yes and the gentleman, count, commenced, 'I have been sent by the Baroness Tamara in France and...'

"'Excuse me, but what does that have to do with us?' Aunt Katarina declared.

"'Allow me, Madam, I will inform you...Anyhow, the Baroness is the sister of this girl's mother,' and he pointed at me.

"'What of it?' Aunt Katarina suspiciously inquired.

"'Forgive me, sir, but there is nothing exemplary, nor beneficial, for this girl here, nor for myself due to that fact,' and she further professed, 'Do you not see, Count, how we live? I am struggling and barely making ends meet with my earnings and an added inconvenience is the Occupation we are under presently. We hardly have enough food to survive on and you came to inform us of this?' Aunt Katarina was becoming agitated.

"'Forgive me, Madam, I had no intention of discomforting you, nor insulting you. I had orders to come here and locate the sister of the Baroness. I had been to the White Monastery, with expectations of information regarding Zoya, but left them with the information of the daughter's whereabouts: Olga's that is. I was told she is residing with you, therefore I came here.'

"'I understand, sir...Count, it is correct. I did go to the monastery earlier and had asked permission for Olga to reside with me and gave them my address. Later I heard that Olga, instead of coming here to me from the monastery, had been sent directly home. She remained there until her mother Zoya was taken to the hospital, thus I took Olga and brought her here. It is all tangled, Count, all tangled.' Aunt Katarina had subsided with her frustrations and inquisitions now and was more serene.

"She asked the count, 'Tell us, how is the Baroness?'

"'Well, my dear friends...the Baroness had left Russia for France and, once there, she had met and married a Baron from Spain. The Baroness did have adequate means, the items she had taken with her from home in Russia. She was now moving in aristocratic circles and was doing quite splendidly, until her husband the "Baron" had abandoned her and took whatever he could from her.

"'Unfortunately it was later found out that he was in fact not a Baron at all and had purchased that title. Ultimately, the Baroness, Tamara, was devastated, but had chosen to keep the title, since she was already known by her friends and acquaintances as such. She did not hide the matters at all, in fact even confessed it. Regardless, all her friends and acquaintances urged Tamara and supported her decision in keeping the title de facto.'

"'Count, would it be correct to assume that perhaps you, yourself, are an imposter?'

"'In fact, dear Madam, you are quite correct in your accusation. I am not a count at all. To shorten a lengthy explanation, I had to travel incognito and, due to the fact that the Germans and Italians were allies, I had to assume this personage, thus enabling my travels through Italy, arriving here.'

"'I understand. Where is the Baroness that is Tamara, momentarily?'

"'She is in Paris and she has remarried a former colonel of the Tsarist's guards, who now is simply a taxi driver in Paris. They are happy together and have no children of their own, thus I was to locate her sister Zoya and seek permission to bring one child, at least, back to Paris with me. I hadn't located Zoya, but rather her daughter, and was hoping of an elaboration with you, Madam, and am grateful for the information you provided me with as to the location of Zoya. I understand she is not well, thus you and I might come to an agreement.'

"'How, sir, could you possibly do such a thing? She is not a parcel to tuck away in your suitcase and simply leave the country!'

"'Rest assured, I had already arranged the possibility of adding one child to my passport, you see here,' and the count displayed his passport and continued, 'I have arranged all the necessary paperwork ahead of time and it was just a matter of retrieving the child. The paperwork would be taken care of here by my connections.'

"Needless to say, Aunt Katarina was very quiet, listened keenly to all that the count had to say, finally exploding into demands of his immediate departure, followed by threats of calling the police, had he the intention of returning to us. She wouldn't hear of it. To trust a stranger? Why he could be a notorious criminal, a pathological liar! The man, Vitya, had left without so much as saying good-bye; he fled when he heard all the cursing and threatening of Aunt Katarina. I don't think he was frightened, he was more frustrated than anything.

"And there you have it. The entire dubious affair. Do you know that I haven't left this room since that man visited us? It is terrible. I feel I am becoming claustrophobic. I am in dire need of a walk in some fresh air. I think…Hope that Aunt Katarina is less paranoid now."

"Olga, it is an intractable incident indeed! It is curious as to how he knows of our family? I am not certain if it is quite an obscurity, but it is to an extent enigmatic. He must have spoken some truth, after all, how would he know that we have an aunt in Paris, France? He also mentioned our mother's name as for the rest of his story, I cannot vouchsafe, it would be audacious.

"Frankly, Olga, I don't feel you should worry about it, for if he hasn't returned yet, it is presumable that he won't, especially after Aunt Katarina's berating." I had just finished my sentence and at that instant the door unlocked and Aunt Katarina came in.

"Vitya, it is late, son. Perhaps you should go now?" she politely suggested while holding the door open. I had no intention of verifying matters with her and was tired, thus I left them.

The visit I had with them did benefit me. I was not concentrating on my catastrophic problems and was consumed in Olga's story. How odd. Our Aunt Tamara was looking for our mother; in addition to that, she wanted one of us! How amusing! I was strolling back home with these thoughts and chanced upon some strangers discoursing on the corner of the streets.

I heard one of the men claim that the Red Army had invaded Belgrade. Agh…Let them come, I have enough problems of my own, rather than dwell on that issue. I arrived home safely. As usual I went to bed directly, for sitting alone and contemplating was not on the agenda for that night.

October…much colder now. The grey, overcast and melancholy day with dark, bare tree branches swaying, couldn't possibly enhance a person's countenance, let alone an already depressed being. That morning I had awoke to gunshots. Everything shook. Yes...that's right, the Red Army! I heard of that last night on the street! I wonder if it is them that are shooting? I was tremulous, no doubt. The stories I had the opportunity of hearing of them did not portray them as cuddly bears, but vicious tyrants. I sat there on the kitchen chair, stared at the dirty wall and pondered. They are Russian, though. I am Russian. I don't know what to think. Half the day went by in this manner and in continual gun shooting.

I noticed that our neighbour flew by my window, hunched! Was he dodging bullets? He was either hiding, scared or actually dodging bullets! This spectacle aroused an even greater timidity in me.

Our neighbour, who lived just above us, had a wife and a daughter of my age. Rarely were they visible. I only knew that he had worked at the Ikarus factory as a machine operator and his wife worked there also. Their daughter was rather haughty and snobby. Whenever she would pass by my home, she would hold her nose, signifying that my home was smelly. What a snob! I knew my home was not clean any longer, but even if it had smelled, which I couldn't grant nor deny the fact, I had always kept everything closed, window and door.

The murky silhouette of my neighbour, due to the dirty, smeared window, had caused me to remain indoors a while longer—that and the gunshots. Looking over to our icon in the corner, with the votive hanging in front of it, which I couldn't light for lack of oil, I decided to pray a small prayer. In this escapade—the war, the invasion, the gunshots, the loneliness, the hunger and depravation—I implored God to help me and guide me and give me courage to leave the security of my empty, sullen abode.

The streets seemed to be abandoned. Seldom a person might appear and then quickly disappear. Gunshots were incessant. Perhaps I could go to the bakery, maybe it was bombed or shot? I was reminiscent of the earlier days with Alex, when we sought food as scavengers after the bombing.

Who knows, I might have luck? I went to the nearest bakery.

Very soon, my dreams of bread vanished. The bakery wasn't shot at, nor broken into. I had no alternative but to seek food elsewhere, or a job, whatever was feasible and available. I went toward King Alexander Street.

At the corner of King Alexander Street, I observed clusters of crowds. There was a gathering of many people. As I came up closer, I noticed that the entire street was filled with masses of people shouting, waving, celebrating. My howling stomach as a wolf in a forest was demanding food, but I ignored it and was enthralled by the commotion. I wove through the crowd, which was easy, and suddenly saw a colony of tanks parading down the street. There was no end to the colony of tanks. I observed a soldier protruding from the shaft of the tank and gleaming with a smile and waving to the hysterical crowds, while flowers were being tossed at him.

The tanks were heading toward the centre of the city and, as they were doing so, the ground shook as if an earthquake was occurring. Aha! The war is over! That's why the celebration! No more rationing, no more begging, but food! Now I can obtain a good job! Excellent! I was overcome with ecstasy!

I was carried within the massive jubilant crowd, practically floated amongst them. I spotted a tank that was turning away from the colony and now headed toward the sidewalk. Oh no! Will he run over the people? Noticing this, the crowd began dispersing. The tank didn't run over the people, he only pulled off to the side. Once that was realized, the crowd continued rejoicing and the masses grew larger. The air was painted with hundreds of colourful flowers, flying everywhere as if it were raining flowers! I looked up at the windows of the buildings and saw that every window was filled with people dangling out of them, waving flags and even rugs! Shouts were heard and there were more flowers flying from above and below! The atmosphere was ecstatic, jubilant and celebratory. What a scenery! I wasn't exactly certain as to what they were celebrating about. I assumed the ending of the war.

What exactly was happening I was unaware of and couldn't put a finger on; nevertheless, I joined in the festivities, for the exuberant crowd with its magnetic enthusiasm had lured me in, thus I, too, was happy. Another relevant and beneficial circumstance was that they were so wrapped up in their celebrations, they didn't even notice, nor care, of my pauper appearance. All eyes were glued to the tanks and the liberating forces (which I later found out about).

Courageously, I walked up to the tank that had pulled off to the side of the street and I put my foot on top of the caterpillar and climbed right on top of the tank with full authority. Wow! I was now standing atop the massive fifty-two-ton vehicle! I had a panoramic view of the street, the colourful crowd and the long trail of the colony of tanks. The young and old were pushing forward toward the tanks, they even looked at me and smiled at me as if I were a part of their cause of celebrations and I didn't mind that attention, for I was swept up in the occasion, nearly floating of joy.

Fully absorbed in the festivities, I now felt like a hero! I began daydreaming and thought of how the masses of people were saluting me and throwing flowers at me, until a loud voice broke my moment in the limelight. "Hey you! Who are you? Get down!" I observed he instructed me in Russian!

Aha! Russians! How pleasant that sounded to me, my mother tongue. I missed speaking my language with my family, save for Olga and Aunt Katarina. Even his scolding was endearing to me.

The soldier, seeing that I didn't move an inch, erupted, "Did you here me, boy! Get down right now!" For some reason, I froze, I couldn't move, nor speak. I was frightened, yet pleased. I heard that if a person is caught in such a situation, they should pinch themselves and snap them back to reality. I did. I pinched my leg and yelled out, "Ouch." It did help, for the next word immediately flew out of my mouth, "Zdravstvuitse." The soldier looked at me in surprise.

Chapter 15

The soldier who was angry and yelled at me was suddenly interested in having a conversation with me and stated, "Kid, how is it that you speak Russian so clearly?"

"Yes, sir, I do. I am Russian. I speak just as you do."

"What's that you say? Hmph, look at yourself, kid. You can't be Russian!"

"I am, sir. Listen, sir, my parents came from Russia, when...I mean, they are Russian and I was born here, but we only speak Russian amongst ourselves. But, sir...may I tell you, I am hungry, very hungry." I held my stomach as I was claiming this. "Please, sir, if possible, may I have some bread?"

At once the soldier bellowed out, "Comrades, give me some food here. There is a hungry child here and he's Russian, too! See what you have."

The Russian soldier looked at me and then reprimanded me for addressing him as a "sir." He instructed me that from now on, I should address everyone as "comrade."

At once, emerging from the shaft of the tank was bread, mushrooms, canned goods, even cigarettes! He gave it all to me! As he was handing the articles, I was shoving them in my inner pocket of my jacket. Soon, my bosom was full. I nearly fell off the tank, from the joy and gratefulness I felt. I wanted to scream! Why, these are my brothers! They are of my blood! I won't be hungry anymore! My family...My family won't be hungry and we could be together! Oh, the joy!

Once I settled down and restored my equanimity, I pulled

back from the crowd, who were still revelling and I recalled a time when the gathering of such people, the crowds on the street occurred. Although, it was not a celebratory occasion, rather a sombre one. A black assemblage.

The city was mourning a loss very dear to them. Ladies dressed in black, with black veils over their faces, crying. Men, too, were not excluded from this exhibit of sorrow. Even little children watching their parents cry had, for that reason, begun to cry as well. The people began to drop to their knees as did Mother and she pulled me down on my knees, too. I was not aware of the cause of this sorrow, nor of the parade? All of a sudden I saw the most beautiful horses ever! One huge, white horse lead two other white horses, which were pulling the wagon containing the casket of King Alexander. The procession was long and elegantly sorrowful. "Mother, look! Those horses, they are beautiful!" I exclaimed and Mother quickly shushed me. The funeral procession was headed toward Oplenac, located on the mountain, where most of the Karadjordjevich dynasty was laid to rest. The day was bitterly grey and sullen as if ordered to be so, particularly for the sad and historical occasion.

Few days later (I was sustaining myself on the gifts I received from the soldier), I decided to revisit my new friend the "tankist." I marched outside confidently and intended to go directly to my new acquaintance.

The day, cold, but unusually bright and sunny, which brightened my already pleasant mood. People were outside, I even greeted a few on the way; they, on the other hand, looked me over and turned their heads. Regardless, I was in too good of spirits for even that insult to weigh me down. The people were walking freely and with an air of relief as they scrambled to complete their duties as if it were previously on hold, during the occupation and now with this new liberation, they were bustling about, determined to continue their once calm and normal lives.

It was the first time I had seen the Partisans. They wore uniforms and were heavily armed, with tracks of bullet casings draped over their shoulders. They wore a peasant's cap with a red star on the front. On their feet some had the traditional folk shoes (with a curled tip at the front of the shoe), made of pig skin. One of these soldiers (Paritsan) was escorting a German prisoner, who had his arms in the air. Some passers-by stopped to observe this, some began cursing and some even tried to hit the prisoner. The crowd began to gather around the Partisan and the prisoner.

Now the people were becoming an unruly and rebellious mob, seeking their revenge on the prisoner. The Partisan soldier, once realizing the scope of the matter, had summoned more soldiers to assist him. He was now pushing back the horde of angry people who were shouting, "Where did you find that monster?! Kill him! Who invited him here!" The Partisan, now unable to control the madness, began thundering, "Step back, I order you to step back!" A boiling confrontation was about to ensue between the crowd, the prisoner and nearly the Partisan, too! The German captive pulled in his head like a turtle, he was indefinite whether he would receive protection from his Partisan captor.

Three more Partisan guards came to the rescue and assisted the first Partisan soldier. They encircled the prisoner, thus protecting him from the raging mass. In this manner they went to the school where the German prisoners were held. This school was located behind a factory called "Boston," later renamed "Proleter."

After the unusual exhibit, the crowd dispersed and I was left to seek my new friend, my "tankist." He was nowhere in sight. There goes my aspirations and assumptions! Where do I look for food now?

I was at Olga's previously and gave them some food and the such. I triumphantly recited my adventure to them, regarding the tank, the soldier and the gifts I received. Of course, Aunt Katarina was thunderstruck and reprimanded me. She was reminding me of what horror those "Reds" did in Russia. I didn't know what to say to her.

My hunger and desolate state persevered and my pride was defeated. It was a difficult dilemma, when the opponents hunger and pride were in dispute and hunger being the omnipotent of the two, won. Naturally, I agreed with Aunt Katarina, but did have a valid excuse and told her so. She softened her tone, but persisted on displaying her displeasure. I reasoned with her, "When we were under German occupation, Aunt Katarina, we had no food, save for the horrendous stew at the Russian Centre. Now I was given food. In hunger, political opinions and idealism are secondary discernment."

"Vitya, I had informed you before that these 'do-gooders,' as you might think they are, killed my entire family in Baku and I barely saved my head!"

It was of no use to further rationalize, thus I simply nodded. Curiously, in retrospect, she did accept the articles I gave them, knowing very well where they were derived from.

I casually slipped out of Aunt Katarina's home that day and her irrefutable declarations. It was cold outside and, looking down at my shoddy pants, full of holes, thought I must somehow replace them with new "used" pants, before the snow drapes our city. I shrunk within my coat, thinking I might hide from the snapping winds.

As I was walking home, I noticed a Russian tank, surrounded by soldiers. On the streetcar tracks were more of these tanks. I came up to one of the soldiers, who was busily searching for something within his sack.

"Zdravstvuitse!" I greeted him with a tone of familiarity.

The soldier casually looked up, back down, and returned the greeting nonchalantly. Determined to begin a conversation I started, "Where are you from, brother?"

"Me? Do you not see? Russia!"

I realized that he wasn't amused at my Russian speaking, nor of my non-accent. Nevertheless, I continued, "I see, yes I see."

The soldier, now agitated, "Well? What of it? Go away, kid!"

Agh! I accomplished exactly nil. I turned around and began to drag myself away. I spotted an army truck behind him and estimated a more beneficial meeting there.

"Stop! You...kid, come back here!"

I turned around and the nonchalant soldier was now summoning me back. He had an implorative expression to him.

"You speak fluent Russian!"

"Yes." Now he notices?

A brief discussion was held. I informed him of my family, well at least partially, and he informed me of his. He asked me where my parents were now and I told him exactly as is, my father abandoned us, my mother was ill in the hospital.

"Who feeds you, kid?"

"I do. I eat when I have food, when I find food."

I then told him of the incidence with the previous soldier, who gave me food. He now understood what I was looking for. I felt nauseous from hunger and all the talking. The soldier began poking into his ruck-sack and fumbling things within it. He pulled out a can and then another and told me to stand there and wait for him. He went to the army truck.

The canvas was flipped over to one side on the back of the truck. Two young female soldiers were calling me. Their soft, harmonious voices rang in the air. I went to them and they began handing me cans of food. I received three more cans from them in total. One of the girls even threw me a loaf of bread! My amazement was unsurpassed! Again, my bosom was full. I started immediately to bite and chew on the bread, which was a little dry, but tasty. They were equally amused spying on me and began giggling amongst themselves. In that escapade, I suddenly saw them become stiff as statues. They stood erect as candles. I looked at them in bewilderment.

"What is this here! Is this a circus or an army?!" A very loud, deep and thundering voice behind me demanded. I slowly turned around, only to find a mountainous human towering over me. He was enormous! He had a motley assortment of medals pinned on the chest of his uniform. He had a belt criss-crossing his chest and a holster for his revolver. His uniform was heavily starched and pressed. His riding pants were tucked into two large and tall, shiny leather boots.

"Who's that? Why are you gathering here? This is not a social event here!" The officer was obviously annoyed and brushed me away with his hand as he finished his sentence. I looked at the soldier that was previously nonchalant, now erect, in a saluting position, his hand trembling. Poor soldier, I thought.

What will be of him now? My poor friends, how they will suffer now? What a mean and arrogant officer! Perhaps it was officers like these that caused all the slaughter and chaos in Russia during the revolution?

Why was he so exasperated? Did I really look like a threat to this monstrous convoy? I was hardly standing on my feet, weak from hunger and my mendicancy couldn't possibly offer intimidation. I left them and headed home.

A drizzle began to fall, I hurried home and as I did so, the cans began jingling in my pockets. I took a short cut home and soon arrived. I instantaneously marched into the room and went to bed. I despised sitting alone at home, thus I avoided being there, except of course, to sleep. The morbid silence was menacing. Between the dirty, torn rags I lay, even they won't talk to me. Tomorrow I'll go to the centre of town. Yes…Tomorrow, downtown.

The next morning I awoke with the thoughts of rent. I had food now, sufficient for a week, but the rent must be paid. I heard that people were losing their homes and businesses. Who cares? I don't own anything anyway. The previous occupiers currency was worthless now. Not that I had any to begin with, thus these facts were not particularly bothersome to me.

I tossed the rags about on my bed, searching for my pants. It was dreadfully cold outside. It was November, but I wasn't certain what day it was. I'd find out when I leave home.

I went to the Stari Djeram Piazza. Some peasants were already setting up their food at the kiosks, though, many were empty. There were plenty of vegetables and fruits, but meat was still scarce. I perceived that I had no interest at the piazza, thus I began aimlessly wandering.

A Russian soldier was bargaining with a peasant woman, or at least attempting to. His intention was to purchase a bottle of plum brandy. He planned to barter his boots. She complained and stated, "Yosh pare!" He was dumbfounded and lost. Obviously, I went over to the two of them. I informed him that she wanted money in addition to the boots. He understood that she meant, "It's time for a change!" When he learned of the error, he laughed heartily. The woman was puzzled. They exchanged the goods and both were satisfied. I walked away.

The bargaining soldier I interpreted for, called me back. The usual discourse ensued. Once we ended this perfunctory elaborations he patted my head and blurted out, "What is it that you want?"

"Nothing. I have food right now." I hesitated on replying, since I assumed that these soldiers were only able of providing canned goods.

"Kid, you look like an urchin! Look at yourself! And, and...Your shoes! They're falling apart; that thin wire you have wrapped around it isn't doing its duty well!"

"So what! There are worse you know!" I offensively snapped at him.

"Come with me, I'll dress you and we'll begin with the shoes!"

We left together, in spite of my contempt. My dire need for clothing was insuperable, therefore I yielded to the soldier.

We went to the school. The school where they kept the prisoners. They didn't look very mighty now, rather pathetic. They had no more ties, shoelaces, belts or other accessories. They were all sullenly content just sitting there.

"Pick the shoes and pants you want!" the soldier commanded, while pointing his finger at the prisoners' shoes.

And they, the prisoners, were now gawking at us in a nervous state, completely anxious. I was beguiled at their humbleness, especially when considering my own wretched appearance. Why were they frightened of me, when I looked worse than they did?

"Pick! Go on, pick the shoes you want!" the soldier restlessly commanded.

"Listen, sir...I mean, comrade, what will be of the one who I choose the shoes and pants from?"

"Ugh! You really want to know everything, kid, don't you?!" He pointed his forefinger at his temple, forming a shape of a gun and uttered, "Boom, boom."

I shivered. "No! No, I don't want the pants, nor shoes, thank you anyway. I really don't need them. I have some at home, really!"

Lord! For a pair of shoes and pants to have someone killed? Never! Regardless of who they were and what they did to me, I would never have peace with myself. It would be torture!

"Listen, comrade...thank you for your help, but I must go!"

"Go then!" he shouted as if I had insulted him.

I ran. I couldn't bare to be there another second, in that bleak and foreboding atmosphere.

A month ago, these same prisoners were revelling and boasting of authority, now they were half-naked and hungry, just like me. It was true, though, who invited them? Regardless, I still held the belief that every soul is not at fault. Some soldiers were forced to abide by the rules and orders, yet some were thrilled to control and cause affliction. It was not for me to surmise, nor to contemplate.

Now in the centre of the city, Terraziye, were many pedestrians, all rushing about doing their own business and I intertwined amongst them. "Yok!" an elderly man shouted as yet another Russian soldier was participating in an exchange of goods. I came closer to them and observed the situation.

The elderly man wasn't aware of what the soldier had wanted. The Russian soldier was attempting to trade his watch for a bottle of vodka, though it was plum brandy he received in the final result, for plum brandy was commonplace and peasants were noted for their excellence in producing the finest plum brandy. When I explained to the elderly man that the soldier wanted a bottle in exchange for his watch, the man proclaimed, "Well why didn't he tell me he wants brandy?" I left them satisfied.

I walked over to the building named Albaniya. At that time, it was the tallest building in Belgrade. The large, gaping hole at the side of the building was still present and reminding all of the previous bombardment and occupation. While I stood there reflecting and staring at the hole, I felt someone's hand on my shoulder. It was the Russian soldier who bartered his watch for the brandy.

"Where are you headed, little guy?"

"Nowhere."

"Come with me, I'll introduce you to the major, since you were good enough to help me back there with that old man."

I had nothing better to do, thus I agreeably left, besides, it isn't often one gets to meet a major!

"Who's the major?" I asked, while skipping alongside the soldier.

"That you'll find out."

We were headed toward Kalemegdan. At the foot of the park, I noticed a Cossack, that is, a man in a Cossack's uniform. The soldier told me to stand there and wait. He approached this "Cossack," they saluted each other. The Cossack stood up and they both walked a few steps farther from me. Then...The soldier turned to face me and was waving for me to join them. I came up to them, looking at one, then the other. The soldier introduced the major to me and further informed me that the major decided to enroll me in the army!

Because I was too young to be a soldier, I was to become an assistant to the major.

"Do you know the duties of an assistant?" the soldier inquired of me.

"A little, I once was listening to a conversation between some people and they were discussing exactly this. It was regarding some soldier named Shveg, and the responsibilities he had to carry out orders."

"Indeed...Well, now you will serve the major."

"Will I get a uniform?"

"Wait and I'll go find out."

The soldier turned and proceeded toward the major who had already returned to his previous position. In a matter of seconds, the soldier returned and announced that I should be come back at the park tomorrow, at ten in the morning and I would receive a uniform.

"Do you understand, little guy?"

"Yes, yes I do! Thank you, sir...I mean comrade, thank you!"

The soldier had also instructed me as to how I was to greet another soldier, by saluting with my hand to my forehead. I was also instructed to address him as lieutenant, for he was just promoted a minute ago. I was astonished at this expeditious promotion and of all places, here in the park! Not bad, I mused, perhaps I will also receive a promotion quickly. I asked the soldier regarding the possibilities of my own promotion.

He answered, "Not so fast, little guy. First you must serve him for years as I did."

"Agh, that's a long time!"

"What do you want, kid? You haven't even smelled the gunpowder yet and you are aiming at a promotion?! Be glad and overjoyed that he is accepting you in the service!"

I nodded in agreement. Am I ever lucky! A uniform! How gallant, how prestigious, how wonderful I will look! From rags to a uniform! I was now admiring the major and his uniform. What authority he has! He raised the rank of that soldier to lieutenant in minutes and right there before me, in this park! The soldier wasn't attired exactly as one would expect, though; he would probably receive his new uniform once he returns to his quarters, I guessed.

The lieutenant suggested I leave now and pointed to the direction from where we came. Immediately I saluted him and uttered, "Understood, Comrade Lieutenant!" I left them and nearly bounced back home from joy. I knew it. I knew it would be beneficial to visit the centre of town today!

Ha! I am a soldier! I won't be hungry now! I won't be thirsty either! I won't be dressed shabbily! I will have shoes, too! Oh the joy! Now I can proudly prance in front of the landlord in my uniform! My head was swelling from all the pride and dreams of revenge. Why, when Olga sees me! We are going to be happy, no more begging! Uff! This does not happen to everyone! Who should I tell? What will Mother say? No! I can't tell her. There's a thing with mothers and armies. They don't mix well.

I walked by our neighbours as I entered the courtyard of my home. They stated that the war was still in force? I thought that the war was over! The Germans were battling continuously. Hmm...what about me? Where would I be sent? Luckily, I won't be at the front, for I am serving the major. Perhaps I'll become a staff sergeant? No, that would take many years. My mind was swirling with all these marvellous thoughts.

At home, I sat down to continue my gloating. I couldn't help to wonder how the major raised the rank of the soldier to lieutenant in the park and without ceremony? As far as I know and what I've heard from the tiny shreds of information from my father, when he did actually talk, usually was of the army and the ceremonies, etc. After all, he was an officer of the White Army, thus I had learned, actually overheard a little about the methods of obtaining a higher rank.

It was through training, experience and knowledge that one would earn and receive a higher rank.

Nevertheless, that didn't interfere with my daydreaming. I decided that perhaps, because we were in a state of belligerence, the major had raised the soldier's rank unceremoniously and in the park, at that. The main thing was that, I was a soldier now and I wouldn't be hungry, nor poor.

It was six in the morning, the crack of dawn. I was on my feet, ready to report and receive my much awaited for, uniform. I no longer was in a desperate need of my alarm clock, for my late friend Judas (Mr.Vlado), taught me how to get up in the morning without a clock. I was to tell myself what time I wanted to get up the next day. Surely enough, it worked. Once I had mastered this technique, I used it often.

I left my home at seven. The air was brisk, fresh and smelled of burning wood. I hurried along the ascending street to reach King Alexander Street. I noticed that people were already bustling about. I hardly paid any attention to them, for I, too, had a mission, an appointment and a place where I had to be. I was drunk with the thoughts of my new uniform and duties.

"Agh!" Did the wire have to break now? Now my shoe was flip-flopping as I rushed to the park. With high hopes I limped, dragging my shoe to the park, knowing that soon I would be rid of these ridiculous annoyances and replace them with decent shoes. I was not too far from the park, when a pedestrian stopped to light his cigarette in front of me. Good! I could use a break and obtain a light from the man, too. After all, it was still early and I had to repair my shoe. I yanked out a cigarette butt from my pocket, a good one, with plenty left on it to smoke.

"Excuse me, comrade, may I?" The man who was simply dressed as a worker and wore a katchket (cap) on his head, looked me over from head to foot. He didn't seem to be annoyed that I addressed him as comrade. I noticed and learned that people were no longer using the terms "sir"nor "madam" when acknowledging each other on the streets.

It is said that there was no longer a distinction of classes. No high society, no middle class, no lower class, all equal. Judging from where I stood, I couldn't agree with this "new" temperament and state. With no real inclination to consider the facts, since I was now a soldier and proud of it. I pulled a heavy drag of my cigarette and pondered.

With a sudden burst of authority I demanded, "Listen, comrade, what time is it?"

Momentarily the man's eyes shot a piercing gaze at me, his eyebrows joined and he retorted, "You, kid, didn't have the common courtesy to thank me for the light and now you demand the time and in such a tone? Go away, you scoundrel!"

Quickly, I regained my senses as I was slapped with this statement. I floated back to earth and earnestly implored, "Forgive me...comrade...I mean, sir...Forgive me! I became confused, sir, I mean comrade, in this new situation, I am not certain of how to address you! You know, sir, comrade, not long from now, I will become a soldier! I am headed right now to the park to receive my uniform. I am to meet with the major and lieutenant!"

The man took a step back, with an amused look on his face; he most likely thought of me as insane. He quietly replied to my foremost question, "It's nine," and he left in a hurry.

At the park, the bare trees stood upon the leaf-covered ground. The smell of these leaves were pleasant and I was standing there, alone, with no one around me. For a few seconds, I thought of my crassness with that man and I flushed of embarrassment. That didn't last long, for I was becoming worried of the non-appearance of my uniform and the men who were to bring it. I shivered, and the wind blew its cold autumn air, directed from the river nearby.

Where are the men? Where are the people? There's no one to be seen! Will my dream be only a fantasy? There goes my uniform! There goes my new life! No...no, I must be patient and wait. Yes, I must not jump to conclusions, I must wait. Of course, I mused, they must have obligations to fulfill and then will come here. As I stood there consoling myself and staring at the pebbled path, which led to the factory producing military uniforms, I remembered Aunt Katya, for she worked at that factory.

I wondered where she was now? I hadn't seen her in a long time. The last time was when she took George to the orphanage. Speaking of aunts, I recalled that I didn't visit my Aunt Nina either. Was she still selling flowers in the tavern since the liberation? When I receive my uniform, I will search for her. This train of thoughts led me to a mournful scenery I had encountered....

A mother wrapped in black was discussing the state of war and her loss of her son at the "Sremski" front, but a few days ago. Here I thought that the war was well over, with the arrival of the Russians. Yet the war persisted and the year was 1944. I surveyed the area around me and observed flags with red stars in the centre, dangling from windows of the apartments. Was the entire city under this influence? Was it a facade? Who knows.

While I was immersed in these thoughts, I saw my Russian comrades approaching. The lieutenant was carrying something under his arm. I was waving to them frantically. They came! They actually arrived here to meet me and my uniform is here, too! The major stood before me as a hero, with his hands on his hips and a cape draped over him, displaying his revolver and sword. He was gallant in the Cossack's uniform, though the star on the uniform didn't compliment it much and seemed actually, rather odd. The lieutenant was still modestly attired, save for his cap.

The lieutenant handed me the parcel he was carrying, it was wrapped in this greyish paper. "Here, take this. Later, you will receive the remainder of the uniform." I shook as I took the package from his hands. I was speechless, nor did I know what to say. I held this object close to my chest with terror and reverence.

"Tomorrow, report here for duty!" the lieutenant broke the awkward silence. We saluted each other, though the lieutenant did gently reprimand me, for I was not to salute with a bare head, but with the cap on. I nodded in compliance, without uttering a word, save for, "Understood." They walked away as did I, nearly tripping over a branch on the ground, for my eyes were glued to the package.

I ran home, still clutching onto the package, hugging it, lest someone takes it, or I drop it. I flew through the courtyard and straight into my kitchen. I turned on the lights, pulled the rags on the windows, for no one to peer inside and placed the treasure on the table. Gawking at the package, I began to think...Now I must leave the family, not that they are here, but I mean I couldn't visit them. I had important and serious duties now and obligations! My hands quivered as I began to unwrap the greyish package.

An army coat, a cap with a star on it and a bayonet. No shoes, no shirt and no pants. But the lieutenant did say I would receive the remainder of the uniform at a later time. I tried on the overcoat, it was too big and too long, just about two fingers off the floor. I had no belt either. Where would I hang the bayonet? That, too, resembled a sword, for it was long and I not tall enough. I found a rope to use as a belt. I placed the cap on my head, which also was too big for me and fell over my ears. I had to gather my shoulder-length hair and shove it underneath the cap. Ironically, I was now fully and impartially dressed in uniform. I yanked the bayonet from its case. Agh, it was a rusty old bayonet! I found a cloth and began to wipe it, not much rust came off.

It was a tragic-comic situation, I was wearing this uniform and my torn pants were somewhat covered by the size of the overcoat, but my shoes! At least if they had included the shoes! I must be patient, for I know I will receive them, eventually. In this state, I decided to go to Olga's and show off my new uniform, my new status...A military authority! I decided to avoid gloating in front of the landlord, until I received the rest of the uniform.

I walked to Olga's and I provoked some stares, some giggles and some untactful comments, which did not bother me, for I believed that they were most likely jealous of my uniform. Arriving in front of their door, I began to bang restlessly, eager to present myself.

Olga opened the door, then slammed it shut, in my face. Why did she do that? I tried again and received no reply. Hmm. "Olgaaaaa! Open the door! It's me, Vitya!" Finally, she recognized my voice and opened the door.

"What's with you? Why did you slam the door?"

"Sorry, Vitya, I didn't know it was you."

"Look at me, Olga! Look, I'm a soldier!"

"Get in, Vitya, hurry up, Aunt Katarina isn't home. I don't think Aunt Katarina would be in a congratulatory mood when finding you dressed like that! Vitya...Why are you wearing that?"

"Olga, we suffered enough! And we begged enough! Now, I will be able to support us all!"

"What are you babbling about, Vitya? You are too young!"

"Stop, Olga! Don't speak that way!"

"What's this whole army thing, Vitya?"

"Olga, sit down and I'll tell you exactly what occurred and how I became a soldier!"

I recited the matter to Olga and she didn't say much, except for a few "uh-huhs," and a few nods. The matter was already settled and I wouldn't hear of any negative lectures. I ended my discussion with her, by instructing her to return home, of course, after she visited Mother. We hugged and I left.

Now...Aunt Nina's! I went directly to her home and was escorted with the same jeers as when I had left for Olga's. Regardless, I walked quickly, it was enough that I was proud and felt honourable. After pounding on Aunt Nina's door for a few minutes, a neighbour opened her door and poked out her head to see who the disgruntled pounder was.

She was a rather hefty lady, with a black handkerchief tied around her head and large dark eyes that were gawking at me.

When she noted my cap, she suddenly inquired in a soft-spoken voice, "Who are you looking for, comrade?" Was it the cap on my head, or the bayonet that summoned respect, I was not certain, but I was surprised at how her comportment had quickly changed.

"Where is Nina Nikolaievna?"

"Oh, she is at her friend's home. She had to go to tend to her friend, for her friend is ill."

"Do you know her address?" I inquired in a rougher manner and deepened my voice purposely, thinking it would deliver me all that I asked for.

"No, comrade, she didn't give me the address. She has only been home a couple of times since you Russians came, and very briefly at that."

The hefty lady was now hanging on to her door knob, signalling that she meant to close the door and the conversation was over.

"Wait!" I ordered. "If she returns home, tell her that her nephew was here looking for her and that he is now a Russian soldier!"

For some reason, I wanted to portray that my aunt had military protection from the Russian army, and what kind of impression I had imparted on her I wasn't certain of, for she simply and hurriedly answered, "Fine," and vanished behind her door.

I was now trekking along Groblyanska Street and found a convoy of wagons of the Russian army. I also discovered that there was an outdoor kitchen. I was hungry. I decided to go to them. A huge, herculean army pot was stewing over a hot plate. I reasoned that since I was a soldier, they must feed me. I saluted them. I walked over to the chef and told him I was hungry.

"Give me your bowl and I'll pour you some soup."

"I don't have a bowl."

"Why didn't you get one from the wagon?"

I began mumbling some irrelevant excuses and he headed to the wagon to fetch me a bowl. With a tin bowl in hand, he began to pour me the soup, right to the rim. "I'm sure you have no spoon either?"

"I don't."

"Here," and he gave me a spoon that he whipped out of his pocket.

I saluted him and went to lean against the wagon and enjoy my meal. Now...It sure is good to be a soldier!

As I was devouring this soup of rice, potatoes and meat, nearly to the point of licking the bowl, I heard a voice behind me.

"What, you like it?" The chef imploratively looked at me.

"Oh, yes, indeed! I do like it, very much! I haven't eaten this well in a long time!"

"Do you want some more?"

"Yes, please. I would very much!"

"Come over here," and he took my bowl and I followed him.

"Them over there, they don't think that I am a good enough chef and that I don't know how to cook and look at you, you would like more!"

He poured me a generous helping again. I informed him that I am not with this division and that I was recruited yesterday by the major and lieutenant. I strived to depict an air of authority to myself, by mentioning major and lieutenant.

The chef analysed me with his eyes and then asked, "What are your duties?"

"Adjutant, that is...One below."

The chef waved his hand in the air and left me to continue his cooking. I was now thinking to visit Mother.

To visit my mother would entail a good amount of travel time. I simply could not hang on to the traffic as I did before, not with this uniform. I had no money for the fare either. What to do? I walked up to Vuk's Monument. The darn bayonet kept hitting the side of my leg, causing it to bruise. A fiacre was passing me by and I was debating whether to hook on. The fiacre stopped right in front of me. One Partisan soldier came out and gave the coachman a piece of paper while he stated, "Charge the Army Command Headquarters!" Aha! A stroke of lightening just hit me! I know what to do now! That fiacre had already left, but another soon arrived. I waved it over to me.

I went inside and declared, "Drive to the city hospital," and he did.

When I had arrived at the city hospital, I did as I had earlier seen the other soldier do. I asked him for a piece of paper and pen. I wrote on the paper, "For the service of driving a Russian soldier," and I signed it. I gave him the paper and told him to charge the Russian Army Headquarters. The coachman took the paper, mumbled something and left. I walked confidently toward the gates of the hospital.

Before I went in to Mother's room, I had taken off my coat and cap. I had no intention of announcing to her of my new status. Mother was delighted upon seeing me and we spent a good several hours chatting about anything and everything, except for my new title. I left her, parting with a gift of some canned food and cigarettes. I was satisfied of the day's events; I was tired and happy, most of all eager for the next day to arrive and my duties to begin.

The next morning found me fresh, exhilarated and ready for the duties I was to receive at Kalemegdan park. I washed, dressed and left my home to the meeting place of my commanders.

We all left together heading toward the bridge called "Zemunski Most," meaning, "Zemun Bridge," for the bridge over the Danube River led to the suburb Zemun. I was seated at the rear of the truck and my two comrades in front. The lieutenant instructed the truck driver to take us to a city called Novi Sad. He (the truck driver) took us only to Beochin town, informing us that he was not going any farther than that. This town was known for owning the largest cement producing factory. The truck driver dropped us off at the train station in that town.

The major and lieutenant were sauntering along the platform of the train station, deliberately leaving me behind, so that they could engage in some kind of discussion. The lieutenant came toward me, where I was leaning against a post, with an air of determination as he approached me.

"Kid, you have orders from the major to go down that street," and he pointed to the street visible from the platform, "and obtain a truck for us. It is necessary for the deliverance of food and necessities for the army. Meanwhile, the major and I will venture to obtain the provisions. When you locate a truck, let the owner know that it is in the name of the army that you are requisitioning the vehicle."

"Understood, Lieutenant!" I importantly left to undertake my orders.

Strutting along the road toward the centre of town, I came across a five or six ton truck, which was parked in front of a little house, not far from the station. The chauffeur was engrossed with fiddling around with the motor of his truck. Now that I was fully uniformed, had boots and the rest of the matching garb, I was elated with my validity. Thus I marched right up to the chauffeur, determined to carry out my mission.

Authoritatively, I ordered the chauffeur to drive the truck to the train station and informed him that that was the order of the major and lieutenant, who needed the vehicle for the transportation of necessities to the soldiers. The chauffeur looked at me and replied that he would oblige as soon as he reported to his boss. I was overwhelmed with the fact that I had carried out my first duty with ease and success. I was floating with pride and neglected to notice the mud on the road and the vehicles that were splashing me. From a distance I discerned the major and lieutenant surrounded by two heavily armed Russian soldiers.

Look at that! I opined, the major found two more soldiers to assist us! I was approximately five steps away from my comrades. I stopped, holding my breath and standing as stiff as a pole, I saluted them as was expected.

I began, "Major, the order you had given me has been accomplished! The truck is on its way here now," and I pointed to the road from where I just came from.

The major, not thanking me, nor acknowledging my first successful mission, had signalled me with his finger to his mouth to be silent. Hmm, maybe I erred? Perhaps I was to address the lieutenant and not the major regarding the completion of my task? I bent my head and frowned.

Suddenly, the two other heavily armed soldiers demanded that I walk ahead of them. I considered this was ordered, due to their important discussion and probable arrangements needed to be made for the provisions. We walked back to the bridge.

Underneath the bridge was an awaiting commercial boat. We were instructed to board the boat and proceed down the stairs, into the lower deck of the boat. I was tragically confused. Why were we boarding this boat? And why were those soldiers commanding the major and lieutenant!? I was in no position to start questioning. I was nearly shoved down the stairs, into the lower deck, the major and lieutenant directly behind me.

Once we were in there, I surveyed the premises. Nothing of interest, save for one table, a chair and a Russian captain seated on the chair. Now it was even more curious, for how can it be that the captain did not stand and salute the major? Well...There would be a lot of discord now, when the major begins to rebuke! Oh, what a dilemma it will be!

Nothing. The major was silent, to my surprise. Suddenly the captain ordered one of his soldiers to undress the major! If that weren't enough, he was also instructed to empty all his pockets and place everything on the table. Unbelievable! I was near delirium as I stood with my mouth hanging open, my eyes bulging at this horrific display of revolting disobedience! With what authority did the captain have to do such humiliating things and to a major! I was beside myself.

When the frisking of the major was completed, the lieutenant was next in line! While the lieutenant was undressing, the major, in his underwear, came up to me and whispered, "Don't say a word! These are our enemies! Just be quiet. Don't tell them who or what you are. If you rat on us, I'll kill you!"

The major's eyes were as I'd never seen them before, glossy and foreboding. A cold chill ran down my spine. I was thunderstruck. It was now my turn to undress. I took off the rusty bayonet, which was instantaneously seized. They stripped me to my underpants. Once they were done, they threw back the overcoat to me and took the star off my cap. The interrogation commenced.

First, they asked me my name, then inquired where I was from. Throughout their inquisition I remained faithfully silent. From the corner of my eye, I noticed the major was observing me. I lowered my head and thought whatever happens, happens. I had my orders. I nearly saluted the major, but recovered my senses, lest I be punished. Now, I was wondering when the major's battalion would arrive and save us from this hounding.

The captain ordered that we sit on the floor near the hull of the boat. There was hay strewn all over the wooden floor. The soldiers brought a petroleum lantern. There were approximately ten more soldiers on the floor beside us. The major and lieutenant received plain overcoats and caps without stars on them and boots without laces. The two of them were sitting on the opposite side of the boat. I lay down on the hay and analysed the situation. How and what to do? As I was ruminating, an hour lapsed.

The soldiers were now bringing us food. A large, steaming pot and bowls. Good! I was famished. The last time I had eaten was during our journey on the truck and we had stopped at this village en route and lodged at a peasant's home, in the name of the army of course.

The major and lieutenant frightened the poor peasant woman to tears, with their commanding voices and bold insinuations. They practically accused the woman's husband (who was absent) of being a traitor and collaborating with the Germans! The woman was speechless and petrified. She tried, all the harder to please and accommodate the major, the lieutenant, including myself. She presented all she had to us. Cheese, wine, breads, smoked meats and other treats were laid on the table before us. To complete our sumptuous meal, we were given dessert and coffee.

After all that pampering, we were each given a room that was a little chilly, nonetheless clean and tidy. The most wonderful, soft down comforters were upon the beds and many over-sized down pillows as well. It was paradise!

Morning came. Another pot was brought down by a soldier. This time it was tea and cornbread for breakfast. We passed several days like this, below deck, on the floor, just waiting.

One day the Kalmistsi arrived, armed to their teeth and now in union with the Russian army. We were forced out of the boat, ordered to march as they strode on horses alongside. Behind us was a wagon, which contained the pots of food, probably intended for us. We marched like this for a long time. I stared at the muddy path we were on, where tracks could be discerned from previous trucks passing on them. Because we were sufficiently rested, we marched rather quickly without the commands from the soldiers. I encountered some difficulty, for my boots were large and I had no laces on them, regardless, I marched as quick as possible, lest the horses trample me.

The heavens were grey and heavy, but no rain fell. We were surrounded by vast terrain. I thought about my empty home and how the rent needed to be paid and I wasn't there. Agh, the landlord will just have to wait.

We marched all day without stopping and the soldiers riding upon their horses had no obvious intention of doing so. My legs were beginning to wobble and give out. One prisoner stumbled and had fallen ahead of us. The guard immediately galloped to investigate the cause of our delay.

Approximately fifty metres ahead of us and on a barren field stood a lonely wall, once a part of a peasant's house. The guards ordered us prisoners to go behind the wall, including me.

"Lie down! Lie down!" they roared.

What were we to lay down on? The cold, weedy grass? I lay down. We all did. Right next to me was a prisoner bearing a long beard, his eyes were barely visible. He was studying me and at once asked, "From what division are you from?"

"What division? I have no division," I answered to his inquiry.

"What happened to your division? They all perished?"

What was this man talking about?

"Who perished?" I had to ask.

"Your division! My division perished. I was left stranded, abandoned and left to wander. These here troopers found me and consider me a deserter, of all insults!"

Whatever, be as you please, I thought. At that instant we heard an explosive command, "Quiet. I don't want to hear any talking. Do you understand?!"

"Yes," I replied. My neighbour said nothing and turned his back to me and tried to sleep.

"Are we to sleep out here, in the cold, under the stars?" I asked my neighbour who immediately retorted, "Quiet! Do you want the Kalmiks to fix you?!"

"No, of course not, but I am cold."

"If you want to be warm, bundle your feet well, not so much your head as your feet and you'll be warm."

I took his advice and took off my boots to use as pillows and I rolled the overcoat around my feet. Well, at least I am not alone. I have this "accused" deserter beside me.

For some reason we were not given any food for the entire day and night. I detected that some of these prisoners were chewing on something. I nudged my neighbour, who snapped, "What now?"

"What is everyone chewing on?"

"Kid, you are insane! Everyone knows that food is not given out when in travel. You received a piece of cornbread this morning, right? You eat half of it and save the other half for later, like right now for example."

"I didn't know that!" I lowered my tone, for I saw the guard approaching us.

"Quiet!" the guard howled. He hears everything, just like a rabbit! Now I had nothing, no food. I had no alternative, but to sleep. I bundled myself up as best as I could and tried to sleep. I gazed up at the sky, the stars were brilliantly spilled all over the heavens. It was a spectacular sight. I closed my eyes and tried to forget I was hungry.

"Get up!" These were the first words we awoke to. We were commanded to form a line. One Kalmik came with a pot of hot water. We were given a tin cup and this sweetened hot water, along with a piece of cornbread for breakfast. We quickly drank the sweet, hot water. Now I knew better, I ate half of the cornbread and the other half I shoved into my pocket.

"Depart now!" the command fell and we commenced our journey. In the distance I heard continual thundering.

I turned to my fellow cohort. "What's that? Looks like it will start to rain."

"What rain! That's the front! Those are canons you hear, not thunder!"

"Are we going to the front?"

"No, not to the front, but at the back. See, kid, these fellows in the first row are all deserters and once they gather enough of us, we are the forefront. Therefore, who is killed is killed, and who isn't is a hero."

"I as well, at the front? What do you think?"

"You? I don't know. You are small and skinny. Maybe a spy."

"What is a spy? What division does that belong to? The artillery, navy, tanks or troopers?"

"Why there, there is my major and lieutenant now, in the front! They are ignoring me now!"

"Be quiet, little guy, just walk. Walk while you can. Forget about them."

That day passed exactly like the previous one. Many more days were to pass in such a manner. Endless walking, thunder never ceasing and now...The snow began to fall.

Chapter 16

Our convoy proceeded for days, in a pensive state, braving the white, snowy winds that woke us from our meditative trans as we marched forward. We passed by mini villages, farms, forests and terrains. Finally arriving at a little village the commanding officials decided on. In this village we were herded into a large hall, where many new captives were to join us. My new colleague just informed me that we were approximately twenty kilometres from Budapest.

"What did you say? That's the capital city of Hungary!"

"Yes, what did you think?"

"Nothing, I think that after walking every day like camels, it is with no amazement that we have arrived to such a distance."

During our march, we were forbidden to talk, nor ask questions, only walk! My rags were falling apart on my feet, the ones I used as socks. I had trouble with the walking, but succeeded. At sporadic intervals and during sleep overs, where we were given bland soup and the dreaded horse meat to eat and we ate fervently.

We were placed in the basement of this hall and ordered to sleep. It was nearing dawn and I bundled my feet as per the advice of my cohort and was adjusting myself in a comfortable position for sleeping, when a guard came to me. I was ordered to dress and follow him. I did so and nearly ran after the guard, who was several paces ahead of me. I followed him into a room where the captain was sitting and waiting. The guard pointed out the chair to me that I should sit on.

Now the captain started, "Good. Now, son, tell me the truth!" He hypnotically stared at me.

I informed him of myself and answered all his questions as he put them to me. I told him of my recruit into the Russian army by the major. The captain gazed at me, not knowing what to say. After I had decidedly spilled everything out, in spite of my warning from the major, I asked him, "Would you accept me in your army? I could be at the lowest rank, just instruct me of what to do?" The captain chuckled and instructed me to leave. I regarded the magnanimous captain and was immensely relieved of his pardoning me. I was free! I bowed and left the room.

Outside, I welcomed the cold, snowy wind and breathed in deeply and satisfyingly. I looked to the right of me and there was the cellar where the prisoners were and to the left a gate, which was wide open and led to the open road. I walked nonchalantly right by the guards at the out post and began my journey back to Belgrade. I believed I was headed in the right direction, for I heard the thundering canons behind me, thus that was the front and I was to go in the opposite of that.

On my way, I saw trucks heading toward the front and none in the direction I was going, to Belgrade. I was praying at least for one to appear and my prayer was answered. I waved and waved and yelled, but nothing.

"Stop! Please!" They laughed as they drove past and I wanted to cry. As they sped by, soldiers were sarcastically waving at me from the back of the truck.

Deafening silence, the snow was all around me, the road empty. I walked alone. How much walking would I have to do? I could not calculate it properly, for I was with the convoy earlier, plus we made stops and now I am confused. I was very hungry, I skipped breakfast, for the captain had summoned me to his office. Thus while the others ate, I was being pardoned. I was terribly hungry. No living soul around. I thought I saw smoke in the distance. Was it from a chimney? I began to run, to investigate. Hoping that it was not a snowy mirage, but an actual house. It was!

The poor peasant's white-washed single story house stood alone, with no other houses nearby. The roof, being thatched, gave the house an appearance of a shack. Behind the house was a barn, in no better condition than the house. I banged on the door twice.

An elderly peasant woman opened the door. She was completely attired in black. She stared at me. I began to show her that I am hungry and with my hands I gestured that I wanted to eat. She said something, but I simply didn't comprehend. I then showed her by grabbing my elbows and shivering that I am cold. She stood there, irresolutely. I heard a man's voice from within and I no longer had the patience for the charades, thus I walked in, uninvited.

Their very modest home was cozy, neat and welcoming. I looked over to the side where there was a wooden table and chairs and on the chair, an elderly man sat. He had yellowy-white hair, beard and moustache, from which a pipe was protruding. He was clad in worn out black pants, black shirt and on his head he fashioned a lambskin cap. He just sat there, undisturbed and not surprised at my intrusion. He looked at me and I at him. He didn't move an inch.

The same way I entered, uninvited, the same way I sat at the table. Then, in an awkward method, I tried to explain to them that I was not a criminal, nor was I there to harm them. This I did by hand gestures and announcing, "No boom, boom. No boom, boom!"

I believe I succeeded, for in that moment the old man said something to his wife and she went over to the cupboard took out a bowl and poured whatever she was cooking in the pot into the bowl.

I had a bowl of undercooked bean soup before me and a piece of bread. I ate very quickly. They were silent and observed me. Obviously, we couldn't engage in small talk, for neither of us understood each other. Thus I finished my meal, humbly bowed to the both of them and left. They must have had other visitors such as myself, for oddly enough, they were not the least bit perturbed.

I was back on the long, lonely road to home. I walked for a

very long time and I was surrounded with nothing but snow covered fields, endless fields to the left, right and ahead of me. It was becoming colder and I walked faster. When I turned around to take another look at the little house, it was not visible any longer. I realized I had walked a good distance.

In the peaceful serenity, the sound of a motor was heard. To my pleasure it was a truck! I began to wave frantically, praying, hoping that this time this truck would stop. He did.

"What is it?" was the most pleasant yell I heard. The driver undoubtedly was tipsy, for he slurred his words.

"Drive me! That's all!"

"Go to the back of the truck and hop in. I have a load of cabbage back there. Try to fit in. You can go to the army transportation station at the village we arrive at, if you plan to go farther that is?"

He obviously assumed I was a soldier, due to my overcoat. I climbed onto the back of the truck. Agh! This cabbage seems to follow me wherever I am and throughout my miseries!

I tumbled in the rear of the truck amidst the cabbages for a considerable time. Once we came to a halt, I heard the driver, "You can get off now! We're here!" I slid out of the truck. The driver stumbled out of his seat, rocking to and fro, until he came to me and pointed out a soldier, who was holding a sign and directing traffic. He advised me to go that person and inquire regarding transportation. I gave him my thanks and more so to God, for getting us to the village safely, for the driver was in more need of a bed than a seat behind the wheel.

I strolled up to the traffic controller, who was wearing an army uniform.

"What do you want?"

"I would like, if possible, that you would stop someone heading for Belgrade, who could take me along for the ride."

"Who are you?"

"Who am I? Well...It's like this....I was imprisoned earlier, then released and sent home. I am seeking a method of transportation to Belgrade."

"Aha, I see...May I see your documents?"

"What documents?"

"Your identification papers!"

"I don't have any."

"Is that so? You must come with me then!"

"Certainly!" Great! This kind man is willing to help me! "Where are we going?"

"You'll see."

In a victorious and stoical manner I followed this traffic director. Not too far was a building in which we entered. Another soldier had now taken me over from the previous traffic director, "Come with me," he said.

We went down many sets of stairs. I was unaware of where I am, for the sign outside stated *Seksard*, and was unfamiliar to me. When we came to the bottom of the stairs and into a corridor, where there were many barred cells, the soldier unlocked one of the cells and pushed me in, locking the door behind him.

"Hey! Wait! I didn't ask for sleeping arrangements, I asked for a ride! Come back! What did I do?"

"Quiet! Tomorrow you will be interrogated," the Russian soldier professed and vanished.

Why was I imprisoned again? The captain just released me. Agh! Nobody to ask, nobody to discuss with, nobody to share my misfortune with. And in this incontrovertible and forlorn state, I lay down on the withered, wooden bench (again) in the dreary cell and tried to sleep.

I woke up, uncertain whether it was morning, afternoon or night. There was no window in the cell, able to tell me. I heard heavy footsteps and a clanking noise. A new guard appeared, unlocked the cell door and ordered me out and to proceed following him.

"After you," I politely stated, when the sudden roar of the guard stated, "Go upstairs, you scoundrel!" I shook and brushed by him and quickly proceeded up the stairs.

It seemed like eternity before we reached the top of the stairs. Through serpentine hallways we trekked, finally reaching a room where, yet another captain was to interrogate me. I was ushered into this room and pushed to sit down right on a wooden chair, directly in front of the captain. He was approximately middle aged, clean shaven and had a serious aura about him. There was silence in the room for about a minute, I surmised that this was due to his studying me.

At once he spoke, "Talk!"

"Talk about what?" I innocently inquired.

"Everything!"

"All right." I wasn't sure where to begin, I didn't think he wanted to hear a lengthy monologue of my life story, thus I began with the most recent. "It happened like this, sir, comrade...I mean Captain...I was imprisoned earlier and later released. Thus I began journeying back home to Belgrade. I hitched a ride on a truck carrying cabbages, brought to this village and instructed to ask the traffic director for further transportation to home. The traffic director, instead of obtaining transportation for me, had brought me here. And...Well, that's about all there is to it."

"Mhhmm, I understand. Now, young man, start from the beginning...Who are you? Who are your parents? How did you end up here, in Hungary?"

I was in a foreign country?! That sign outside should have told me so, but I was too involved with the traffic director to have paid better attention. And...Those people that fed me, they were Hungarians! I assumed that because I was in a different village they had spoken differently.

Studiously thinking at this sudden revelation, I had neglected to answer the captain, even forgetting about him for an instant.

"Young man! Did you hear me?"

"Oh...Yes, yes...Of course, my name is Vitya and..." I told the captain all about my experiences, my recruitment, the major and the lieutenant, my imprisonment, my release and so forth...

"Who took your laces, Vitya?"

"Some Kalmitsi that escorted us and marched us to the village where we were held in a basement hall."

"I see." At that instant the captain picked up his phone, talked to someone and in no less than a few seconds, a soldier appeared in the room. He instructed the soldier to take me to the community room. The captain told me to follow the soldier and nothing else. I was not aware of where I was going, nor why I was being sent to the community room. I followed the soldier, this was now a habit.

Unusually, Seksard was a large commune, with many houses. Though, there were mostly army personnel and little, if any civilians. The picturesque village's houses had iron fences in front of them, with very large entrances to the homes. Antique, iron lamp posts, were akin to the ones in fairytales. The streets, were not of cobblestone, but large cement tiles.

While I was admiring the scenery, I failed to notice that we had arrived (the soldier and I) at this large building, most likely a school at one time. It was of four levels and owned many windows. The soldier opened one of the double doors and we entered. We walked through an airy corridor briefly, until we came to a large hall, perhaps a gymnasium. Another soldier stood guard there and after an exchange of words between the two, I was handed over to him, a very familiar pattern, which I was becoming unfortunately accustomed to.

In this prodigious hall, were many beds, perhaps forty, if not more. They were equally divided on each side of the hall and in the centre was a large coal furnace and pathway. Later, I learned that it was the inmates responsibility to fetch the pails of coal from the basement and feed the hungry furnace. The hall was not only divided by the beds to the sides, but also by the inmates themselves. On one side were Russian inmates and on the other were Hungarians.

I observed that the Hungarian inmates were suspicious of their fellow Russian inmates and would usually behave indifferently when the need to communicate with the other arose. I sat with the Russians and listened carefully to their stories, for there really wasn't anything else to do there. Many stories were told and I would pretend not to listen for fear of being scolded by the older inmates' accusations of prying and snooping. Thus I would blankly stare at the ceiling while lying down on my bed, or close my eyes as if I were asleep, or at least trying to. Regarding the food...It was good, we were allowed repeats and, thankfully, were not hungry.

One morning, an officer came in to the hall and had ordered all the civilians to form a line and were informed that they were being transferred to another location. I was just becoming accustomed to this atmosphere and the established routines. Well, I thought, I wouldn't be included in this transfer, after all, I am not a civilian, I was a soldier. Thus I thought, but worried nonetheless.

The civilians were soon emptying the hall in an orderly fashion and the soldiers remained. I didn't budge. Lo and behold, the soldier came over to me. "Come...You, too!"

"No! No, I am not Hungarian!" I matter-of-factly declared.

"I know that, but you have been called to visit the major, a real major this time!"

I waved to my fellow captives and followed, again, the soldier. Snow was falling and there was plenty of it on the ground when we came out of the building, and the brightness of the white snow had caught me off guard. I had to stop for a few seconds to regain my sight and to adjust to the brightness; it was also sunny, but cold. I walked alongside the silent soldier, with no intentions of striking up a conversation myself.

We walked for a long time in silence and it suited me, for I was observing my surroundings. We walked this way, right to the outskirts of the village. Along our snowy route, I reflected on what the captain had said and on what I had said.

This major, the one we were about to visit, might be the one providing me with transportation back home? After all, this one is a real major, unlike the previous imposter that recruited me. I was informed by the captain that "my" major and lieutenant were frauds. How foolish of me to have believed them! But...In the situation I was in, it was an affable opportunity to escape destitution, or at least I thought.

We turned on a little side road and took a few more steps until we came to a large wall, with a gate attached to it, similar to the one I saw in Panchevo. The soldier hit the gate twice and a young, beautiful woman appeared.

"What do you want?" she asked him in Serbian. Well, how interesting that she speaks so abruptly to the soldier? The soldier answered in Russian, "The captain sent us."

The woman waved her hands in the air, shrugged her shoulders and stated that she didn't understand what he wanted. Naturally, I, knowing both languages, came to the rescue and informed her of what the soldier stated. She was stupefied. She saw I was attired in Russian dress and didn't expect me to speak her language.

She informed me that the major was unavailable momentarily, but that the soldier could leave me with her in order to see the major as soon as he becomes available. I translated the matter to the soldier, in agreement, he saluted and left us.

The pretty lady told me to come with her and we went through the gates and into the kitchen, through a side door. She instructed me to sit at this very long and narrow table and wait. I sat there and studied the kitchen. It was clean, partially white and had many utensils scattered about. I was becoming tired of waiting. I began to fiddle with my fingers and whistle, though quietly.

In ten minutes, which seemed like hours to me, a man walked in, he was a soldier as well. "Are you Vitya?"

"Yes, I am."

"Good! Come with me!"

I followed the soldier. I found myself in a laundry room. "Take off your clothes!" I took off my overcoat and held it in my arms as the soldier was aiming to pick it up with a long stick. He took my coat and swung it over into a large boiling pot of water.

"What! Hey! That's my coat!"

"Quiet! Now take off the rest of your clothing!"

I had no choice. I obeyed and soon was standing in my undershorts. My clothes had joined my stewing overcoat in the large pot.

"That, too!" he pointed to my underwear.

I took it off and that also united with the rest of my simmering garb. I stood there stark naked and shivering. I, of course, covered my privates with my hands and was terribly ashamed. My uniform was now gone! I was cold.

"You look like a plucked chicken!" The soldier chuckled. "Go over there in that barrel."

I looked around and saw a large barrel in the corner of the room. I was not only naked, but ashamed, tired and humiliated and spilled out, "Why now the barrel?"

"Go wash, that's why! Wash that long hair of yours, too. I will be cutting it!"

That was good news to me. I dragged myself sideways, awkwardly so, and climbed into the barrel. "Aaahhhh! The water was actually warm! There was soap, too! How splendid! I plunged into the barrel and delightfully soaked for nearly a half hour as the warm water hugged me. I scrubbed and scrubbed and dug my nails into my scalp and made sure that I was thoroughly clean. The water became murky and I became lighter.

"Get out now! Vitya, is it? Is that your name?"

"Yes, it is." He already forgot my name?

"They call me Vova." The soldier appeared to be in a lighter mood as I was in a lighter state myself. Vova threw me a rough, but clean, towel and I dried myself. "Sit here, Vitya, you're getting a haircut!"

I did. I was grateful to be rid of my shoulder-length hair, which was burdensome and hung in numerous knots. Ha! The lice won't be celebrating now, I rejoiced. I had a crew cut and was overjoyed, for now I truly resembled a soldier!

I received a new set of clothing. Everything was included: underwear, pants, shirts and socks and army boots! I now had a very clean and complete army uniform! A Russian soldier I was! This is unbelievable! I never entertained the idea that I would be recruited again, actually for the first time, not counting the false recruitment by the fraudulent major and lieutenant. If I had wings, I would've flown off the ground from sheer happiness. I dressed in my uniform and then followed Vova into the kitchen again. We were met with new faces sitting at the kitchen table, some of these were happy, some solemn.

"These people here are Partisans and you are to speak to

them in their language, thereby translating for us and for them. You are an interpreter now, Vitya. This is why you are here. The major does not understand them very well and needed an interpreter and here you are."

Vova gave me the initial instructions and I was to begin my new duty soon. I carefully and non-judgmentally looked over the Partisans. Curiously some were wearing German shirts, some wore Yugoslav shirts and some Hungarian shirts. They were all clean, clean shaven and tidy. Vova seated me at the side of the table.

Ten of us were at this table. I surveyed the kitchen again, now it was uncluttered, smelled freshly washed and I noticed the frilly, white curtains which I hadn't before. The lemon yellow floor was lustrous. The woman must have cleaned while I was bathing, I surmised as we all waited for the major to arrive. Suddenly everyone rose as did I, upon the major's entry.

He was not an old man, rather young. He had an amicable appearance and very large sky blue eyes. He was as handsome as a prince. His stride was charming and gallant. He came to sit at the head of the table. He wore a marvellous uniform, fully decorated. Once he sat, he advised the rest of us to do the same. Dinner was commencing.

The young, beautiful woman was rushing back and forth bringing all the necessary utensils, plates and bowls full of deliciously fragrant food. The major looked at her and informed her that he was expecting guests the next day and wanted the dinner served in the next room. She not understanding all that he said, looked at me. Immediately I made myself useful, simultaneously flaunting my abilities before the major, by translating what he said to the woman. The woman graciously replied and agreed, but needed to know how many guests would be dining? I turned to the major, who was apparently delighted in this course of conversation and did not disguise his agreeable expression, when I translated the woman's question to him. "Six," he stated. The woman understood, for the word "six" in both languages is identical, save for a slight dialect.

After we dined, my duties began and I translated all that was necessary to the approval of the major. I was pleased with my new assignment and I was treated justly. I had the commodities necessary to human sustenance. Vova informed me that we were soon to go to the large hills, by motorbike, for the purpose of obtaining wine.

I was given an empty jug of ten litres. I sat at the back of the motorbike and Vova and I departed for the hills. We ascended up the snowy trail, surrounding us were vineyards, protruding from the snow. Before reaching the top of the hill, we stopped in front of a door, recessed within the hill. I was dumbfounded. Who would have expected a wine cellar within a hill? I watched Vova attempting to break the latch on the locked door as eagles were flying above us as if berating us.

It was pitch-black within this mini cave within the hill, but Vova came prepared and he took a flashlight from his bag on the bike. We were inside. An amalgamation of earth, wine and dampness scented the frosty air. I was looking toward wherever Vova was pointing with the flashlight, following the trail and was astounded at the discovery of colossal wine barrels.

It was unfathomable to try and explain the size and enormity of these gargantuan barrels. Each of them had a tap at the bottom of it. Vova's eyes sparkled. Vova tried the tap and ruby red wine began to flow out of the tap. "Quick, Vitya, hand me the jug!" I gave him the jug and it was filling. Halfway through, Vova couldn't suppress himself of the temptation and tasted the wine from the jug. "Delicious!" He chugged a while, then handed it to me. I took three sips and agreed on its favourable taste, thus handing the jug back to Vova.

"What's the matter?"

"Nothing. I can't drink anymore, that's all."

"Fine." Vova placed the jug beneath the tap and the refilling began. "You know, Vitya, Seksard is known for its wine!"

"I didn't know," I calmly replied, while watching Vova appease his thirst.

Many more times Vova and I were to visit this hillside wine bar, although we did visit different locations of the hills at times, all of them were mini caves, recessed within the hill. How Vova knew of their exact locations was beyond me. We were amidst the wine district in Hungary.

Vova and I became quite friendly, even though he was relatively older than I, but we got along well. One day, Vova instructed me to guard the entrance of our building (where we lived), at night. He gave me a rifle, taught me how to load the rifle and what I was to do upon noticing suspicious intruders. I was not to permit anyone at all to pass through the entrance. I took my obligation very seriously and reverently. However, I did wonder, it must have been Vova's duty to guard at night and he simply passed the duty to me.

Vova took me outside to show me exactly where I was to stand guard. "Here, you stand right here and you may pace if you like, but beware, do not permit any soul through this entrance!"

"Understood!"

Vova left me. I felt important. I held the rifle with honour and began pacing. Suddenly I heard faint footsteps in the distance.

"Who goes there?!" No one answered, but the footsteps were all the more audible. Again I shouted, "Who goes there?! Halt! I order you to halt!"

I cocked the rifle, prepared it for firing. My hands were trembling. Did this have to occur now when I was on duty? I was annoyed at Vova for granting me this honourable, but unfavourable, position which I found myself in.

At once I heard, "I stopped!" The footsteps now owned a voice. "Who goes there?" I roared.

"Captain!"

Captain? What should I do now? How can I be certain it's the captain? I began to yell, "Turn and go forth!" The "captain" turned around and then began toward me again. I couldn't discern him, nor he me, for it was a very dark, black night. Again the footsteps.

"Halt!"

"What now?" the voice asked.

"Turn and proceed!" I commanded wearily.

My goal was to have the person, or "captain," cross over to

the opposite of me and thereby pass me, but instead he had made a 360 degree turn and proceeded straight toward me! I was becoming frustrated at how stupid this person was for not obliging and doing as I asked.

Very irritated and ignorant as to how to proceed with the matters, in anxious anticipation I hollered out, "Turn to the left!" The captain, equally annoyed and distressed, now demanded to see the sergeant.

"Where am I to find the sergeant now?" I strictly asked.

"I demand to see the sergeant right now! That's an order!" the captain thundered with anger and fury.

I heard more footsteps, but behind me now, "Who goes there?!" I demanded.

"Sergeant!"

Wphew! I recognized the sergeant's voice and was overcome with relief. The sergeant came to me, didn't ask me any questions at all, but simply ordered me to return to the building at once. I gave him my rifle, and explained that it was loaded and ready for shooting.

"Good, good. That's fine. Go now," was his simple reply.

After that "guarding" incident, unfortunately, I had never seen Vova again. I presumed he was dismissed due to his disobedience and entrusting me, an inexperienced soldier, with such a task. It was a despairing occasion.

In a week's time, I was loaded onto a truck, accompanied by the Partisans and left for Belgrade, or so I thought, with no dismissal, no good-byes to the major, nor anyone else for that matter. We travelled the entire day, stopping at the town of Subotica. In this town we were stationed in front of an attractive building, seemingly owned, or once owned, by a wealthy personage. We were ordered out of the truck and lined up against the wall of the edifice. Interestingly, the captain was now standing before us. He studiously examined us and in a blink of the eye, we were joined by ten more Partisans, not much older than myself, roughly fifteen to sixteen years of age.

The row I was in was slowly dispersing, due to their report of what brigade they adhered to. I, being of no brigade, was left there like a withered leaf. Obviously conspicuous, the captain moseyed over to me and inquired my name and the usual necessary questions ensued, which I had heard too many times. Thus I informed him that I was in the Russian army, a soldier, actually an interpreter for the major.

"A Russian! You are a Russian then?"

"Yes."

"Good. Do you want to work here for us as a courier, or...You have the option of being imprisoned, since you lack any proper identification papers."

"Work! Yes, indeed work. No prison, thank you."

"Very well. Report directly beside this building. That's where the couriers are."

There, in Subotica, I involuntarily became the courier for the Yugoslav army. It was either that or prison again. I preferred the former. I worked there for six months. Us couriers, used bicycles to deliver mail and orders to the soldiers, battalions and various government offices. I was given a Yugoslav Army uniform and was performing my duties as ordered.

We ate in a large staff dining hall (kitchen) and the food was plentiful and tolerable. For some reason, the courier was considered a higher rank than that of a regular soldier, which suited me perfectly. Thus, I was treated amicably.

One day I was summoned by the captain. What now? What did I do? Did I deliver something incorrectly? To the wrong person? Oh no! I began to recollect my work and think of what I could've done wrong. There was a time I was given the task of monitoring the telephone on the second floor, in case that phone calls came in to the headquarters, but I don't recall any wrongdoing there, nor mishaps. I was shaking as I entered the office of the captain.

I was now standing in front of the captain and my co-worker was standing right next to me. I was listening to the orders given to my colleague by the captain. He was ordered to be transferred to the Army Aviation Academy. I trembled. What if I were sent to an academy?

My colleague saluted the captain and took leave. The captain now turned to me. "We have decided to demobilize you, because of your age. You will be given a piece of paper and a ticket for the train to Belgrade, that's all. You are dismissed." I nearly fainted. I saluted, nearly embraced the captain, but withheld.

The Germans capitulated, it was spring 1945. I was permitted to keep the uniform, for I had no other clothing. I was given nothing regarding compensation for working, nothing at all, save for the train fare for the ride back to Belgrade. All the same, I was in dire need to depart from this town of Subotica and go home, if I still had one that is. I missed my family, my wretched two-room home with its stained walls. I was going home. I was finally going home!

Chapter 17

During my train ride, I lapsed into memory lane, recalling my adventures and misfortunes I encountered, while absent from home. Yes...The war was over! While in Subotica, all the people celebrated, including myself. We ran out spilling onto the streets, yelling and shouting. Laughter was heard, gunshots in the air, the crowd was jubilant, relieved and grateful. Many things had changed since I left. The government had implemented a five year plan to reconstruct and repair the city of the damages caused by the war.

At the station in Belgrade, not much had changed. The platform was semi-crowded. I got off the train and began my course toward home. I didn't know, or rather expected, not to have a home anymore, for the rent...Long overdue. The landlord must have re-rented it to somebody else. Regardless, I'm going there, whatever the result may be.

Every step closer to home, aroused many memories...Mother, I need to see her. I didn't know what do first. I must settle the "home" issue first, for I wouldn't have a place to retire that night. I walked by herds of people, who didn't look twice at me, all accustomed to having uniformed soldiers walking to and fro. The people and atmosphere were more relaxed now and everyone was continuing their lives, rebuilding their homes, while children played on the streets. The air was filled with the scent of fragrant flowers.

The day was warm and sunny. A little more and I'm home,

maybe. I went through the familiar courtyard, not encountering the landlord, nor neighbours. I went directly to my home, but knocked, just in case. Surely enough, a stranger opened the door to my kitchen.

"Yes?"

"Olga? I mean, is Olga here?"

"No. Olga doesn't live here anymore. She moved across the street, over there," and the lady pointed in the direction of Olga's new home. "You see, young man, she exchanged this apartment for a one-room dwelling. But, I can tell you...That she is not there either. She married."

"Oh...I see. Well...thank you." I was shocked. Indeed, a lot had changed, including Olga's status...Married!

I wandered out of the old, memory trigging courtyard. I guessed approximately where this "new" home might be, according to the pointing of the new tenant in my home. I guessed correctly. I walked through the new courtyard, passing by homes, which obviously were not occupied by Olga, for other people were entering, leaving and some had their doors wide open, with children running in and out of their apartments. I walked straight to the end of the courtyard. I found it. The last door. It seemed abandoned and wasn't even locked. I opened the door.

Inside there was not much to be found. Our stove was not there, just a little round stove on three legs. Our old iron bed was there, though. The one Mother slept on. It was in the corner, at the back of the room. One lonely table and one chair. Upon the table was one glass, one fork, one small pot. No other dishes, nothing.

I lay down on the bed. I began to think, what was I going to do now? I was not quite sixteen yet and I needed to find a "legal" job, pronto! I tried to devise a plan of all the things I needed to do and people to see. Starting with Mother.

After a brief rest, I got up, splashed some water on my face and left to visit Mother. I was ecstatic to see her and she was overjoyed upon seeing me. Needless to say, hundreds of questions poured out of her. I noticed she was not quite well. I wanted to take her out, but I knew of the answer I would receive. I answered her questions the best I could and, after many hugs and tears, I left.

I was back on the street. I had no food. I had no money. I had only the sealed envelope from the captain for work purposes and a scrumpled piece of paper in my pocket. I took it out and read it. Oh yes...Now I remember! The clerk who worked with me at Subotica, he was in charge of censoring the mail. He gave me his address in Belgrade where his parents lived and invited me to come there once I left Subotica. I hadn't seen him upon my departure from Subotica and wasn't certain if he had left as well. Anyhow, I thought I might try to visit them.

I came to the address which he gave me. The home was clean and modestly furnished. His parents were affectionately welcoming and insisted I had dinner with them. Naturally, I didn't need to be asked twice, I accepted their gracious offer. We ate and I told them of their son and how we met and of my work while in Subotica and then the discussion regarding the war ensued and the liberation and the ending of the war.

I had a splendid time with them and they escorted me to the door, with assurances from me that I would visit them again. I was very glad to have visited them, for their benevolence was highly appreciated and accepted. Just as I was about to take my first step out, over the threshold of their home, the lady pushed a hundred dinars into the palm of my hand, I tried to return it, for their company and the dinner we shared was complacent and I simply couldn't. They forced me to accept their gift and said that they hadn't seen their son in such a long time. Perhaps I reminded them of their son and they felt inadvertently obliged. Nevertheless, I accepted it with many bows and thankfulness. I left them waving at the their door as I retreated home.

New hardships had begun. I was job-hunting. I went to numerous factories, begging, pleading for work, and the only reply I received was, "Nothing." I was desperate and near hysterics. I needed food and money for the rent. Every morning I rose at the crack of dawn in tune with the roosters and marched to every manufacturing establishment and then some. Where was there work? In a devastated state, I dragged myself to a factory called "Proleter," previously known as "Boston." It was a shoe factory. I thought to try my luck there.

Inside this establishment, I was greeted by an elderly man. I must have had the most piteous comportment and my sorrowful expression, combined with my pathetic clothing and ripped shoes, might have caused him to sympathize. I was in dire need of work.

"Do you want to work, young man?"

"Do I! Yes! Please!"

"Excellent! Tomorrow morning, bright and early, be here. You will work in the cutting room."

"Thank you! I humbly thank you!" I flew out of there like a bird. I obtained a second wind, was refreshed, revitalized and euphoric. The timing of becoming employed was precise. I was skimping and saving the last of the hundred dinars I had received from the generous family I had previously visited.

I became the cleaner of the cutting room where men's and ladies' shoes were manufactured. In one year, I gained a promotion: a shoe cutter, cutting the uppers for the shoes. I had received a working card with the letter "G" on it, the lowest possible rank. With this card I was able to receive dinner at the "menza," the staff cafeteria.

Everyone was still rationing, even with the war being over. I also was entitled to receive 200 grams of bread per day. For lunch, I would occasion the private kitchen, across the street, where a humble elderly couple had set up a few tables and provided various modest meals cheaply. It was similar to a food bank. Usually, it costed me half my day's wages for the lunch.

The second year of employment I received a promotion again, the same occupation, though now I was paid by piecework. In spite of this new promotion, I still had the same amount of provisions.

At the local piazza the kiosks were filled with produce, such as potatoes and other vegetables, meats and cheeses and lard. All that was available for purchase without the rationing card, but at astronomical prices.

One evening I was sitting at home, attempting to mend my torn garments (my shoes were mended by my colleagues at work), when I had heard a knocking at my door, which was very unusual. In three steps, I was at the door and opened it. What a shock I received! It was Alex!

He shoved me back in the room and demanded, "Quick, let me in! Turn off the lights!"

"Why? Alex!? Wait!" I was overcome with joy, confused at his attitude, but relieved...He was alive.

"Silence! Do as I say and I'll tell you everything!"

Alex's apparel did not excel my own apparel, although his shoes were in a better condition. He was dishevelled and very worried, near hysteria. He stormed in and was quite roused. I didn't turn off the lights as he suggested, but I did draw the curtains (rags) on the window. He sat on the bed and stared at me in a restless and confused manner. Eventually he calmed down and began to enunciate and address all the difficulties he had encountered. I learned of his misfortunes, his escapes and so forth. I told him briefly all the escapades I experienced.

Alex then informed, "Vitya, I live with Gypsies, not far from here you know. I also obtained a job recently as a city janitor. Agh, hmm, I barely survived, Vitya, barely. Now, I have more news for you and plans for us, but I must leave and I'll return tomorrow.

I was ecstatic of reuniting with Alex again, I sympathized with him for his suffering during his absence. Impatiently I awaited for the next day to arrive, to see Alex again. At work I was nervous and restless, all the while thinking of Alex, the news he had and the plan for "us." The day went by slowly and the hours exaggerated. Finally, the time came to punch out and head for home!

As a loyal dog, I stared at the door, waiting for Alex. Several times, I opened the door, thinking I heard a knock, or some kind of shuffling at the door. I paced the room, thinking, wondering what could his plan be? True to his word, the knock finally came and Alex was standing at the door. He came in, not as flustered as yesterday, but not even-keeled either. "Vitya, we must leave Belgrade! It's a fact. It's not an option."

"What's with you, Alex? I can't leave! I have a good job, not a prolific one, but substantial. Besides, I had enough travelling, I even went to Hungary! Therefore, I'm not going!"

"Where's George, Vitya?"

"You know where he is, at the orphanage."

"Where's Olga?"

"She's married, remember...I told you that last night," I reminded Alex. He didn't ask about Mother, because he had been to see her.

"Alex, why all the questions?"

"We must leave! Vitya, listen...The Communist Information Bureau arrived. President Tito and Stalin are no longer collaborating. Most, nearly all of the White Russian immigrants, are fleeing Yugoslavia!"

"What is this you tell me? Where am I to leave, Alex? I do not have money for such luxuries as travelling. My income barely suffices for the most base of needs."

"I know, I know. Listen, I will go get George from the orphanage and I'll arrange the papers. You obtain some money! We are heading west!"

"What? West? Alex, I don't have money, nor do I know where to obtain some. Secondly, why west?"

Alex's eyes were ricocheting across the room as I observed him in bewilderment. His gaze stopped at the door, where my winter coat was hanging. "I see you have a winter coat?" Alex sarcastically alluded.

"What of it? I ate only beans for six months, no meat, to save for that coat, which I purchased on the black market. I am not parting with my coat!"

"You don't need it, Vitya! Where we are going...It's warm, sunny and you simply will have no use for it! But...We do need money, and urgently!

"Vitya, in Trieste it's beautiful, figs and olives grow there! And the bread! Well, there's no limit of it! Now, do as I tell you! I am older and you must obey!"

"Well, if it isn't the song and dance! Alex! I am older now and am supporting myself!"

"That's good, Vitya, but I am still older! Therefore, do not argue with me, and, Vitya…Not a word to anyone, absolutely no one!"

"Who to tell?"

"Good. I'll be back!" Alex left like the wind.

Alex didn't appear the next day, nor the day after that. In fact a week went by and I accepted that he forgot the entire matter. Nevertheless, perhaps out of habit of obeying Alex, I had sold my coat, for half of what I initially paid for it. Now I wondered whether it was such a good idea to do so and was annoyed with myself for obeying. When would I learn!

Nightfall and I sat at home eating beans of course. A knock on the door. There stood George and directly behind him was Alex! Alex shoved us inside and began, "Good! We are all here!"

"What do you mean all here?" I asked Alex in a state of confusion, excitement and joy of seeing both my brothers with me, finally united.

"I mean the three of us!" Alex answered and pulled out some papers he had in his inner pocket. It was a travelling pass for the three of us, enabling us to enter Trieste, Italy.

"Here, look, Vitya, the three of us are named here in these passes!"

Suddenly we heard a shuffling in the corner of the room. Alex pulled my arm. "Vitya! Do you have someone here?"

"Yes, Alex, the neighbourhood rats!" And true to my word, an enormous rat ran by us and into a hole at the other side of the room. We jumped back, but were far too involved with the "new" plans to be disturbed by this appearance.

"Listen," Alex continued, "the both of you sleep now, for we are leaving tomorrow morning!"

Alex left us. The next morning, we were up at six. It was still dark outside. Alex lugged some kind of baggage on his back. He took all the money I obtained, including my last pay cheque from the factory I worked at. "Alex? How much money do you have on yourself now?"

"Enough, it's not your concern."

"What do you mean it's not my concern!"

"Now, now, come, just listen to me, Vitya, and we'll be fine!"

Here I was travelling without a single dinar to my name and I had to trust Alex's words, for after all...He was older!

We got to the train station. George and I stood on the platform, while Alex went to purchase the tickets. The train was already at the station and waiting for its passengers.

"Come, let's go in," Alex ordered. We were seated in the third class car of the train. It was empty.

"We have room!" Alex jubilantly announced.

"Of course we do, it's empty!" I shot back sarcastically.

"Yes, but it will soon be full!" Alex wisely commented and instructed us to sit at the rear, near the rest rooms. His logic was that when the car became full, we needn't push and shove to get to the toilets.

We sat on the wooden benches and waited. An hour lapsed, we waited, becoming nervous and agitated. Finally, the whistle blew, the train jerked and we began to move slowly, crawling, until the train reached its normal travelling speed.

"Alex? How long are we to travel?"

"Quiet! Why do you ask? If you are so curious, then...This train is going to Slovenia."

"Oh, then I suppose we will be travelling through Croatia?"

"Yes, we are."

I noticed that Alex was not inclined to engage in a conversation, therefore I snuggled up to George, who was already napping. I looked out the window; villages were passing us by as we departed from Belgrade farther and farther. Now the telephone poles were zipping by, hypnotizing me. I closed my eyes to rest.

I awoke to Alex's shaking of my arm. "Vitya, we are in Zagreb."

"How can that be? We just left Belgrade?"

"Indeed, many hours ago and you slept like a baby."

"Good, Alex, let's go out and take a look around!"

"No looking around. Sit here and be quiet."

"The car is nearly empty, Alex."

"Yes, many had unboarded here."

"Where are we headed to now, Lyublyana?"

"Quiet already!"

I looked at Alex. "Alex, I'm hungry!"

"I was waiting for that," Alex cleverly remarked and switched his seat; now he sat opposite of George and myself. He took his rucksack and began scrummaging through it. He pulled out a loaf of bread and some greasy paper.

"Well...Look at him!" I was surprised and commented, "You thought of everything!" He simply nodded in recognition of his cleverness. He then took out a paring knife from his bag and proceeded to slice three pieces of bread and then unwrapped the greasy paper. He brought bacon, too! He sliced some bacon and handed it to me. We woke up George and I shoved his share of the food in his hands. We ate. Whatever was left, Alex neatly stored it away back into his rucksack. We drank water from the fountain at the station.

In one hour we departed for Slovenia. In our car, nearly empty, save for an elderly couple a few benches ahead of us, who were also chewing on something as they quietly chatted, we felt the train jerk. The whistle blew and we commenced our journey. Again the hypnotizing poles and the train's lulling put us fast asleep.

We were woke by the sudden jerking, tumbling and screeching of the train's wheels. "What's that? Where are we?" I drowsily inquired. Alex opened the window and stuck out his head to find out.

"In a forest," he proclaimed. He pulled his head back in and closed the window; with that, the door of the car opened and an armed border patrol guard entered. He demanded to see our passports.

"Aha, we are at the border!" I joyfully exclaimed. Alex gave the guard our papers, who glanced over them for a minute or two and handed them back to Alex.

The guard then looked at us and announced, "Your car will be transferred to another set of tracks, which will be taking you to Opachina."

Alex jumped. "No! We are not going to Opachina, we are going to Trieste!"

The guard then informed us that it's as far as the train goes and the Italians would take us over from that point to Trieste.

We fell silent. The wagon was loaded now with new faces and we left.

The train, after a brief ride, stopped again. Now an Italian border patrol guard entered our car, armed with a Karabinka (a special Italian-made short rifle, exclusively used by the Italians).

"Passaporte! passaporte!" a heavily accented demand fell. Alex again handed our papers to the guard, who scrutinized them and handed them back. All went well and we were soon crawling again. At approximately 150 metres we were at a halt, again! Now the conductor waltzed in and stated, "Tuti fori! Tuti fori!"

"What's he saying?" I nudged Alex.

"I don't know," Alex replied softly.

"Look...The people are leaving the car, Alex!"

"Yes, I see. Let's go, too."

Once we left the train, we envisioned the passengers walking by the wagons, toward a small building. When we entered this small building, we were met by many people. It was filled to its capacity. There were four doors at the far end of the room and on each door a list was posted with names listed alphabetically. I turned to a lady who was standing beside me, also observing the doors and their lists. "What's that?" I asked her.

"That, son, is for the passengers. If you find your name on that list, you enter through that door."

"Oh, I understand, thank you."

The three of us looked over the lists and found our names and we proceeded through the corresponding door. In the area we had entered, we had our pictures taken and were fingerprinted and then interrogated. In one hour this inquisition ended and we commenced into yet another area, a large auditorium.

Hundreds of people were there and some were eating. Yes, we had crossed the border. This was Opachina. Whether this was the name of the station or a suburb was unknown to me; all I knew was we were out of Yugoslavia, never to reside there again.

We were given lunch as the others, with loads of bread, small

Italian rolls. We gladly ate and then we were summoned to exit this building onto the road, where we were to board upon an autobus. Just as we were leaving on this bus, we observed the arrival of another train and hundreds of passengers, new faces were filling the platform quickly.

We were engulfed by forests. Surrounding us was the thick and lush greenery, calming and pleasant to the eye. "How long do we travel now, Alex?" I inquisitively asked.

He looked at me angrily and strained the words through his teeth, "Am I your tour guide, Vitya?!"

George was quiet and was content observing the scenery; he hadn't much to say, for he saw that I had to obey Alex, for he was older and I was older than George, thus he remained quiet. We spent two hours on that bus, before it turned into little side streets. We noted the happy dispositions of the habitants of that town and how lightly they were all dressed. The women wore light, summery dresses and sandals upon their feet. The men were short sleeved and the children in short pants. "You see, Vitya! It's warm here! And you wanted to save your winter coat, ha!"

"True, Alex, but don't forget, we did a good deal of travelling, thanks be to my winter coat!"

"That's not important now! We are in the west!"

The bus entered through these large iron gates and we were in a yard of some sort. We exited the bus and followed the other passengers. More buses were arriving and, in the centre of the yard, with the buses encircling, a hill was forming, compiled of luggage, bags, trunks, blankets and what-nots. Suddenly we noticed ten sharply-dressed Italian men walking to and fro with lists in their hands. They were separating and categorizing the people, determining who goes where.

Behind us was a monstrous edifice, once serving as a warehouse for rice and other products needed for the city. The Italian men assigned the three of us to the third floor of this titanic building. We entered and ascended these wide, wooden stairs easily, for we had no luggage nor trunks to carry.

The building had three floors and on each floor were three sections, each equipped with washrooms and shower stalls, located near the exit. The sections contained army style beds, with army linen upon them, tightly made up.

Immediately we took three beds near the window. The many windows were relatively high and were barred. In the centre of the floor was a long, narrow table and benches.

"Well, it's nice!" Alex proclaimed as we lay down on our beds and rested until we were called for dinner. "Let's go down," Alex ordered, seemingly curious of our new residence.

"What if somebody takes our beds?" I worried.

"Put something on it then."

"What? I only have my jacket, Alex."

"Well, put your jacket!"

"What if they take my jacket?"

"Agh! Who will take your torn jacket, Vitya?!"

"Fine."

I placed my jacket on the bed and we left. As we were descending the stairs, we were now paying more attention to our surroundings and the people within this enormous building, people like us, except that some of these people owned suitcases and trunks; we didn't.

The name of this camp was San Sabo, located on Via Rio Pri Mario #1. The head, or the president of this camp, was a Mr. Lampe; he was easy to recall for he had a port wine mark on the half of his face. The meals and accommodations were provided by UNRO (United Nations Refugee Organization). We were free to come and go as we pleased from the camp. I surmised that approximately there were nearly, if not more, two thousand souls in that camp, the majority being White Russians, a very low percentage of Romanians and Bulgarians. This colossal edifice was extended to a block's width.

On the first floor was an enormous hall, more like an arena. Endless rows of tables and chairs were before us. Near the kitchen, at the door, were oversized pots filled with spaghetti and macaroni. We filled our plates and sat down at one of the long tables to eat. We ate and ate and nobody prevented us from doing so. Pots were being brought one after the other, replacing the empty ones. Baskets upon baskets of bread were placed on the tables: little Italian rolls. Habitually, the three of us filled our pockets with these rolls and departed to our section.

We unloaded the rolls on the bed and covered them with a blanket. We then decided it was high time for a shower.

In the shower stalls, soap was plentiful, thus we needn't "steal" the soap from an unobservant patron of the shower stall. Since we had no towels, the three of us sat on the wooden benches within the showering section, naked, to dry. We then dressed and proceeded to bed. Needless to say, we slept well, after we first shared our thoughts, insights and reminiscences.

We discussed our father, who we hadn't heard from at all, while we were in Belgrade. Vechislav vanished for good, we never saw him again. Mother was still in the hospital and we discussed visiting her once we settled our lives and were able to help her. Olga we were in touch with; she was married and had no alternative but to stay with her husband.

Noise, shouting and commanding woke us the next morning. We saw an American sergeant yelling something out. At once, an elderly man with glasses on approached the sergeant and told him something. The sergeant turned and left. Of course Alex had to go and find out what the noise was about, thus he walked up to the elderly man in glasses and inquired. When he returned he told us that the sergeant was aiming to form an army garrison there. The elderly man told the sergeant that the camp was filled with women and children, it was a civilian family camp, not a military one. He advised him to go to the military camp.

We spent the day as the day before; we ate, washed and talked. The next day a commotion was heard within the camp. Carpenters arrived with wood and tools in order to partition the floor by constructing cabins, rather than having the open rows of beds on the floors.

The beds were removed and the construction began, section by section. In each cabin (as we called them) were four beds, or rather, two bunk-beds, adequate for four persons per stall. Amusingly, there were no doors, thus people created doors by hanging the army blankets, providing some kind of partial privacy.

We were assigned to a cabin in the centre of the floor. George and I remained in this cabin and camp, unfortunately Alex had to transfer to another camp called San Jesuite. It was a camp for single persons, not family. Since George was still a minor and I younger than Alex, we were allowed to remain. The San Jesuite camp was located in the older section of the city, to the dislike of Alex.

Our days were passing by quickly. One day we went downstairs in the dining room and began fumbling through boxes that were laid out for the refugees in need of clothing. I found three shirts and two pairs of pants. The box was brimming with old clothing and shoes. In my life I had not owned three shirts and two pairs of pants at once! After we finished with the boxes, we discovered a new tenant in our cabin upon our return.

An older lady was assigned to join us in our cabin. She took the lower bed. We didn't communicate much with her, for we were seldom there and now more so, providing this lady with privacy we thought she wanted.

Time was rolling and we were now occasioning the city and often roaming about. We collected cigarette butts as we did in Belgrade, though we were careful not to smoke in front of the ladies, who would scold us upon noticing. Some of the women at the camp were obsessed with making themselves up, why? We couldn't comprehend. We would complain as we walked past by the heavily-perfumed air and the clouds of powder on the way to or from the cabin.

San Sabo had now organized a voluntary security post at the entrance of the building. The refugee—volunteer—would stand guard and not permit anyone to pass through without questioning them first. Thus Alex was thoroughly questioned before he was permitted entry, and when he did enter, he found us still asleep in our beds. "Get up! You have work to do!" Alex shouted, startling us...We got up. I looked at Alex, who was agitated. Alex informed us of the hardships he faced at the singles camp. The refugees there were single males; they were curt, rude and obnoxious. He had a difficult time with them. Anyhow, Alex continued to instruct me regarding a new task I was to partake in: From a paper bag, Alex yanked out a metal last, a hammer, pliers, a box of small nails and pieces of leather.

"What do you need that for, Alex?"

"For you!"

"For me?"

"Well, you did work in a shoe factory, did you not?"

"Yes, but I didn't construct, nor repair shoes there."

"You will here!"

"Where did you get the money for all of that, Alex?"

"I borrowed it."

And, it was determined that I was to become a provider of shoe repair. We later went outside, around the building, where there was a scenic view of the gorgeous, green hillside. Right after the hill, along Via Rio Pri Mario, was farmland and flat terrain. It was the most beautiful sight. Well...We went outside to obtain empty orange crates, which were discarded by the kitchen staff and very much needed by us for our new endeavours.

I was instructed to visit the partitioned cabins and ask for any shoes in need of repair. "Tell them, Vitya, that there is now a shoemaker here and able to repair any kind of shoes," Alex professed.

"Who will pay for the repairs?" I naively asked.

"They will! You return their repaired shoes, only upon their payment of your services, not before. Do you understand?"

"Yes."

"Good. Tomorrow, I will return with shoe polish, cloths, sandpaper and you can begin to work!" Alex stated confidently, turned around and left.

I began my new line of work with enthusiasm. George, of course, was included in all this work. I assembled the material in our cabin (this was possible now, due to the transfer of the lady who was with us earlier. I assumed she requested a cabin with only females in it, which of course was quite understandable). Alex came with a box full of shoes in need of repair. I noticed that on many of the shoes, the soles were ripped off, almost as if purposely done so. I reattached them with the tiny nails I had. There were plenty of shoes and sandals with the heels broken and I repaired them, too. I then polished them and, finally, admired them; they looked almost new. I completed the repair of three pairs of shoes, when I asked Alex, "How much do I request of them?"

"Ask for 100 liras per pair," Alex decided.

"Fine," I answered, completely consumed in my work and admiration of my work.

We all worked splendidly, the three of us. Each of us had his own task to fulfill, to bring the shoes, to repair the shoes, to deliver and accept payment for the shoes.

Our enterprise was successful and we were accumulating plenty of liras! By nightfall, we were tired and, naturally, Alex would collect the income and leave for his camp. We bought cigarettes now and had enough to purchase items we needed. For a month we toiled at this task, until the administration ruined our project.

Unfortunately for us, they decided to equip the building with a "Free shoe repair service," located on the first floor of the building. The "shoemaker" was provided with a little area all his own, specifically for that purpose: shoe repair. To our dismay, our venture ended. Alex was bitterly disappointed and angered. We began to discuss our "business" in detail, now that we had free time to do so.

Articulating as to how many shoes we repaired and the mysterious unattachement of soles on many of the shoes I repaired, I asked Alex, who seemed to know almost everything!

"Yes, Vitya, that was due to the people's craftiness! They cunningly hid their valuables within their shoes: gold and jewels!"

"Really?!" I was amazed at their aptitude and skill and Alex's immense knowledge.

We spent hours discussing, musing and collecting cigarette butts again. Our money was at an all time low..Again! Christmas was around the corner. Children were happy and eagerly awaiting the special occasion. Downstairs, beneath the stairwell, kiosks were established. Because the nearest piazza was not of a walking distance, wise merchants decided, with permission, to set up their kiosks and sell their goods. Sausages, salami, sugar, milk, cheese and other delicatessen products were now readily available for those able to purchase them. The aroma when walking by these mini-kiosks was overwhelming and lured many customers to purchase.

I was lying down on my bed. I was alone. George had went somewhere and Alex didn't arrive yet. I began to daydream, but was interrupted by the loud cheers of the children next door to me. The children were singing and banging and then demanding that their parents decorate the cabin for Christmas. The parents answered their children sharply, "What would we decorate with? Downstairs there is only macaroni and bread rolls!"

The parents were not in a favourable temperament, due to their status and the inability to provide a memorable Christmas holiday for their children.

It struck me, like a lightening bolt. Decorations! They need decorations! But...Where to find decorations? While in Belgrade, it was different during the holidays. There was snow, first and foremost and secondly the parading Santa Clauses and Christmas trees. Wait...That's it! Trees, yes trees! Christmas trees! A plan was now formulating and brewing in my mind.

I promptly informed George and Alex of my new idea. They were inspired and enthusiastic. We began to devise methods, conceiving ideas and conjuring up a system. Alas! We had a new venture!

Again, we each had our own mission to fulfill. These missions consisted of gathering branches off of various evergreens, meaning firs, pines and anything that proved to be most sturdy and adequate for our purpose. The collection of empty crates and the dismantling of them provided us with strips of wood, which we used to construct little stands for the branches.

We dedicated ourselves to the assembly of these mini-trees and very soon we marched through the aisles of the floor by the cabins and observed the children tugging their mother's or father's sleeve, entreating them to purchase a "Christmas tree." Downstairs in the dining hall, our sales soared! We had prospered! We had money for Christmas, too!

Mirthfully, we bought ham, cheese, salami, pastries and a pack of "Alfa" cigarettes. They were the cheapest brand, but for us it was gold. Alex was so ardent at the outcome of our aspirations that he maintained to embark on the project again. "Alex, today is Christmas day and the people would not be zealous to purchase little trees, for the holiday is nearly over." Alex dismally agreed.

A few weeks after Christmas and we were back to cigarette butts and had exhausted our supply of money. I went outside for a short walk as did George, though he went his own way. I was pacing outside of the building...Hmm, how to earn some money? On my way out of the camp, I passed by the "Free shoe repair service," argh! They blissfully took my income away, at least that is how I felt!

Frugalness wouldn't sufficiently merit, thus I strived to concoct a project. I trudged a little farther from the entrance of the camp and to the yard, where I perceived a clumsy construction of cardboard boxes, akin to a chicken coup. Most naturally and inquisitively, I pried through the cracks of the cardboard to enable myself a better view of what was within the coup.

An old Russian man, also a camp resident, was blowing on something. I decided to go around the coup and enter. I came to the man and probed, "What are you making?"

"Well, can't you see? Ducks!" Indeed there were many brightly-coloured ducks, which the old man was making out of plaster of Paris. He was blowing on the ducks, in order to dry the paint. "Ahem, excuse me, but may I know whether you are able to provide a slot in the middle of these ducks, for example, to enable money to slide into?"

"Yes, I can," the old man brusquely snapped.

"How much do you ask for one duck?"

"Fifty liras!" he maintained.

"Whew! That's a lot!"

"I can't sell it for less than that!"

"I see. Well, can you make me fifty pieces, I mean ducks? And...How much time would you need for that?"

"Yes...And three days."

"Fine. I'll be back in three days."

"Agreed!" the old man stated as he rubbed his hands together.

In three days, George and I went back to the old man. The old man proudly unveiled the ducks. They were pleasant to look at in an assortment of colours: green, red, blue and yellow. "Do you have a cart by any chance?" I inquired of the old man.

"Yes, of course I do, how do you think I bring all my material?"

"May we borrow it please?"

"Fine," he hesitatingly answered.

We loaded the ducks onto the cart (a homemade cart made of a plank of wood, with four wheels attached to the bottom and a handle to pull it) and George began to lug the cart away from the man. Instantly, the old man yanked me by the arm and with his other hand shoved his palm before my eyes, demanding, "Two and a half thousand liras! Pay up!"

"I don't have that kind of money! I'll sell these ducks and come back with your money!"

"No, no, that won't do! Pay now!"

"Look, if I leave here without the ducks, not you nor I would have any profit, but if I sell them, we both win. After all, you do know where I reside!"

The old man made grimaces, grabbed his head with both his hands and turned around, while grunting something. He retreated to his coup and I accepted that as his agreement of my conditions.

We left with the ducks. We trekked along the street, heading toward the centre of the city, which wasn't that close. We took a short cut through a tunnel. One and a half hours of walking we did. George was becoming tired of lugging the cart and asked me, "How much more walking, Vitya?"

"A little more and we will arrive at the piazza."

"How will you sell, if you don't know that language?" George asked.

"Don't worry about that, I have learned enough."

By now I had learnt quite a few words in Italian by listening to conversations on the street and in the piazzas. I explained to George the words I knew: "porto" meant "bring," and "chento" meant "hundred," and "via porto tua mama," meant "go call your mother." Along the way I was thus practising the few words I had picked up.

Arriving at the piazza, we went farther from the merchants' kiosks, not to intrude, nor provoke any arguments with them. We found a spot on the sidewalk and lined up our ducks in neat rows and they looked splendid, shining brightly in the sun. In a matter of ten minutes we were enclosed by children of all ages.

Clusters of children kept approaching us, gleefully admiring the duck-piggy banks. I announced to the children, "Via tua mama, porto chento lire, per una, per una!" The children immediately dispersed and reappeared hauling their mothers behind them.

Realistically, a hundred liras was not an extravagant sum. One thousand liras was the day's wages for a common worker. Thus, my duck-piggy banks was not an exorbitant amount. In one hour we had sold our entire stock and had earned five thousand liras!

"What success, George!"

"Indeed it is!"

"Let's go back to the camp now!" I triumphantly declared.

Upon our return to camp, I directly paid the old Russian man my debt and simultaneously ordered another fifty ducks to be made, in three days. We picked up those ducks in three days and sold them at the market as well. We repeated this system another three times. On the fifth day of our marketing, we had encountered some difficulties. We saw that there were duck merchants scattered throughout the piazza and we were not the sole merchants of this product anymore, to our disappointment. Due to this mushrooming effect, we barely managed to sell ten ducks that day and gave up on that business altogether.

Obviously, the old Russian man was now producing and selling these ducks not only to us, but to others as he conveniently neglected to inform us. Angrily we marched back to the old man, intending to return the unsold ducks, recover our money and tell him to sell them himself! Thus, we did.

Back to the drawing board. I needed employment. George had found some part-time employment and I was left to devise another scheme for profit. Soon enough, a new project was underway.

George and I went to the piazza early in the morning. I observed there were loads of paper trash strewn about in the piazza. We began to collect the trash and thrust it in the empty potato sacks we picked up back at San Sabo. We filled our sacks to the brim. We hauled these sacks approximately three streets away, where we had heard of an old man in a barn who had habits of purchasing old items, recyclables, including paper trash. We ventured in this old, worn out barn and amidst all the junk we found the old man.

Because I was blessed with an ear for languages, just like my mother, I had absorbed many words in Italian, especially since we were there for already five months. I asked the elderly man, "Comprare? Comprare?"

"Si! Si!" he declared and instructed us to place the sacks on the scale to weigh them. After we had placed the first one on the scale, he announced, "Chento lire," and did the same for the next sack. We had two hundred liras in our pockets! Enthusiastically, we ran back to the piazza, to collect more trash and return to the man for the sale. That day we accumulated eight hundred liras! We had no objections from the staff, nor the merchants at the piazza, for it was exceptionally clean and tidy and, retrospectively, we gained a reasonable profit from this tidiness.

Two weeks we laboured in this manner and were thrilled of having money in our pockets again. One morning, upon arriving at the piazza, confidently aimed to commence our work, we were faced with a shock. Not a single piece of discarded paper was on the ground, nothing! The piazza was spotless! What horror! We were tricked again!

"Look! There's the lady from our camp, across from our cabin! Look, she's pulling the potato sack full of trash!" I remarked astonishingly.

"Yes and look over there! There are more like her, doing what she is and what we were!"

"Oh, rrr! That's ridiculous!"

How did they pick up on this system? I must have thought out loud, for George answered, "They probably followed us." That was the most inevitable explanation. They must have noticed that we suddenly had money for purchasing cigarettes and other items at our local merchant's kiosk, beneath the stairwell. Thereby, they clandestinely followed us! No secrets could be kept at the camp. The nerve!

I sat in the dining hall, faced with unemployment again, brooding, thinking and devising was now common practise for us. While I was sitting there observing some of the residents and attempting to ruminate, Alex appeared before me and then sat down. Alex was now in the custom of obtaining financial assistance from us, thus his visit that day.

"Alex, I don't have any more money."

"Well, the two of you are working and should share with me!"

"What! Why don't you work for yourself, Alex?"

"Vitya, there are well over two thousand refugees and you think I will obtain work?"

"Alex, where there are people, there is work. If you were stranded in a forest where there were no people, I would understand, but here?"

Meditatively, Alex left and headed back to his camp, this time without any money, for in truth, I hadn't any to give.

I went upstairs to my cabin and decided to look through the

garments I had collected from the boxes in the dining hall, courtesy of the Red Cross. I chose the best outfit I had and dressed accordingly. I found an old, worn out attache case and took that, too. I had surmised a plan.

Dressed somewhat smartly, briefcase underarm, I began to call on each and every cabin, inquiring the inhabitants whether they had any goods to sell. It was astounding to envision what some of the people had for sale and were willing to part with! I soon had a motley assortment of silver trays, flatware (cutlery), unspun pure wool and other gadgets. I thrust all the items into my briefcase, which even though was not of exquisite appearance, served the purpose nonetheless, and embarked on selling these items. The margin of profit was 15%; the remainder was to be given to the owners.

I took the streetcar to the "older section" of Trieste and, whenever I did go there, I would always be enthralled by the charm of that part of the city. It was truly beautiful! The top part of buildings were in resemblance to castles and forts. In these structures were little cozy shops. The houses were constructed of grey stones and the antique lantern lamp posts added much charm to the cobblestoned streets.

Within the structures were stairwells, which led to the floor above, where spot lights illuminated the quaint city streets at night. It was a strikingly pretty scenery. The streets were small and narrow and it is within these little narrow streets that I had come across pawn shops.

I had no trouble selling the items, save for the unspun wool; I had much difficulty selling that item. The earnings I made were abundant, nearly two to three thousand liras a day. I worked this way until the people had run out of merchandise to sell.

I was lying down one particular evening, simply relaxing and allowing my mind to rest, when I overheard the discussion next door, which wasn't difficult, for we had no ceilings, nor doors, only the partitioned walls. The volume of the neighbours chatting also attributed to my eavesdropping. One lady began, "Did you hear that President Tito wants to confiscate Trieste?"

"Yes, I've heard, but the Americans prevented this from occurring. Trieste is considered 'F.F.T.' (Free Territory of Trieste)."

"True. Many foreign ships dock here, it is an important and busy port!" a man professed.

"What if Tito takes Trieste? What will become of us?" the lady asked in a worried tone.

"You should have thought of that twenty-five years ago when you gave up Russia! Now you can scramble across the world!" another deep-voiced man articulated.

So it is...Here I am and what of my ancestors? Where are they? What happened to my grandfather? What about the rest of the family? What about their possessions and property? Who has that now? Here I lay, on this army bed, in a refugee camp in Trieste, without a country of my own, still poor, though not hungry, with no family, save for my brothers. Why did our parents create us? Why, I asked myself.

Chapter 18

Nine months we had spent in Trieste. I had learnt the language and spoke it fluently. After considerable deliberation, I had decided to apply for immigration papers for Australia. I was unable to obtain them, due to the quota reaching its capacity for that country. I then applied for the United States of America, but had no luck there either, with their quota also reaching its capacity. My final application was to Canada and, gratefully, I was able to obtain papers for that country.

Once that had been established, I had to undergo the necessary procedures, which included a medical examination. I travelled by train to Bremen, Germany via Italy and Austria. We, the refugees, being only men on board, no women or children, were already assigned with employment once we arrived in Canada.

We boarded the ship, *Miss Nellie* (which was once a commercial cargo ship) and travelled for eleven long and sickening days during the month of May.

On the ship, I was placed below deck at the tip of the nine thousand tonne vessel, in a cabin. The bunk bed was fastened to the floor with screws, thus preventing it from tossing around in the cabin. The nightmarish sea-sickness I had experienced was unfathomable. I didn't and couldn't eat and begged the kitchen staff for an orange or a lemon.

Through the porthole, I only saw water, huge waves, and a glimpse of the sky. There were approximately a thousand of us on board, all from the same camp, San Sabo in Trieste.

Journeying over the Atlantic Ocean, we finally, gratefully, docked at the port in Halifax. We were immediately put on a train, which took us directly to Princeton, Ontario. There we were assigned our duties to work on the Canadian National Railways. The year was 1951.

We ate, slept and lived in the train and travelled across Ontario removing and repairing the railroad tracks. There was a car specifically designated for the purpose of cooking and providing us food, which was a type of kitchen attached to the train. There, the beef (when they purchased half a stead) was placed with two large blocks of ice on top, for there was no refrigeration. Flies were abundant and I had suffered from stomach problems for two weeks.

Every morning we rose at five, had breakfast and commenced work at six. We travelled from our destination via mini-wagons on the tracks (similar to those used in mine shafts), to our location of work.

We were expected to purchase our own work uniform, shoes, linens and blankets from the canteen. We were obliged to pay two dollars a day for room and board. Our wages were fifty cents an hour. We were given credit at the canteen and, usually, once we paid room and board, the canteen debt and the tax deduction, we were virtually left with nothing. I had spent a year working like this, until scrimping and saving enough enabled me to settle in Toronto, Ontario.

I had left my two brothers behind when I decided to come to Canada, but most fortunately we were reunited within a few years. Both of my brothers had established themselves families. Alex, before I brought him to Canada, had spent five years in Brazil, South America. Terribly, Alex had fallen ill in his middle age and passed away in Toronto.

I recall when visiting him in the hospital we would reminisce regarding our past; he would merrily laugh when I mimicked him of his bossiness and his commandments during our childhood. That tragic loss occurred in 1975.

Several years had gone by. I worked (ironically) in a shoe factory in Toronto; the company was called "Carrier." After many wonderful stories I had heard from friends and acquaintances who visited the beautiful city of Los Angeles, California, I had finally decided to embark on yet another journey and experience the splendid city.

I travelled by train to Los Angeles, which was quite comfortable. The train had an observation deck directly on top of the car, easily accessible by means of stairs where, once seated, one could view the magnificent and invigorating panorama of the picturesque vista.

Four days I had spent travelling across the United States and observed and delighted in the wonderful landscapes. Truly awe-inspiring! I was recalling many of the agreeable and pleasing stories of the country and the city of which I was headed to, told by acquaintances who had the opportunity of visiting. Their stories were like fairytales to me and I simply had to travel myself and experience all they had told me.

True to the stories I had heard, it was spectacular for me! I was greeted by the sun-filled city, where magnificent palm trees gently swayed in the light, warm breeze and the people, in summer dress, were strolling along the streets. I walked amongst them and soaked up the warm kisses of the sun. The sky was heavenly blue, not a cloud in sight. I was completely fascinated. Not to suggest that Toronto had not fascinated me, for it had, but the weather and the palm trees in Los Angeles made me feel like I was in a fairytale!

Orange trees! Lemon trees! I was enjoying all the sights and sampling the foods. Mexican stands that sold tacos and enchiladas were around me and I sampled all. I visited the Central Market and many other notable locations. I had thoroughly enjoyed my visit to Los Angeles and, by the work of fate, had met my future wife there.

Soon, my future wife and I travelled back to Toronto, where we had established a family: two daughters, who are now married and have families of their own. We lived in harmony for fifteen years before the events took a turn, thus we divorced and each went on our separate ways.

Regarding my mother…Sadly, I was not able to help her, none of my siblings were. Her health was deteriorating and she was not able to leave the hospital she was at, let alone travel. Our sister Olga had visited her and kept us informed through letters.

Our dear and beloved mother passed away in the month of April, 1960. It was also through Olga that we had heard of our father's passing in Austria, several years after our mother's passing.

Father had never bothered with us, nor with Mother; we believed he formed himself a new life in the country he chose to reside in. As mentioned before, Vechislav, we had never heard of again, missing in action during the war. Our Aunt Nina had vanished. I tried locating her in Switzerland, for I had heard through the grape vine that she and her new husband had went there. I had no luck in my search.

My childhood thus slipped away, including my youth, in hardship and hard labour. Now, memories were left, mostly tear-provoking and painful, some tragically comical. I had began anew, in a far-away country, a new life, new acquaintances, new experiences. In Toronto, I frequented the Russian church, which had tremendously helped me acquire basic commodities and settle into a new life when I had first arrived.

In this church I had the honour of meeting the son (Grand Duke) of Her Imperial Highness Grand Duchess Olga, who was a very pleasant man. I had the opportunity of a lifetime...Which I will never forget...I personally met the Grand Duchess Olga at her home in Campbleville, Ontario:

An acquaintance of mine had some matters to tend to considering the Grand Duchess; he had a package to take to her and had asked me to accompany him on the long ride. I agreed.

We arrived in front of the modest home, where we immediately observed the Grand Duchess herself in her garden, tending to something. She was modestly dressed, but when she approached us upon noticing our arrival, her majestic carriage was instantly discerned. Her refined manners and comportment instilled an everlasting impression on me. My acquaintance had introduced me to the Grand Duchess and she momentarily concluded, while warmth emitted from her eyes, that she new of the name very well, because her own regiment was the "Ahtyrsky regiment," which incidentally is my surname. She had also stated that she was the colonel of her regiment. Our meeting with the Grand Duchess Olga concluded with the deliverance of a parcel by my acquaintance, and with reverent bows and humble greetings we departed.

I didn't think of it then, but many years later, when I reflected on that momentous and advantageous occasion regarding the humbleness, yet proud acceptance of fate and the obvious stance of Highness and nobility the Grand Duchess maintained. She possessed the perseverance and determination of continuing with her life...In spite of the horrific hardships she, too, encountered, the loss of her loved ones, her home, her friends, entwined with her own struggles she had imparted on me an admiration and an understanding and realization. Realization of the possibility of perpetually achieving one's aspirations and not withering and succumbing to the ironies of life, rather gaining strength and wisdom. These traits impressed and imprinted on me the qualities of a human being and the tolerance and abilities of people. I was sheerly affected by the visit to the sister of Tsar Nicholas II, Grand Duchess Olga. At times I visit the resting place of the Grand Duchess Olga, where not far from there, my brother Alex rests as well.

I have been left with the many scars of endurance, memories and realizations through research that, ironically, my siblings and I are: The Noble's Pauper Children.

1901 года Августа 19 дня, я
нижеподписавшийся, даю
нижеследующую подписку Приставу 1 стана Курского уезда
в томъ, что отношеніе Канцеляріи Ея Величества Государыни Императрицы
Маріи Феодоровны отъ 4го
Августа ..., за N 3338 объ оставленіи безъ послѣдствій просьбы
моей о пособіи, мнѣ сего числа
по содержанію объявлено, въ чемъ
подписываюсь. Крестьянинъ —

Константинъ Андреевичъ Кипринъ

Прошеніе Краснухинъ

Printed in the United States
31727LVS00004B/46-204

9 781413 759419